HOME OF LOVE

A Short History of the Papal Seminary, Kandy-Pune

(1893 - 2015)

HOME OF LOVE

A Short History of the Papal Seminary, Kandy-Pune

(1893 - 2015)

Mercês de Melo Carlos, SJ

Updated & Edited by
Kurien Kunnumpuram, SJ

Christian World Imprints™

&

Papal Seminary

First Published in 2016 by

Christian World Imprints™
Christian Publishing & Books from India
H-12 Bali Nagar, **New Delhi-110015**
info@christianworldimprints.com
www.ChristianWorldImprints.com
Phone: +91 11 25465925

&

Papal Seminary
Ramwadi, Nagar Road, **Pune-411014**
papalseminarypune@gmail.com
www.papalseminary.in
www.papalseminary.org
Phone: +91 20 41036222

ISBN: 978-93-5148-154-6 (HB)
ISBN: 978-93-5148-155-3 (PB)

Printed in India.

Contents

Introduction

This book is basically the work of Father Carlos Merces de Melo, SJ. On the occasion of the Centenary of the Papal Seminary, he wrote the history the first hundred years of the existence of the Seminary: 1893-1993.

Now we are celebrating the Diamond Jubilee of the existence of the Seminary in Pune. The staff and the students of the Seminary thought that Fr. C.M. de Melo's book should be revised and updated. And I have been asked to do it.

As I carefully read de Melo's history, it became clear to me that it is remarkably a good book. All I sought to do was to correct a few mistakes and cut out some paragraphs which I thought were unnecessary.[1] I also added one chapter to the book, narrating the story of the last twenty-two years.

It is my fond hope that this revised and updated history of the Papal Seminary will appeal to the staff and students of the Papal seminary, past, present and future.

I wish to thank all those who helped me in the revision and updating of this book. I would like to place on record my grateful thanks to A. Francis for his competent secretarial assistance.

Kurien Kunnumpuram, SJ

Pune
December 3, 2015

1 The original book of Carlos Merces de Melo still remains authoritative. Those who are interested to get the original work of Carlos Merces de Melo may be provided with a softcopy. Requests may be made to: papalseminarypune@gmail.com.

Preface

Papal Seminary is one of the Oldest Seminaries in India today. It was started in Kandy, Sri Lanka, in 1893. It is already 123 years old and it has its own wonderful history. On the occasion of the Diamond Jubilee of the shifting of Papal Seminary from Kandy to Pune, I am very happy that Fr. Kurien Kunnumpuram, SJ has taken great trouble to update the history which was written by Fr. Carlos Mercês de Melo, S.J. in 1993 on the occasion of Papal Seminary Centenary Celebrations. Fr. Carlos had taken great pains to bring out the history in 1993. Fr. Kurien has made some corrections of the existing history and has added one more chapter giving the history of Papal Seminary from 1993 to 2015. I really appreciate the hard work that is put in by Fr. Kurien. Fr. Kuruvilla Pandikattu, SJ and his team were entrusted with the job of bringing out the book on the History of Papal Seminary on the occasion the Diamond Jubilee of its shifting to Pune. I thank them for their efforts to bring out the updated book of Papal Seminary History.

History is very important for every individual and institution. Studying the history of Papal Seminary gives us an opportunity to come to know the great personalities who shaped Papal Seminary. It also tells us about the various attempts made over the years to form effective priests for India and abroad. The present has to be built on the past. Therefore, unless we know what has gone in the past, we will not be able to mould the present and the future in a meaningful and constructive way. Those who don't learn from history are doomed to repeat the same mistakes.

Papal Seminary has a glorious history. Over the last 123 years it has been able to train thousands of priests, sisters and lay people. Until it was shifted to Pune, Papal Seminary (Papal Athenaeum) was catering almost exclusively to the Papal Seminarians. After it was shifted to Pune, it started accepting students from other religious congregations and lay men and women.

Four Cardinals and 72 Archbishops and Bishops have gone through the training in Papal Seminary. At present, there are one Cardinal, 23 Archbishops and Bishops and 16 Archbishops and Bishops Emeriti. We are happy that we get students from large number of Archdioceses and Dioceses from all over India. At present, we have 178 Seminarians and 16 Staff members from 59 Archdioceses and Dioceses and 3 Religious Congregations. Among the students 58 study philosophy and 120 study theology.

Papal Seminary aims at producing efficient and effective leaders for the Church in India and abroad. It tries to provide an atmosphere of freedom so that the seminarians can interiorize the values that we try to inculcate in them. Seminarians usually call it a 'Home of Love'. The seminarians are divided into small groups of 12 or 13 and a staff animator is assigned to each group so that the group members get a chance to come to know each other better and establish close relationships. Over the years, it has been found very beneficial for the holistic formation of the seminarians.

Fr. Jose Thayil, SJ
Rector, Papal Seminary

Pune
December 3, 2015

Foreword

It is befitting that as the Papal Seminary completes 100 years of its existence its history should be recorded. This work would mean hours of painstaking research into documents available, interviews and correspondence with former Papal seminarians and finally the compilation of a book that would make interesting reading.

The magnum opus was entrusted to Rev. Fr. Carlos de Melo, S.J., who was given just a few months to complete it. Though some might think that Fr. de Melo being a professor emeritus would have the time required, but he is as busy as any of the other professors in the Papal Seminary. He kept aside nearly all his other commitments and took up the challenge.

The term "Home of Love" which was formerly used frequently to characterize the Papal Seminary in Kandy inspired Fr. de Melo to make a "Work of Love" of what he has undertaken. I have had much experience of this in my recent visits to the Papal Seminary. His conversations were full of what he had discovered in letters and documents, on how many chapters had been written already, and what difficulties he was facing.

This book demonstrates how the vision of Pope Leo XIII in establishing one general seminary for the whole of India has been realized. So great was his prophetic thrust and the trust that on one side of the medal struck in 1894 on the occasion of his sacerdotal silver jubilee was the inscription "Filii Tui India, Administri Tibi Salutis". The sons are now bringing salvation to people in many parts of the world.

For us the saying "Bloom where you are planted" is important. But equally if not more important is to "Bloom where you are transplanted". Transfers, as we priests and bishops know, are an uprooting and transplanting, and can be painful. The transfer of the Papal Seminary from Kandy to Poona in 1955 was not different. What would become of the "Home of Love" and the "Kandy Spirit"?

The lush greenery of Kandy gave way in 1955 to the brown aridity of Ramwadi, Poona. I joined the Papal Seminary in 1955 and sensed that it was faith and obedience that prevented the professors and students from behaving like the Israelites in the desert and yearning for a return to the past. They grasped the present and looked with hope to the future. The luxuriant vegetation around the Papal Seminary now is but one sign of how well they worked towards and achieved their goals.

Fr. Carlos de Melo helps us to realize that the "transplantation" did not bring barrenness but only a change in the fruitfulness, for the "Kandy fruit" has to be different from the "Poona fruit". Both are excellent.

Rt. Rev. Valerian D'Souza
Bishop of Poona

Pune
September 1993

Prologue

Seminaries in the History of the Church in India

The recruitment and proper formation of her future ministers, her priests, has ever been one of the major concerns of the Church founded by Christ.

The divine Master Himself gave her the lead in this important area of her solicitude. Before sending the Apostles out on their mission of spreading the "Good News" to the ends of the world (cf. Matt 28:18-20). Jesus gathered them together and kept them in close intimacy around himself for about three years. They had left everything to follow Him (Matt 19:27). They were then given a personal experience of Christ's way of life: they listened to his teaching, became acquainted with his mission and his ideals, had the time to reflect deeply upon his message of salvation and personalize it, shared his joys and sorrows, his fears, anxieties and hopes... In this way, during those three unforgettable years of life in his company, they came to grow day by day in their knowledge of and love for the Son of Mary of Nazareth who presented himself to them as none other than the Son of God Himself, true Man and yet true God! Finally, after Christ's death and resurrection, they received the Holy Spirit who was to abide with them for good. This was Christ's final touch to their formation, the Master's parting Gift to his beloved disciples and to his Church.

The Church too, in the course of the centuries, has taken pains to follow the lead given by her Founder in preparing the future messengers of the Gospel for their unique, God-given task in the world.

In the early years of Christianity young men aspiring to the priesthood received special training, intellectual, spiritual and pastoral, under the respective Bishop and the senior members of the clergy, and later on in the so-called *catechetical schools.*

Gradually, especially since the tenth century, these schools began to be thrown open also to lay students. The twelfth and thirteenth centuries saw the rise of the Studia Generalia, later called Universities. Many of these were already run by the Church, but side by side with seminarians or clerics, lay students too flocked to these centres of learning. Such familiar intercourse with the general run of the laity in class and in the boarding houses - aggravated by the lack of adequate spiritual guidance, possibly also of careful selection and discernment of vocations - proved in the long run detrimental to the spirit and the proper formation of candidates to the priestly life. The bishops took note of this danger and began to look for ways and means of counteracting it, but it is from the ecumenical Council of Trent that the decisive came in this area.[1]

Actually, ever since the rise of the "Reformation" which severed from the Church entire sections of the People of God, the formation of candidates to the priesthood had been a matter of anxiety and preoccupation to the entire Catholic world. In this connection, we know, for instance, how deeply St. Ignatius of Loyola the Founder of the Society of Jesus, was interested and involved in this matter, and how he did his best to have the idea of seminaries for the training of future priests endorsed by the Council. He did so through his confreres, some of whom like Le Jay, Laynez and Salmeron took an active part in the Council sessions of Trent. Even before the Council met, but having it inview, Ignatius sent Claude Le Jay to Germany with instructions tomeet personally the German bishops and win them over to this project which he considered to be vital for the future of the Church in his time. The same Le Jay worked in union with Laynez and Salmeron, who took part in the council as the Pope's theologians, to diffuse this idea among the Council Fathers.[2]

The Council of Trent opened on 13 December, 1546. It took up for discussion the topic on the formation of candidates to the priesthood, on 10 May, 1563, during its second sitting.[3] Two months later, it approved a decree on the formation of future priests in the general session on 14th July.

Among other things the decree prescribed that "every diocese, according to its means and the size of its territory must erect and support a seminary for the training of a certain number of clerical students chosen from the episcopal town and from the entire diocese or from the entire province".

This decree came to be promulgated through the Bull *Benedictus Deus et Pater* by Pope Pius IV on 26 January, 1564, which confirmed all the decrees of the Council.[4] It has since remained the basic law of the Church on the education of students for the priestly state, and it certainly had an impact also on the formation of the clergy in India. Nevertheless, it is opportune for us to remember that the establishment of seminaries or centres of ecclesiastical training for future priests was nota novelty in India, for such institutions were already in existence in our country long before Trent, as we shall see.

"Seminaries" in India before Trent

A first attempt in this direction seems to have been the College established by the Franciscan Friars in Goa in the year 1540.

This year, as Father (later Bishop) George Anathil, SVD, remarks is "one of the most important dates in the history of theological formation in India" as "it marked the beginning of modern seminary training in India".[5]

A second similar college was founded also by the Franciscan Vicente dos Lagos in 1540 or 1541 at Cranganore, in Malabar, but this time for the benefit of the St. Thomas Christians. Saint Francis Xavier speaks of it with great hope in one of his letters to St. Ignatius.[6] As Anathil observes, "It was the first Attempt ever made among the Saint Thomas Christians to give their clergy a systematic training".[7] Till then the Syrians followed the ancient Malpanate system which corresponded rather closely to the Hindu *Gurukulavasam.*[8] An elderly priest gathered around himself a number of young men showing inclination to the priestly life and trained them for their mission. The instruction they received was necessarily somewhat deficient, but they gave due importance to the study of Scripture and the Liturgy.

Near the city of Goa, at Verem or Reis-Magos, the Franciscans founded a college in 1555. The best students were chosen to learn Latin and cases of conscience and were eventually ordained priests, so that they might serve in the parishes of the Archdiocese and help the European Fathers in the ministry of the confessional.[9] The Franciscans had still another seminary for the same purpose at Bassein, near Bombay. It lasted till 1759.[10]

Side by side with these there was the famous Colegio de Santa, founded in Goa by two zealous Portuguese missionaries Diogo da Borba and Dr. Miguel Vaz. Begun in the year 1541 as a Pious Association or Confraternity for the conversion of non-Christians, it soon - that is, by the year 1543 - developed into a training centre for future priests. After the death of its founders it passed into the hands of the Jesuits who continued to run it till they were expelled from Goa by the Marquis of Pombalin, 1759.[11] Its students came from the various countries of the East. The proportion fixed for each country was as follows: 10 for Goa, 6 for each of the following countries: Malabar, Malacca, the Molucas, China, Bengal, Pegu, Siam, and from 6 to 8 for Sofala and Mozambique in Africa. By 1614, according to the testimony of the Jesuit historian Sebastiao Gonsalves, this college had produced many priests who "with great edification and spiritual progress worked among the souls entrusted to their care, without forgetting the zeal for the conversion of their native brethren which they had acquired during the years of training in the Seminary".[12]

The Jesuits also directed a college or seminary for the Saint Thomas Christians, at Vaipicotta, in Kerala. Fr. Francisco Roz, S.J., the future Archbishop of those Christians, started there classes of Syro-Chaldaic which were a great success.[13] In a letter written to his Superior General in 1644, Andrew Lopèz, S.J., gives the following instructive details regarding the functioning of this seminary. He writes: "In this seminary are received the sons of the Christians of St. Thomas. They learn the Syriac language taught by the rector himself, with a view to their being ultimately ordained priests, for Mass is said in Syriac... The seminarians learn not only Syriac but also Holy scripture in the same language. Every Saturday they attend conferences on matters of faith, the administration of the sacraments, devotion to our Lady and the Saints, each session ending generally with an exhortation. Those among the seminarians who are not yet in Holy Orders recite every morning the Christian doctrine, while those who are in Orders say Matins at 5.00 a.m. in the church, and Vespers and Compline in the evening. At night, before going to bed, they recite all together the litanies of our Lady, or of the Most Blessed Sacrament. The Blessed Sacrament is reserved in a small chapel, where they make their examen of conscience, and then retire for the night".[14]

"From this seminary many priests came forth fairly well instructed", Fr. Anathil tells us. "Its end was tragic. The growing tension between Syrians and Latins, especially after the Synod of Diamper, led at the end to the Coonan Cross revolt, and this swept away also the seminary of Vaipicotta. In 1652, the seminarians were forced by the angry mob to quit the seminary and it was closed down".[15]

These seminaries - of which all except the last one were pre-Tridentine catered to the formation of young candidates to the diocesan priesthood, but they were all run by the religious. In keeping with the practice of the time, the local Ordinaries had no direct jurisdiction over them. The need was now felt of new types of seminaries that would be technically diocesan institutions entirely under the control of the local bishops, in keeping with the decree of Trent. There were no such seminaries as yet in India, and this explains the first decree of the First Provincial Council of Goa (1585) which says: "... As in these parts of India there is as yet no seminary whatever, and the need of a seminary being greater here than elsewhere, because of the great scarcity of priests coming from Portugal, and because of the need of native priests for the conversion and instruction of the natives, this Synod ordains that, in keeping with the dispositions of the said Council of Trent, seminaries be established in all the dioceses. And if it is not possible to doso in each diocese, let at least one common seminary for the whole province be erected in this city of Goa, for the instruction and education of the young men sent by each of the Bishops, both sons of the Portuguese and sons of the natives, fit for that (way of life)..."[16]

After the Council of Trent all the existing seminaries in India continued their mission with renewed zeal and fervour. Foremost among them was perhaps Rachol, in Salcete, Goa. It started at Margao as "St. Ignatius College" for the education of the native children. Later, in 1574, it was transferred to Rachol. Eventually, in the course of the years, it became a centre for the formation of future native priests.[17] After the expulsion of the Jesuits by Pombal in 1759, it was continued by the Goan Oratorians, and then by the Fathers of the Congregation of the Missions (or Lazarists) till, after the expulsion of all Religious Congregations from Portuguese territories in 1583, it passed into the hands of the native diocesan clergy who have been running it efficiently upto now.

Instructions from Rome

Rachol was situated within the jurisdiction of the Portuguese Padroado. Outside Padroado, however, various foreign missionaries were also engaged in the meritorious task of the formation of the native clergy. The Sacred Congregation de Propaganda Fide seemed never tired of reminding them of their obligations in this regard. To give but one instance: in its famous *Instruction of November 23, 1845*, the Congregation had these significant paragraphs in this respect: "2. Let them also be very diligent and see to it that from among the native Christians, or the Christians living in those parts, worthy clerics are duly trained and initiated into the priestly life. In this way, as the faith goes on spreading in the country, and the number of the faithful increases, the observance of ecclesiastical discipline will be fostered and so the stability of the Catholic religion better safeguarded. It will therefore be very helpful, even necessary, to establish seminaries, in which young men called by God to the priesthood may be properly brought up and instructed in the sacred doctrine".

"3. The native Levites should be well trained in all knowledge and piety, and exercised in the sacred ministry, in such a way that - as the Apostolic See so greatly desires – they may be fit for all ecclesiastical offices, not excluding the higher offices of the government of the Church, nor let them hesitate gradually to appoint them as their Vicars".

"4. Consequently, the custom of appointing native priests only as auxiliaries (of the European clergy) - a practice which they rightfully resent - is by all means to be abolished. On the contrary, it is the following rule that should be gradually and with due prudence adopted everywhere, namely, all other factors being equal, the order to be followed in promotion, both regarding the natives and the Europeans, should be the years of service in the Mission. Honours, offices, and grades should be conferred on those who have served in the sacred offices longer".[18]

The instructions from Rome were clear and emphatic, as we have seen. Nevertheless - whatever may be the reasons for it - the response on the part of our Prelates in India failed to come up to the expectations of the Roman authorities. This is what the Apostolic Visitor sent by Rome in 1859, Bishop Clement Bonnand, remarks with much regret, namely that the Ordinaries in India did not pay due attention to their duty of promoting the native clergy.[19]

To be more concrete: apart from the Padroado dioceses of Goa, Damaun and Diu, there were in all eighteen Vicariates in India, and yet even as late as 1859 seven of them had not even a single native diocesan priest. There were no seminaries for the formation of native diocesan clergy in the following Vicariates: Agra, Patna, East and West Bengal, Madura and Jaffna. Seminaries did exist in Coimbatore, Bangalore, Bombay, Vizagapatnam, Verapoly, Puthenpally, Mangalore, Trichinopoly and Pondicherry, served by the Foreign Missions Society of Paris, had a Minor and a Major Seminary run more or less in line with similar institutions in Europe. From the latter, 14 or 15 native students had been ordained priests, and 13 were preparing themselves for the priesthood.[20]

Still later, in 1893, Propaganda enjoined on all the ecclesiastical Provinces in India to hold Provincial Councils between November 1893 and April 1894, under the presidency of the Apostolic Delegate, Msgr. Zaleski. One of the points they had expressly to investigate, and inform Rome about, was precisely the question of the native clergy. In his letter of convocation, Cardinal Ledochowski, Prefect of the S.C. of Propaganda Fide wrote expressly: "Since the formation of native diocesan clergy is, in the opinion of this Sacred Congregation, a matter of greater importance than others, let the Fathers participating in the synods not refrain from discussing it. They will thereby be able more easily to decide by common agreement how, in keeping with the decrees of Trent, they could establish in each diocese, or at least in each ecclesiastical province, seminaries in which native clerics can be safely instructed in the necessary disciplines".[21]

This then was roughly the situation in India till the end ofthe 19th century regarding the recruitment and formation of the native diocesan clergy. Efforts were, indeed, being made here and there in that direction, yet Rome was far from satisfied, and thought that more could still be done. There was no National Seminary for the nation as a whole; the first one, as we shall see in the following chapter, would be the Papal Seminary of Kandy which came to be established in 1893.

Notes

1. Carlos M. de Melo, SJ, *The Recruitment and Formation of the Native Clergy in India*, pp. 113-128.
2. M. Berbera, SJ., L'Origine dei Seminari a norma del Concilio di Trento in *Civilita Cattolica*, 1940, vol.III, 25 July, 1940, pp. 215-221. At the same time Ignatius set about taking practical steps in this direction. In 1551, while the Council was on, he founded the "Collegio Romano". A year later he established, again in Rome, the "Collegio Germanico" which was a real seminary in which German students were trained for the priestly life and ministry while they attended classes in the "Collegio Romano" (the present Gregorian University). Ignatius undertook this foundation at the request of Pope Julius III, and in compliance with the wishes of the same Holy Father, he wrote the rules and statutes of the College. As Cardinal Steinhuber informs us, Ignatius did so without having any set model before his eyes, but eventually produced a document with norms and guidelines that later served as models for countless institutions of the kind. Moreover, within the space of ten years, he founded other similar colleges in Italy, France, Spain - thirty-three in all during his life-time, from the College of Gandia in 1546 to that of Billou in France, opened in 1556, a few days before his death. St. Peter Canisius, called the second apostle of Germany, inherited Ignatius' zeal and was, in turn, responsible for the establishment of some 22 seminaries in Germany. When Pope Gregory XIII asked him what he could do for Germany, Canisius promptly replied: "Found seminaries that will give to the Catholic Church, year after year, priests according to the heart of God, well founded in doctrine and exemplary in their life".
3. *Concilium Tridentinum* IX, p. 483. The 16th chapter carried the following heading: "*Ut in cathedralibus ecclesiis certus initiatorum numerus educetur, ex quo tanquam ex seminario eligi possunt, qui digne ecclesiis praeficiantur.*
4. *Bullarium Romanum* VIII, p. 244.
5. George M. Anathil, SVD, *Theological Formation in India*, Poona, p. 14.
6. Epist. Xaver, I, p. 254, pp. 17, 26, 43, 74.
7. G. Anathil, *Theological Formation in India*, p. 17.
8. *Ibid.*, p. 14.
9. J. Wicki, S.J., *Der einheimische Klerus in Indien*, p. 69.

10. Francisco de Sousa, S.J., *Oriente Conquistado a Jesu Christo* P.I.C.I.D.I. p. 48;, Casimiro Christovam de Nazareth, *Mitras Lusitanas no Oriente* I, p. 293.
11. Carlos M. de Melo, *The Recruitment and Formation of the Native Clergy in India*, p. 85.
12. *Historia dos religiosos da Companhia de Jesus nos reinos e provincias da India Oriental,* 1614 (Mss kept in the Archives of the Jesuit Curia in Rome), ch. 6. In the opinion of Fr. Joao da Lucian Vida de S. Francisco Xavier I, p. 144), confirmed by Fr. Alexander Valignano Historia del Principio y Progresso de la Cia. de Jesus en las Indias Orientales, p. 55), it might stand comparison, as regards the dimension of the building, the number of the students, and of the professors, and the soundness of the instruction imparted there with the best and the most famous colleges of the Society in Europe.
13. A. Brou, S.J., Les Origines du clerg dans l'Inde, in *Revue d'Histoire des Missions*, VII, p. 49.
14. Andrew Lopez, A Short Account of the Missions under the charge of the Fathers of the Society of Jesus of the Malabar Province in the East India, Trichy, quoted by Anathil, Ibid., pp. 19-20.
15. G. Anathil, *Theological Formation in India*, p. 20; Ferroli, S.J., *The Jesuits in Malabar*, II, p. 33.
16. *Bullarium Patronatus,* Append. I, p. 77.
17. Carlos de Melo, *The Recruitment and Formation of the Native Clergy in India,* pp. 182-183. *Arquivo Portuguez Oriental*,Fasc. V, p. 699; .C.C. Nazareth, *Clero de Goa,* p. 716.
18. *Collectanea S.C. P. Fide*, I, p. 541 ss.
19. Rome was convinced that an essential condition for the promotion of the native clergy in India was the establishment of the ecclesiastical hierarchy. However before proceeding further, Rome felt the need of having accurate and detailed information about the state of the missions in India. It is in view of this that Propaganda sent Msgr. Clement Bonnand as the Apostolic Visitor of the entire mission territory of India. Msgr. Bonnand, Bishop of Drusipara, was the first Vicar Apostolic of Pondicherry. He was a Prelate of great prudence, gentleness and piety and had a long experience of missionary life in India. Hence the choice. (cf. C. de Melo, *The Recruitment and Formation of the Native Clergy in India,* pp. 277-305).
20. cf. C. de Melo, *The Recruitment and Formation of the Native Clergy in India*, pp. 282-284.
21. *Acta et decreta Conc. Prov. Bombayensis Primi*, p. 1.

Chapter 1

The Foundation of the Kandy Seminary
The Pioneers

The training of its future priests, as we have said, is a matter of vital importance for the existence and progress of the church in any region of the world. It could not be otherwise in India. We now begin to trace the early history of what has come to be known as the Papal Seminary of India.

Three distinguished personalities were called upon to play a leading role in the establishment and growth of this unique institution: Pope Leo XIII, the founder, Archbishop Ladislaus Michael Zaleski, the organizer and chief support, and Fr. Sylvain Grosjean, S.J., its first Rector. No history of this ecclesiastical institution would be adequate without a word about each of these three outstanding personalities.

I. Pope Leo XIII

Gioacchino Vincenz Pecci, descendant of a noble family of Carpineto, Frosinone, in Central Italy, was born on March 2,1810. He did his early studies at the Jesuit College of Viterboand later joined the Gregorian University for philosophy and theology, in preparation for the priesthood. After theology he did civil and canon law at the Sapienza, also in Rome. Ordained priest in 1837, he was in the course of the years assigned to important posts such as Apostolic Delegate at Benevento in the states of the Church, and in Perugia. Appointed Titular Archbishop of Damietta he was sent to Belgium in 1834 as Papal Nuncio. On his return to Italy he was nominated Bishop of Perugiain 1846. As a pastor he took keen interest in the formation of the diocesan clergy. Times were hard for the church in Italy, indeed in the whole of Europe. Liberalism and anticlericalism were active everywhere challenging the Christian Faith. To make the situation more dismal, the diocesan clergy was on the whole illequipped for their task as the intellectual and spiritual leaders of the People of God.

Archbishop Pecci was keenly aware of this painful situation. Already as Nuncio in Belgium he had shown a marked zeal for the cause of the higher training of the clergy. As Bishop of Perugia, realizing thoroughly the need of the times, he sought to make of his seminary as much a seat of learning as a home of virtue. Thus, in 1848, he revised the curriculum of studies followed in the seminary, drawing inspiration from the writings of the Angelic Doctor, Thomas Aquinas. He personally presided over the quarterly and yearly examinations of his seminarians and took a special interest in the philosophical debates periodically held there, as well as in the theses presented by the students as part of their academic work. In 1849 he established in the diocese a Saint Thomas Academy for ecclesiastics in general.

Elected Pope in the year 1878, Leo XIII turned his attention to the vast Indian "continent" so full of promise for the Church. Given his personal experience in the places where he had worked as priest, Bishop and Nuncio, it was but natural that here, too, his first thoughts should go to the clergy and their formation, and so he conceived the idea of one National Seminary for the whole of India. It was a new and daring initiative but the great Pope knew well that "there is nothing that is impossible to God" (Lk 1:37). Well, it is precisely about this time, that is, towards the year 1888 that Providence came to his help through the generosity of an English gentleman who donated the sum of £30,000 expressly for the establishment of a house of formation for priests in India. This gentleman, of whose name we are not quite certain - probably Mr. Woodhouse - took this decision after consulting Bishop Peterson, Auxiliary of Westminster, and Archbishop Stonon, an English Prelate posted in Rome.

This substantial gift could hardly have come at a more opportune time. Only a little earlier, after protracted and careful negotiations, the Holy See had come to a settlement with Portugal regarding the limits of the jurisdiction of the Portuguese Padroado in India. This momentous event opened the way for the realization of a project in which the Holy Father was greatly interested, namely, the establishment of the ecclesiastical hierarchy in India. The Pope made his decision public through his Apostolic Letter *Humanae Salutis* of September 1, 1886. He followed it up with the Bull *Post Initumin* which he designated the new dioceses erected in India, both metropolitan and suffragan.[1]

The Pope's next move was the establishment of a General Seminary for the training of native seminarians for the whole of India. Seminaries, as we have seen, did exist in several places in India, but most of them were situated outside British India, and in any case, they were, each of them, restricted to their own respective diocesan vicariates or regions. There was no National Seminary for the whole country, and this is what the supreme Pontiff was intent upon. This determination to do what he could for the formation of the native clergy in India[2] prompted him to go so far as to write a special Encyclical Letter in this regard to the bishops of the whole world: (*Ad extremas Orientis oras: de collegio clericorum*).

In this encyclical the Pope announced his intention of founding a new, National Seminary for India, and he appealed to the generosity of Catholics the world over for funds in favour of this initiative which he considered crucial for the future of the Church in that vast subcontinent.

More in concrete, he wanted young Indian candidates to the priesthood to be given an intellectual and doctrinal formation that would equip them fully for an active and fruitful ministry among all the faithful of the country, whether native or foreign: (*erudiantur ad omnem elegantiam doctrinae*). At the same time, their spiritual formation was to be such as to prepare them to spread the light of the gospel in the various regions of their immense homeland. As we have seen, this insistence of the Holy See on the formation of the native clergy in India was not something new and unexpected. It was in keeping with the constant tradition of the Church throughout its bimillenial history.

Another singular token of Pope Leo XIII's interest in and Affection for the Papal Seminary of Kandy was the special medal he ordered to be coined in the year 1894 on the occasion of his own sacerdotal silver jubilee. This medal had on one side the portrait of the Pope, and on the other that of St. Francis Xavier with the following inscription below it: XAVERIO AUSPICE ETPATRONO MDCCCLXXXXIV. On the same side but further away from the centre was another portrait of the Pope sitting on his throne framed by an oval-shaped inscription *FILII TUI, INDIA, ADMINISTRITIBI SALUTIS*. The Pope presented the medal, struck in gold to all the Heads of States, while many more, in silver and bronze, were sold all over the world. In July 1894 this medal was also sent, by the Pope's express will, to all the Ordinaries of the Apostolic Delegation.

The project of a General Seminary for the whole of India falls within this historical context. The Holy Father knew well enough that such a proposition was not likely to find immediate favour with the Heads of the Indian missions on the whole. Inspite of the repeated exhortations of the Roman authorities in this sense, the Indian Prelates - as will be seen in the following chapter - were not as yet psychologically prepared for such a step. It is to the credit of Pope Leo that, faithful to his own intuition, he went ahead with his plan. Sounded about this matter, Monsignor Aiuti, the Delegate Apostolic in India, suggested that such a seminary should be situated in Bangalore or Mysore and consequently entrusted to the Fathers of the Foreign Missions of Paris who were then doing missionary work in that part of the country. Pope Leo, however, had made up his mind to take the matter in his own hands for the time being. All that concerned the proposed General Seminary was then entrusted temporarily not to the Congregation de Propaganda Fide but to that of the Extraordinary Ecclesiastical Affairs presided over by the Pope's Secretary of State, Cardinal Rampolla.[3]

The Pope was fortunate enough to be able to find as his right hand man in the execution of this grave design a Prelate in whom he had full trust - Ladislaus

Michael ZALESKI, a Polish Monsignor who was at that time attached to the Papal Nunciaturein Paris. He recalled him to Rome and sent him to India on the "special private mission" of studying in loco the ways and means of founding a General Seminary in India in line with his design, and informing the Holy See about it.

II. Msgr. Ladislaus Michael Zaleski

The ancestral palatial house of the Zaleski's in Lithuania was the birth place of Ladislaus Michael, the son of Leon and Gabriela, of the Polish nobility. Graceful and dignified yet at the same time extremely simple, kind and cordial in his manners, a great friend of the youth and the children who spontaneously flocked around him, Zaleski was a man of broad vision, strong-willed, enterprising, selfless, and zealous for the glory of God and the good of the Church. In addition to his native Polish, he was fluent in Lithuanian, Russian, English, French, Italian and Latin. Surprisingly, he even mastered Tamil and Singhalese.

Before coming to India he had been on a diplomatic mission to Spain. He first came to India in the suite of Msgr. Agliardi, in 1884. On that occasion he had the opportunity of seeing a bit of India, North and South, and was present at the impressive ceremony of the establishment of the ecclesiastical hierarchy in 1884. He also took part in the Synod of Colombo and signed the resolutions passed by that Synod in January 1887.

On his return to Rome he was appointed Consultant to the S.C. de Propaganda Fide. The years 1889 to 1890 saw him in Franceas Councillor at the Papal Nunciature in Paris, but, as mentioned above, in 1890 he was sent back to India on a "special private mission" with definite instructions from Cardinal Rampolla in aletter dated October 31, 1890. He was thereby commissioned to study the ways and means of erecting in India a new, general or central seminary for the whole nation, or to put it in Zaleski's own words, "the creation of a National Seminary in Kandy, for the entire country, a college of higher theological studies for the young clergy in accordance with the programme of the Gregorian University in Rome", of which he had been a student. He was to go about this affair "without detriment to, and with deference to the official mission of the (then) Apostolic Delegate Msgr. Aiuti."

During his earlier stay in India, from 1884 to 1887, Msgr. Zaleski had been deeply impressed by the splendid work being done by the Belgian Jesuits in Bengal and Bihar (Ranchi), where they were endeavouring to promote the native clergy. There he had heard about-perhaps met?-the then Superior of the Mission, Fr. Sylvain Grosjean.

This time, in 1890, he arrived in India just in time to attend the jubilee celebrations in honour of St. Francis Xavier in Goa. This visit, too, was providential, for it confirmed him in his convictions about the problem of the native clergy in this country. Putting down in writing his impression of his visit to Goa, he says in one of his books the following: "We spent the following day in the Patriarchal Seminary of Rachol and I was quite free to examine it from close quarters; it strengthened my conviction that forming a native clergy in India was not such a difficult enterprise as it is generally made to be. True, each beginning has its difficulties, even serious ones, but see, herein Portuguese India, the entire local clergy is Indian, indigenous, and it is in no way inferior to that of many dioceses in Europe. I know of more than one diocese even in Italy, whose clergy is inferior to that of Goa... In this patriarchal Seminary of Goa, the rector alone is European – all the professors and all the students (360 in all) are Indian, native, and I can affirm that this seminary differs very little from those I had seen in Europe."[4]

After visiting Goa, Msgr. Zaleski proceeded to Bangalore to pay his respects to the Apostolic Delegate, Archbishop Aiuti, and acquaint him with the special mission entrusted to him by the Holy See. Aiuti introduced him to the bishops of his delegation through his circular letter of December 8, 1890. On December 30 Zaleski himself wrote a common letter to them about the purpose of his visit to India. Not satisfied with this he took it as part of his duty to contact the bishops personally and discuss with them matters related to his visit. He then sent a detailed report to Rome. He was still busy with this problem when news reached him of his appointment as the Apostolic Delegate to India in succession to Msgr. Aiuti who was recalled to Rome and then transferred to Munich as the Papal Nuncio to Germany.[5] Raised to the rank of Archbishop of the titular See of Thebes, Zaleski was consecrated by Archbishop Goethals, S.J., in Calcutta, in May 1892.

Zaleski filled this office for full twenty-five years and won the respect and esteem not only of Christians but of non-Christians as well, who were won over by his simple and friendly ways of dealing with them all. He took up residence in Kandy, but travelled a lot visiting the various dioceses of the country.[6] In these visits he covered a distance of about 75,000 miles. In addition to this, he greatly promoted the active apostolate of the laity in various parts of India, becoming thereby the precursor of what came later to be known as "Catholic Action".

Known for his love for the poor, the Apostolic Delegate was often seen entering the poorest huts to visit the sick and give them his blessing. His love for children too was proverbial. He wrote from Kandy: "Do not imagine that I live the life of a hermit here. On the contrary, all the children from neighbouring villages have become my friends. A score of them always potter about my garden and a few who can scarcely walk as yet sit with agrave expression on their faces in my verandah."[7] And in another letter: "A few days ago it occurred to me to count the number of children whom I gathered around me since I had settled in Kandy. There were ninety of them not counting the boys from the Catholic schools..." On February 9, 1892 he took a group of children for an excursion to Pidrutallagalla, the highest mountain in Ceylon. Writing to Cardinal Ledochowski on February

15, 1892 he tells him that of the 35 children who had been coming to him from the beginning, 18 had already received baptism. He was to baptize eight more within a few days and eleven of their parents were also getting ready for the sacrament.[8]

All this meant a lot of fatigue and loss of time, but Zaleski considered it an essential part of his mission as it enabled him to be in touch with the bishops, the clergy and the people, to study the situation of the Church in the various regions of his delegation, to encourage missionaries in their arduous and selfless task, and to bring these distant faithful closer to the head of the Church whom he, the Delegate, represented in a very special way. By order of the Pope he also presided as his delegate over the Provincial Synods in various places.[9]

Another important feature of Zaleski's personality is that of a writer. In spite of his busy schedule, the journeys up and down the country, and the hazards of health, he found the time and the patience to write several books - a dozen or more - in English, French, Italian and Polish, covering no less than 7761 pages, with another 6895 pages left in manuscript.

However, Zaleski will be remembered most of all for his ceaseless activity on behalf of the formation and development of the native clergy in India. So deep and personal was his interest in this cause that - as he candidly confesses in one of his letters to Grosjean - not only did he accept his commission to India eagerly and enthusiastically, but he almost solicited it for himself, fearing that otherwise it might be assigned to another person less acquainted with India and less sympathetic towards the Indian people and their beloved country.[10]

Msgr. Zaleski had visited and inquired into several seminaries and ecclesiastical colleges in various places in Europe and Asia, and was therefore well prepared for the special task assigned to him by Pope Leo XIII. One of the first steps he took in view of this special mission was to secure for himself as his right-hand man Fr. Sylvain Grosjean who had only recently been relieved of his office as Superior Regular of the West Bengal Jesuit Mission (comprising Bengal and Ranchi), and had been appointed Rector of St. Xavier's College, in Calcutta.

Once the Seminary was established in Kandy, not very far from the Delegate's own residence, Zaleski continued to remain in close touch with it: in fact, he looked upon it as his own creation. It was he who authorized the erection of new buildings on the campus and even closely supervised the works. He paid frequent informal visits to the seminary and conversed familiarly with the crowd of seminarians who gathered around him and with the members of the staff. He was informed about new admissions and eventual departures or dismissals, sanctioned the selection of new members of the staff, examined the accounts, and in many different ways, controlled the running of the seminary. With all good intentions, and probably without meaning to do so, he to some extent intervened - one would say unduly - in the regular administration of the institution as though he were its immediate head which, indeed, he was not. Fr.

Grosjean mentions this in passing in one of his letters. His own role as rector – Grosjean confesses - is reduced to being no more than a consultor or executor; it was the Delegate who decided everything concerning the Seminary, and he seemed hardly to think of delegating his powers.[11] He kept the funds in his own hands and passed on to the rector, from time to time Rs. 500/- or 3,000/- as need might arise, for paying the workmen, or for other expenses. The rector thus, became just a sort of executor of the Delegate's decisions.

As long as Grosjean was the rector there was no problem, for Grosjean knew well how to forget himself in order the better to safeguard peace and harmony in their mutual relationship. Later, however, one of his successors, probably Fr. Adessi, (as Fr. Ancot narrates in one of his letters), reacted differently. Obviously annoyed at the interference of the Delegate in the administration of the Seminary, he once sent to him a message through one of the Fathers to the effect that the Seminary was entrusted not to him, Zaleski, but to the Society of Jesus. Zaleski, we are told, became pale on hearing this, yet he did not take it tragically. Soon, he composed himself, and graciously invited the messenger to his carriage for a quiet ride around the beautiful Kandy Lake.

Zaleski had a great love for India and its people. It is instructive to see how positive he was in evaluating, for instance, the seminarians he met, hailing from the different regions of India. Thus, he writes: "We have in our Seminary agreat number of clerics from Malabar, very gifted and worthy boys they are..."[12] Again, referring this time to the clergy of Travancore and Cochin, he writes: "The clergy which is wholly indigenous, is little different from our own diocesan clergy. Some of them are well-educated and in behaviour and social relations very gentle and manly. They are ardent, and the best proof of their mettle is the piety and faith of their flocks. The rooms in their vicarages are not only clean and devoid of luxury, but I find them tastefully and elegantly furnished. Every one of them has a picked library of theological and ascetic literature."[13]

In the same vein, he has this to say about the children of the Paravars in Tamil Nadu: "I would have liked to have spent atleast a week in Tuticorin among the Paravars, the children of St. Francis Xavier as they proudly call themselves. There is a burning faith in this, the only totally Catholic tribe in India. Every single child there would gladly suffer a martyr's death for its faith. These boys neither allow me to say my Breviary, nor let me finish my meal. I was permanently surrounded by them, and what satisfaction it was to talk with them, what comfort to be allowed to peep into the depth of their uncontaminated, pious, tender souls."[14] In his visits to the parish priests the Delegate was always very considerate to them and made it a point during his stay with them to take over the Vicarage and become the host, in other words, he paid all the house expenses and "the parish Priest and his Vicar became his guests."[15]

In October 1916, a few months before the 25th anniversary of his appointment as Apostolic Delegate, he received from Rome the news that in the following Consistory he would be promoted to the Patriarchal See of Antioch, which naturally entailed his transfer to Rome. The news soon became public and caused a lot of consternation both among Christians and non-Christians, all of whom had at one time or the other experienced the friendliness and broadmindedness of the Polish dignitary.

Before leaving India he wrote two touching farewell letters, one to his brother Bishops, the other to the priests. To the priests he says among other things: "You know well, beloved sons, how I have always been very solicitous about the cause of the native clergy. The native priests called me their father, and truly, if love makes one a father, then certainly I was indeed a father to you. Now I bid you farewell, with a heavy heart, but ready to accomplish the Father's will. You will no more see my face, you "whom I ardently loved and who were my joy and my crown" (Phil. 3:1). If you truly love the Lord your God with all your heart and all your soul, with all your mind and all your strength, and love your neighbour as yourselves; if you have no other ambition than to restore all things in Christ, if you strive humbly for the salvation of souls, you will always experience the divine help; it will crown your apostolate with much fruit, and the God of peace and consolation will be with you always" (Kandy, November 1, 1916). These are words that reveal to us something of the writer's own interior life.

In his letter to the Bishops of India he says: "...for one fourth of a century I worked together with you in this vineyard of the Lord. I have been a witness both of the zeal and wisdom of the Bishops.... as well as of the zeal and onerosity of the Missionaries working under your direction.

Now I take leave of you, not to return to India anymore; but with my heart I shall remain always with you and if I am still able to render you any service in any way, I shall be extremely happy to do so.

All these years I have endeavoured to do the things that were of God, in faithful devotion to the Vicar of Christ. If I ever offended anyone of you, I now humbly ask him to forgive me. In all my actions and words, I always kept before my mind nothing else but the glory of God. I kept away from me any earthly consideration, mindful of the words of the apostle "If I sought to please men, I would not be the servant of Christ". And now I leave you with a fraternal embrace. Pray for me, so that just as we worked together in spreading the kingdom of God on earth, so we may also praise God together forever in heaven..." (Kandy, November 1, 1916).

Shortly afterwards he left for Rome. He died there nine years later, on 5 October 1925, at the age of 73. In his obituary note the "Catholic Directory" summed up his life in these words: "The best part of his life he had given to these lands, in whose service he had all but exhausted his physical strength...but won the affection of a people naturally ready to return love for love".

In his last will Msgr. Zaleski had expressed the desire to be laid to rest in the little church of Our Lady of Ostrabrama which he had built at his own expense at Ampitya, not far from the Seminary, and he had left a sufficient sum of money for the transfer of his remains to that shrine.[16]

Accordingly, there was a move in 1936 on the part of Kandyans to secure his body for the purpose. To meet the expenses it was suggested that an appeal be made to the Catholics of India, Burma and Ceylon. This suggestion did not meet with the approval of ecclesiastical authorities. It was war time and there were additional difficulties on that score. Zaleski, we learn, was not too friendly towards the British, and to get the thing done with the help of the Italian consul who showed himself willing to help, might lend itself to unnecessary misunderstandings.

In the course of time Ceylon became an independent nation with the new name Sri Lanka. As for the Papal Seminary, in 1955 it was transferred to India, to Pune (then Poona). The See of Poona was then occupied by Bishop Andrew D'Souza, himself an old student of Kandy. It therefore fell to Bishop Andrew's lot to approach the Italian and Polish authorities in Rome with his request for the transfer of the late Archbishop's remains to the Pontifical Seminary now functioning in his diocese. His request met with a favourable answer.[17]

Consequently, all the necessary formalities having been gone through, the "body" of this great friend of India was flown to Bombay on December 1, 1957. On the following day it was brought to Pune by His Excellency the Internuncio Archbishop Ronald J. Knox, who was accompanied by the Vicar General of Bombay, Msgr. V. Dyer. It reached Pune around 12.00 noon. Soon the seminarians carried the casket to the newly constructed large Seminary church. Here, after a short religious service, it was entombed at the foot of the main altar of the church and covered with a marble slab, bearing the following inscription:

D.O.M.

EXMUS DNUS
LADISLAUS MICHAEL ZALESKI
ECCLESIAE ANTIOCHENAE LATINORUM PATRIARCHA
QUI OLIM TITULARIS ARCHIEPISCOPUS THEBARUM
DELEGATUS APOSTOLICUS IN INDIIS ORIENTALIBUS
JUBENTE LEONE XIII SUM. PONT. INSTITUENDO CLERO
ANNIS XXIV CONTINUIS OPERAM NAVAVIT
WIELONAE IN LITHUANIA ANTE DIEM VII KAL. JUN. NATUS
A.D. M.D. CCC. LII
ROMAE III NONAS OCT. A.D. M. CM. XXV VITA FUNCTUS
QUEM EX-ALUMNI KANDIENSES
HUC TRANSLATUM PIE SARCOPHAGO CONDIDERE
A.D. M.CM. LVII

R. I. P.

Recording this event Bishop Andrew made the following statement: "The translation of the remains of Msgr. Zaleski to India is mainly due to the suggestion and effective move in Rome by our Msgr. Joseph Fernandez, Superior of the Missionary Society of Benaras. We old Kandyans are very happy about his success, and grateful to the Poles in Rome for their help" (3.12.1957). To complete this statement we cannot fail to mention the name of Brother, now Fr. Ishwar Prasad, of the Missionary Society of Benaras, who was then doing his studies at San Anselmo, in Rome, and was greatly instrumental in bringing about smoothly the much longed - for transfer.[18]

Archbishop Zaleski left to the Seminary a number of his books on India and Ceylon, and on the East in General; his furniture and crockery; the Crucifix of the Library; a marble clock, a thermometer over the weather chart, the palm trees planted by him around the house, and several other objects.

III. Father Sylvain Grosjean, S.J.

"One of the most outstanding missionaries in India": that is how one who knew him well, Archbishop Zaleski, expressed his appreciation and esteem for Fr. Grosjean. We have already met him in the course of this chapter and he will appear again in this historical account of the Papal Seminary, for this institution is, indeed, heavily indebted to him. For the moment we have only to point out briefly what role he played in the carrying out of Pope Leo XIII's far-sighted project of a General Seminary for the whole of India.

We are in the year 1892. Fr. Grosjean who had been Superior Regular of the "West Bengal Mission" till January 31 of that year was now posted to St. Xavier's College, Calcutta, as its Rector, a post he had previously held. He already foresaw that he was not likely to remain there long, for Archbishop Zaleski was in contact with the higher Jesuit authorities in Belgium and Rome, trying to secure from them Grosjean's services for the Papal Seminary due to be established in the country as soon as things were ready.

Accordingly, on July 1, 1892 Grosjean received a telegram from Kandy: "Reçu instructions; venez, urgent" - Zaleski. On the day following the Vice-Superior of the Mission received a similar telegram asking him to send Grosjean urgently to Kandy.

Fr. Grosjean was personally opposed to the idea of the Bengal-Bihar Mission being put in charge of the new seminary, and he had good reasons on his side. As former Superior of the Mission he was well acquainted with its problems. The missionaries of Chotanagpur were confronted at that time with the marvellous and overwhelming result of the pioneering apostolate of Father Lievens: natives flocked to him by the thousands seeking to become Christians, and the number was continuously on the increase. By this time there were more than 80,000![19] Where then to find enough missionaries to attend to their instruction and formation? Such being the situation how could the Mission take the additional burden of starting and running a National Seminary for the whole of India, and that one, too, situated far away in the South - in Ceylon - where the climate, the language of people, the customs and local usages were so different from those in Bengal or Bihar? Would this not mean the ruin of so promising a ministry as the one they were presently engaged in Bihar? True, Pope Leo and Zaleski had made up their mind about entrusting the seminary to Jesuits and to no other institute. The Holy Father himself had opted for the Belgian Jesuits for this mission, yet Grosjean asked himself whether it would not then bewiser and more prudent to get the Jesuits working in South India to take it up, for instance in Madurai, Calicut, Mangalore or Bombay? Besides, Grosjean was personally of the opinion that a common seminary for the north and south was impractical and destined to fail. Given the marked differences between the two parts of the country and the respective inhabitants, such a venture would never succeed. So he thought. Beside the differences in the language and customs, there were other factors to be taken into account. In the south, the problem of caste was particularly acute; similarly, there was the Padroado-Propaganda conflict not known in Bengal or Bihar. And so on.

True, in accordance with the directions received from the Pope himself, Zaleski had made up his mind to put the Jesuits, and nobody else, in charge of the seminary. Nevertheless, Grosjean, as we have said, asked himself whether it would not be more normal in that case, to entrust the work to anyone of the southern Jesuit Missions. Msgr. Zaleski, however, was adamant in his determination to secure Grosjean's services for the seminary. So, too, the Archbishop of Pondicherry, Msgr. Laouënan who advised Grosjean "blind obedience". They told him that his persistent refusal regarding a project so dear to the supreme Head of the Church might result in its being altogether dropped, and if so, he, Grosjean, would be responsible for this and accountable before God! Writing to Grosjean, Zaleski told him: "If I have insisted with the Holy See that it should be determined before hand to whom the seminary was to be entrusted this was simply in order to close the door to other projects which I could foresee. If I proposed the Belgian Province it is because I had seen you at work in Calcutta and because I was deeply convinced that the foundations you will give to the new Institute would be solid. Besides, the Very Reverend Father General hastened to confirm this choice. But the essential thing for me is that the Seminary should, from the very start, be directed by the Jesuit Fathers;.... The guarantee that the educational system of the Society gives will always be the same. Well, such aguarantee is necessary for our bishops."[20]

The end result of this all was that finally Grosjean yielded to the demands made on him, fearing - so he wrote to Father General - that by persisting in his refusal he might be responsible for jeopardising a work of the highest importance for the Church in India.[21]

This acceptance of a new mission which was so far from his habitual thoughts and preoccupations was a truly hard step which he at first tried to evade as best he could, but finally accepted though at much cost to himself. To make matters worse, his attitude in the whole matter was misunderstood by his superiors in Belgium and even by the new General of the Society, Reverend Father Luis Martin, who succeeded Fr. Anderledy in 1892, and did not know him. To them it looked as if Grosjean settled matters with the Delegate, Msgr. Zaleski, and then communicated to Belgium the result of what had been decided by Propaganda and the Delegate and accepted by him. This, however, was far from true. In reality it was heroic on the part of Grosjean to accept the care of the new General Seminary that was placed on his shoulders, much against his will. It is instructive in this regard, and highly edifying, to read the following passage of one of his letters written probably to his Provincial in Belgium.

He wrote: "... I do what I am told to do. The moment when Msgr. Zaleski made me foresee all this, when he summoned me to Bombay, towards the end of 1890, that moment, I say, was one of the bitterest I have ever experienced in my life. At the time, I was already exhausted after the endless worries and preoccupations of a long term of administration. My only desire and ambition was to go and be of help to some missionary in Bengal, to teach catechism to children and the poor, and do some good in some hidden village in the missions. The Fathers there know this well... Your Reverence knows well how much I tried at first to free the mission from the burden of the Seminary, and in doing so, to also free myself from it. But when I realized that all was in vain I gave up fighting against what might be God's will, and so I set myself to the work of finding the means to render service to the Missions of India in general, and to our Province in particular. This is my one single desire, and this is what sustains me, together with prayer, in the difficult situation in which I find myself at the moment."[22] Truly heroic!

We shall soon see Grosjean at work as Rector of the Seminary, so we can close this chapter with the following testimony of Msgr. Zaleski who had chosen him as his closest collaborator in the foundation of the Pontifical Seminary. Writing to the Jesuit Provincial of Belgium on March 7, 1899, Zaleski said: "Without the energy, the dedication, and the spirit of sacrifice of Rev. Fr. Grosjean, I would never have been able to set up this institution in the midst of the multiple difficulties that we had to face at its beginning. The great wish of our Holy Father would probably remain unfulfilled. The prestige that Fr. Grosjean enjoyed among all the bishops made the seminary popular. It is chiefly because Grosjean was at the head that almost all the bishops and missionaries looked at the new initiative with confidence. He is a man who during his long missionary career rendered enormous service to the Church in India".

Notes

1. Eight ecclesiastical provinces were thereby formed, as follows: 1. GOA, Primatial and Patriarchal See of the East Indies with the suffragan Sees of Damaun, Cochin and Mylapore; 2. VERAPOLY with Quilon; 3. MADRAS with Vizagapatnam and Hyderabad; 4. PONDICHERRY with Trichinopoly, Mysore, Coimbatore and Mangalore; 5. CALCUTTA with Krishnagar and Dacca; 6. BOMBAY with Poona; 7. AGRA with Allahabad and Lahore; 8. COLOMBO with Jaffna and Kandy, all in all 25 dioceses. (Msgr. Leo P. Kierkels, C.P., Apostolic Delegation of the East Indies 1884-1934, "Belmont", Bangalore, pp. 43-44).
2. This is made clear in the Decree of August 28, 1893 by which the Cardinal Prefect of Propaganda convoked the Provincial Councils in India. In this Decree Cardinal Ledochowski writes: "As the formation of a diocesan clergy selected among the natives is, in the mind of this Sacred Congregation, a matter of greater importance than others, let the fathers assembled in the respective synods take care not to leave it aside. They will thereby be able to decide by common consent, in keeping with the mind of the Fathers of the Council of Trent, how ecclesiastical seminaries could be established in each diocese or at least in each Ecclesiastical Province, for native clerics to be properly trained in the necessary disciplines". (Acta et Decreta Concilii Provincialis Bombayensis Primi, p. 1, quoted by Carlos de Melo, op. cit., p. 309).
3. H. Josson, Le Pre Sylvain Grosjean, S.J., Museum Lessianum, Louvain, 1935, pp. 214-215.; S. Grosjean, S.J., Historia Fundationis Seminarii Kandyensis (MS preserved in the Archives of the Belgian Province), p. 2.
4. Voyage aux Indes, p. 312ff.; Carlos de Melo, *The Recruitment and Formation of the Native Clergy in India*, p. 204f.
5. Referring to this matter, Archbishop Kierkels, Apostolic Delegate to the East Indies from 1931 to 1952, has the following remark to make:- "Concerning the Pontifical Seminary, it has been sometimes asserted that Msgr. Zaleski's mission took the matter out of the hands of Msgr. Aiuti, previously entrusted with it. But there is archival evidence that Msgr. Aiuti had no special commission concerning the subject, although Msgr. Zaleski was instructed to act with due deference to the general official mission of the Delegate". (Golden Jubilee of the Apostolic Delegation of the East Indies 1894-1934), "Belmont", Bangalore, p. 50). Be that as it may, it is certain that, nevertheless, whether merely consulted, or officially entrusted with the matter or not, Msgr. Aiuti took it upon himself to try to win over the Bishops of India to his own preference for Bangalore as the most suitable place for the General Seminary of which there was then question. He seems to have done so without any previous reference to Msgr. Zaleski. This is what, as Grosjean informs us, Zaleski himself told him. Besides, Grosjean himself, as well as four other Fathers of his Mission (Bengal-Ranchi) received from Msgr. Aiuti letters in this sense, dated 30 December 1890. The Fathers mentioned by Grosjean are Frs. Lafont, Neut, Lievens and Bruni. This may perhaps, give us the clue to the motives behind the rather sudden and unexpected transfer of Msgr. Aiuti from India in 1891, four years after his appointment to India (S. Grosjean, S.J., p. 23).
6. In a letter Msgr. Zaleski explains the principle behind his frequent travels in India:- "In my position, effective work can be done only by travelling, by visiting missions, by keeping in touch with the bishops, the clergy, the people; to further their apostolic work, to encourage by example and by work those who in their hard and sometimes fruitless work might lose heart; to strengthen their ardour and the faith of the people and, what is also important, to make these distant faithful feel closer to the head of the Church - to the Pope". (The Rev. Dr. Witold Malej, Patriarch Ladislaus Zaleski, p. 30).
7. *Idem, ibid.*, p. 53.
8. *Idem, ibid.*, pp. 54-55.

9. *Idem*, *ibid.*, p. 13.
10. *The Examiner*, 24 October, 1925, p. 510.
11. Actually, it was not a question of "delegating powers". These matters lay within the powers of the Rector of the seminary, they were part of his duty; the Delegate had not to give the powers to him in this regard. He needed no delegation from the Apostolic Delegate. However, that is how Zaleski understood his office. The following letter written much later, that is, in 1910, to the then Rector Fr. Julien Meunier, shows how meticulous Zaleski could be in asking for detailed information regarding the financial matters of the seminary:
    26 Sept. 1910
    JM Tres Revrend P. Recteur
    Veuillez me dire ce qu'il faut entendre par la rubrique "subsides" dans les comptes des accepta du terrain du Seminaire.
    Votre devoue
    L.M. Archev; de Thebes
    Delegue Apost.
    P.S. *Combien de cocotiers au rapport et combien deplantes qui ne rapportent pas encore, approximativement.*
12. Malej, *op. cit.*, p. 20.
13. *Ibid.*, p. 28.
14. *Ibid.*, p. 23.
15. *Ibid.*, p. 33.
16. *The Examiner*, 25 November, 1916, p. 474. The Church of Our Lady of Ostrobrama, Patroness of Lithuania, was built - as we said above - by Archbishop Zaleski at his own expense. It occupied a prominent position, overlooking the lake of Kandy and the town: an elegant temple in the form of a cross, able to hold some two hundred persons. It served as the parish church for the small group of Christians attached to the Seminary, and Fr. Grosjean was appointed its parish priest by Msgr. Pagnani, OSB. The following note found in the Seminary Archives written in Zaleski's own hand witnesses to his sense of humour. It is a sort of inscription apparently to be engraved on his tomb in the little church he built for himself in Kandy:
    HIC JACET HUJUS SACELLI FUNDATOR
    NE PERMITTAS, DOMINE, UT EJUS GHOST
    GEMENS ET SIBILANS IN TENEBROSA NOCTE
    TERREAT SEMINARISTAS.
    (Here, lies the Founder of this chapel. Do not permit, Lord, that his ghost groaning and hissing during the dark night frighten the seminarians).
17. Letter of the Rector of Kandy Seminary to the Delegate Apostolic, of 12 June 1955.
18. In Memoriam, the Most Rev. Msgr. Ladislaus M. Zaleski, p. 14-17.
19. H. Josson, S.J., *op. cit.*, p. 151.
20. Letter of Msgr. Zaleski to Fr. Grosjean 14 February, 1891, Josson, S.J., *op. cit.* p. 219f.
21. Letter to Fr. General (cf. Josson, S.J., *op. cit.*, p. 220f).
22. H. Josson, S.J., *op. cit.*, p. 260.

Chapter 2

The First Beginnings (1893-1898)

As we said above, Monsignor Zaleski came to India in 1890 with definite instructions from Pope Leo XIII to study in loco the ways and means of establishing in India a central or "National Seminary" for the formation of the native clergy for the whole country. This seminary was to be entrusted to the Fathers of the Society of Jesus, more concretely, to the Belgian Jesuits of the northern Mission of Bengal-Ranchi, about whom the Pope had been amply informed by Zaleski himself. The Pope wanted the Seminary to be erected without delay, so that its inauguration could coincide with his own episcopal golden jubilee: it was to be a souvenir of that jubilee, which would occur on February 19, 1893.

During his earlier visit Zaleski had spent several months in India, and had the opportunity to get acquainted with the situation of the Catholic Church in the country. This time he took up residence in Kandy (Ceylon). One of the first things he had to do was to finalize, in agreement with the Bishops, the choice of the place where the Seminary in question was to be situated. Msgr. Peterson had suggested Rome as the place best suited for the purpose. It would be the "Indian College" in Rome parallel to similar existing national ecclesiastical "colleges" in the city: the French College, the Irish, the Portuguese College, etc. The students resided in the College, but frequented the courses of philosophy, theology, etc. at the Gregorian University, or in any of the other approved ecclesiastical Institutes of higher studies in Rome. Zaleski, however, had his own arguments against this proposal. It often happened, he said, that young Indian candidates trained in Rome, did not show themselves too willing, on their return to their dioceses, to take up lower posts: they had a sort of "superiority complex", and this spoiled somehow their relationship with their bishops. Zaleski's own preference was for Kandy. This little township was situated in the island of Ceylon which was then part of India, though separated from the mainland by the sea. Zaleski saw a two fold advantage in this circumstance.

In Kandy

Evidently, the bulk of the Seminary population would come from India. If the Seminary were situated within the Indian territory, it would be rather close to the native dioceses of the students, with the result that they could be too easily affected by the various problems that agitated British India at that time. First and foremost, the entire nation was under the impact of the nationalist movement aimed at securing India's independence from Great Britain. It would therefore be difficult for the young seminarians not to be drawn into this struggle, and Zaleski thought this might distract them from their studies and possibly even have a negative effect on their prayer life and spiritual progress. Secondly, in India, and particularly in the southern part of the country, the caste problem was rather strong, even in Christian families. (It was known, for instance, how, in Coimbatore, parents had forcibly withdrawn their sons from the seminary, when they came to know that they had to take their meals at the same table, side by side with companions of a lowercaste). Such being the state of things, it was thought more advisable to separate the young candidates to the priesthood forsome time from their home environment and give them an opportunity to grow in their priestly training and their spiritual life in a place more distant and free. Kandy was, indeed, well suited for this purpose. It had the added advantage of being free also from the Padroado-Propaganda conflict we alluded to in the previous chapter.

Zaleski had certainly discussed these points in detail with the Roman authorities, perhaps even with the Pope himself, and had received pertinent instructions in this regard. However, he had still to sound the mind of the local bishops and talk matters over with them. This is what he tried to do as soon as he landed in India, this time at the end of November 1890.

Zaleski knew well - as we have said - that the Apostolic Delegate, Msgr. Aiuti was all for Bangalore as the place most suitable for the proposed Seminary, and would naturally like to hand it over to the Fathers of the Foreign Missions of Paris who were already working in that area.[1] Zaleski, however, had different thoughts about this matter. So, on February 6, 1890, he, on his part, sent a circular to all the members of the Indian hierarchy, as well as to the Major Superiors of the religious informing them about his mission and asking them to let him know their considered view on that question. Not satisfied with letters, he made it a point to meet the Ordinaries of each place and discuss with them personally the pros and cons of the places suggested for the seminary, namely, Bangalore, Tranquebar, Poona (now called Pune) and Kandy. He personally favoured this last place, and so convincingly did he present to them the reasons for his preference, that, as a result, most of the bishops were won over to his view. Now it only remained to him to determine the exact locality in Kandy where the seminary was to be built.

Since it had already been decided by the Pope himself to put the new seminary in the hands of the Jesuits, Msgr. Zaleski, with the authorization of Cardinal Rampolla, took the initiative of inviting the Jesuit Major Superiors of India to come to Kandy for a common meeting with him during which they would examine together many of the issues connected with this project.

Of the five Major Superiors only three were able to come: Fr. Hermann Jurgens of Bombay, Fr. Barbier of Madura, and Fr. Grosjean himself, of Bengal-Ranchi. By June 29, 1891, they were all in Kandy, the guests of Msgr. Zaleski. The agenda had been very carefully prepared. Among the points to be discussed were the following: the advantages of Kandy, the choice of the exactsite for the seminary, the programme of studies, the administration, other relevant questions.

The four of them met every morning. As each point was taken up, Zaleski invited each of the three to present his views in all freedom and frankness. Eventually, all agreed that Kandy was an ideal place for the seminary. So, far as studies were concerned, they would abide by the "Ratio Studiorum" prescribed for the scholastics of the Society of Jesus, and followed at the Gregorian University in Rome. However, our students would have a year or two of humanistic studies, Latin and English, before beginning philosophy. Also, it was understood that the intellectual and spiritual formation imparted to the seminarians in Kandy should be such as to prepare them for work and ministry not only among their own countrymen but among Europeans or other foreigners as well. At the end of their meetings each of the three, independently from the other two, wrote his own report of the session and handed it to Monsignor who translated it into Italian, in view of the Roman readers.

Besides, Fr. Jurgens was asked to draw up a Scheme of rules and regulations for the use of the future seminarians. These again were drawn up mostly from the *Ratio Studiorum* of the Society, and from the rules of certain Roman Colleges, such as the Urbanianum, the Pio Latin-American College and the Mangalore Seminary.

The "Schema" was sent to all the bishops of India, and then, after a few changes and corrections, the entire project was forwarded, together with Zaleski's observations, and the reports of the superiors mentioned above, to the Sacred Congregation in Rome, by the end of December, 1891.

The question of the seminary was discussed in Rome on February 1, 1892. Zaleski's report made an excellent impression there, with the result that on March 15 he was appointed Apostolic Delegate in India in succession to Msgr. Aiuti. It is Msgr. Jacques della Chiesa - the future Benedict XV - who in a private letter addressed to Zaleski informed him that "*vous yavez fait belle figure; maintenant on peut le dire, puisque votre nomination en est la conséquence*". Archbishop Aiuti was rather unexpectedly recalled to Rome, and then posted to Munich as the Papal Nuncio to Germany. Soon after, on June 15 Zaleski was informed that the Papal

Seminary would be established in Kandy, "a locality approved by 12 Ordinaries". By Protocol 7903 of August 6, 1892 he was further instructed to communicate hence forward with Propaganda, and no longer with the S. Congregation of Extraordinary Affairs, which had only temporarily and by way of exception taken the matter in its own hands.[3]

The choice of Kandy, so much favoured by Zaleski, was nevertheless, not agreeable to some of the missionaries working in India and Ceylon. Among these were the Oblates of Mary Immaculate. True, Kandy itself was under the Benedictines; yet, due to lack of personnel, they feared they might have to give up the mission. The Archbishop of Colombo, Msgr. Bonjean, who was an Oblate of Mary Immaculate, and his confrères, were aware of this and hoped that Kandy might eventually come to them: they would then be the only missionaries in charge of the Catholic Church in the island. They were therefore understandably rather adverse to the entry of the Jesuits into "their island". This is what Zaleski himself told Grosjean.[4] The Benedictines, on the contrary, together with their Bishop, Mgr. Pagnani, O.S.B., were only too eager to welcome the sons of Ignatius to their diocese. In fact, they were among the first to send their scholastics to the new seminary, as soon as it began to function in Kandy.

No sooner did the news of the approval of Kandy by Romereach Msgr. Zaleski, he hastened to wire to Grosjean summoning him urgently to Kandy. A second telegram to the same effect was sent to the Vice-Superior of the Bengal Jesuit Mission. Accordingly, Fr. Grosjean left Calcutta on July 5, 1892 by train, reached Tuticorin on 11 and was heartily welcomed by Zaleski on 12. Here mained a guest of the Apostolic Delegate up to May of the following year, after the Seminary was opened.

As we saw in the previous chapter, Kandy had been chosen as an ideal place for the future seminary, yet the exact locality had yet to be determined. This is what Zaleski and Grosjean had now to do, before anything else.

Kandy is a little town nestled in a valley surrounded on all sides by hills of 500, 800, even 1000 feet high, by gardens and parks and a beautiful lake which reflects in its waters a goodpart of the town. It had been the last strong hold of the Sinhalese kings before Ceylon became a Crown Colony of the British Empire in 1815. Grosjean arrived there on July 12,1892. From that day on, every afternoon, the two of them were seen walking up and down the town trying to select the most suitable spot for the construction of the seminary, and one that was not too dear. They intended to purchase some 280 acres of land, but without letting the different owners suspect that it was for them, else, as they rightly surmised, the prices would immediately shoot up. So, they had recourse to a stratagem. They contacted a friendly neighbour, one Mr. William Goonetilleke, Municipal Inspector, told him about their intentions, and let him look for a convenient locality for the seminary, and then negotiate with the different owners the purchase of the land.

While this man went out on his err and, Zaleski and Grosjean stayed at home praying. They started a novena in honour of St. Michael, Msgr. Zaleski's Patron Saint. On September 29, the feast day of the Archangel, they offered Mass commending their intention in a special way to St. Michael. On the ninth day of the novena Goonetilleke came to them with the news that he had discovered a place that seemed to him well suited for their purpose: the hillock of Ampitya, belonging to different owners.

As soon as they could, Zaleski and Grosjean went to have a look, taking a walk in the jungle. They were brought to a place that was open and commanded a magnificent scenery. It seemed to them truly an ideal place for an institution of ecclesiastical formation. It was surrounded by hills and valleys, the great river Mahavali Ganga and the streams, the Dumbara Valley, Lizard Point, the Knuckles, Matara-Patara and Hatara. Both agreed that this was, indeed, a most appropriate setting for the seminary. Saint Michael had heard their prayer and they were happy. They then authorized Goonetilleke to start acquiring the land bit by bit, now 6 acres, then 20 or 30, and so on. He had to face difficulties, but Saint Michael came to their aid and so he was able gradually to purchase upto 180 acres of continuous land, to begin with. He then sold it to the Delegate Apostolic in 1893.

Thinking that Mr. Goonatilleke was buying the land for his own use, the owners sold it to him at the normal price, but no sooner was it known that the land was meant for the Apostolic Delegate, the prices began to shoot up enormously. Nevertheless, more land was purchased adjoining the one that had already been acquired, until the total extension of the property covered noless than 250 acres, costing in all Rs. 41,228.

Once the land was bought, the work of clearing it began. All useless vegetation that covered the ground was burned up, fruit-bearing trees were planted all over, paths and roads were opened up in the jungle in all directions. This "operation" went on forfull two years and cost as much as Rs. 10,457. Similarly, the construction of the seminary itself took two years to complete.

Seminary Opened

Zaleski, however, could not wait until then to inaugurate his seminary. So, on March 7, 1893, he sent a circular to the Indian bishops informing them that in his paternal benevolence towards the Indian Missions, Pope Leo would like the inauguration of the Papal Seminary to coincide with his own episcopal golden jubilee as part, as it were, of the jubilee celebrations. In order therefore to conform to the wishes of the Holy Father, he, Zaleski, had already rented a bungalow belonging to a private family, not far from his own residence. The new seminary would temporarily function there, till the proper building was completed. He then requested the various Indian Prelates to send their students to Kandy. As for the courses to be followed there, besides a year or two of humanities, or rhetoric

(Latin and English), they would have three years of philosophy and four of theology.

In answer to this letter, only three students were present in Kandy when the Seminary was actually opened in May 1893: one from Tuticorin, another, a Syro-Malabar by rite from Trichur, and the third, an Anglo-Indian, from Agra.

The first of these, Dominic Swaminather, arrived at Kandy by train, on 23 April, 1893, around midnight. He inquired about the seminary, but no one seemed to have heard anything about it. So, dying of hunger and fatigue, after the long journey from Tuticorin, he knocked timidly at the door of the Benedictine Monastery. Nobody heard the call and so the poor lad had no other choice than to spend the night on the floor of the verandah of the cathedral near-by. There they found him in the morning, and accompanied him to the Delegate's residence where his agony ended when he was welcomed with open arms by Monsignor and Fr. Grosjean. One of the first things they did was to cut off his "uchikudumi" - the little tuft of hair kept in accordance with the local usage in Tamil Nadu. He was also relieved of the gold-emerald ear-rings he wore.

On that very day, April 24, another young man arrived: Joseph Chereath, a Syro-Malabar candidate from Trichur. A third one came a few days later: William Smith, from Agra. He had started for Ceylon earlier than the other two, but due to the distance, was the last to arrive. Evoking this circumstance, several years later, Fr. Swaminather liked to say that inchoative William was the first seminarian of Kandy, but terminative, it was he who could claim the distinction of being the first Kandyan!

The three seminarians took up residence in the bungalow rented for the purpose - Westcliffe House. The meals for all were prepared at the Delegate's residence.

Classes began most probably on May 4 with these three students, plus five Benedictine scholastics, one of whom later became the Bishop of Kandy, Msgr. Beckmeyer. In July more arrived from various quarters, namely Aloysius Ignatius, for Colombo; three of Syro-Malabar Rite Augustine Kandathil, Cyriac Vettikapallil and Mathew Pallikunnel, for Ernakulam and Changanacherry; Andrew Kalathil, Michael Nalavareth, Joseph Suarez and Joseph Chaminikodath, for Verapoly and Cochin; Joseph Maria Aloysius and S. Siluvaimuttu and Jaganather, for Trichinopoly; Henry Norman, Albert Cotter, Joseph Rogers and Henry Fairhall for Agra; Vincent Fernando for Galle; John Ribeira and Karl Fonseca for Quilon, and Jerome Pereira for Kandy. A second house had to be rented to accommodate them all – "Harley House", situated higher up between the Apostolic Delegation and Westcliffe. Given the situation of the two Houses, those who stayed in Westcliffe house had to climb up for their classes, while those at Harley House had to come down for meals.

They had, at the beginning, only one priest to look after them: Fr. Grosjean. For some time, he was the factotum there: rector, professor, spiritual director, etc. – all in one! For lack of professors, he made use of one or the other among the seminarians who happened to be more advanced in studies, to coach their companions in Latin or English. One of them, for instance, was Andrew Kalathil, T.O.C.D. He, however, fell seriously ill in November and expired on December 3, 1893, after an illness borne with admirable patience.

The seminarians also helped as linen-keepers, prefects of the servants, infirmarians, and what not! A fine spirit of solidarity, love, and service united them to gether into one family. Writing to his Provincial in Belgium, Fr. Grosjean had this to say about them: "Given the variety of States, languages and castes, they could expect a lot of difficulties in the common life of the Seminary. Actually the missionaries as well as the bishops could hardly believe that a National Seminary for the whole of India would be able to function harmoniously with Indians coming from such different backgrounds. However, the way things here turned out shows that far from confirming their fears and apprehensions, exactly the contrary happened. No difficulty was experienced at all on the ground of caste, for instance, quite the contrary of what was happening in some of the diocesan seminaries in the south... Kandy was far removed from their home dioceses with the result that such differences seemed not even to be noticed by the seminarians". Just an example: out of precaution, and in attention to Brother Swaminather, Grosjean had warned the cook not to serve him meat dishes. But as soon as he came to know this, it is the Brother himself who, though he came from Tamil Nadu, went personally to the cook and told him not to continue this practice. Their home usages, he said, did not count when they were out of their place, and so he would go along with the rest and follow the local custom, like the other members of the community.

In the following year - 1894 - they all began Philosophy; three years later, theology, with eleven students. On the staff there were, by this time, besides the Rector, two other Fathers, four scholastics, two Coadjutor Brothers, all Jesuits. Together with 27 philosophers and 26 juniors they made all in all acommunity of 73.

The number of students went on increasing till in 1910 they were 99. In 1897 three Benedictines were ordained priests; in 1898 the first diocesan priest received the priesthood, a Ceylonese, V. H. Fernando, for Galle; and in 1900 the first ten, fully formed in Kandy, Fr. Swaminather and his companions.

Seminary Formation

All this made good news, it is true, and yet, more had still to be done in this direction, for even after such constant reminders from Rome, the response from our Church leaders was still rather slow and cautious. Some still thought that Indians were not yet fit for the priesthood. Others were of the opinion that they could be ordained, yes, but only to be placed in subordinate roles, under the direction of Western Prelates. Others however felt strongly that Indians were quite capable of holding posts of leadership in the Church in India, provided they were given a correspondingly thorough intellectual and all-round formation (Capuchins, Salesians, Jesuits).

Incidentally, even as late as the year 1935, Fr. Wladimir Ledochowski, the General of the Society of Jesus, writing to Fr. L'Hoir, then Rector of Kandy insisted on the same idea. He said: "...You will have to find (on the spot) men capable of teaching from now on in the Kandy Seminary. The views of the Holy See are quite clear (in this respect): it is eager to raise the level of ecclesiastical studies. To give an adequate response to this desire of the Holy See, Kandy must have professors numerous and competent enough to be compared to those of a Collegium Maximum of the Society...In the choice you make I would request you not to exclude Indians. On the contrary, it is necessary in this matter to take into account the desire of the Holy See. As you know, it wants to see that more and more Indians are made to enter into the catholic intellectual movement". (Letter of July 21, 1935). Father Ledochowski stressed this point again and again in his letters to Jesuit Superiors in India (cf. *Acta Romana*, 1936). So, too, did his successor, Fr. J. B. Janssens (letter of September 8, 1938).

It is the same idea that is expressed in the Statutes of the Kandy Seminary, of 1940. Speaking of the nature and end of the faculties, art. 2 of the Statutes says: "*Pontificiae Facultates Kandienses eo fine erectae sunt ut Auditores in disciplinissacris secundum doctrinam catholicam altius instituantur atque adfontium cognitionem laborisque scientifici usum instruantur; etsic pro singulari hujus Athenaei ratione excultiores operarii evangelici ex tota India praeparentur ad fidei christinae propagationem et sacri ministerii officia in Indorum regionibusobeunda.*"[6]

Such exhortations coming from the highest authorities of the Church and the Society ended by producing tangible results to the extent that in the course of the years the Kandy Seminary acquired among other institutions of the kind a certain reputation for academic excellence.

However, not only studies but other aspects of the formation of future priests were also duly attended to. Regular discipline was enforced. A fixed time-table regulated the actions of the day, with time marked for rising and going to bed, for the prescribed exercises of piety, for classes, study, recreation, meals and sleep. Silence was insisted upon, not just as a prescription, but as the atmosphere demanded by a life of prayer, recollection, study, spiritual growth and fraternal charity. No student could leave the premises without due permission. Cleanliness and tidiness regarding both each one's person and one's belongings was insisted upon. Seminarians were not allowed to go home during the entire time of their priestly formation that is at least seven years, except for very grave reasons, at the discretion of the Rector. They were ordained priests at the end of their theology and they could go home only after celebrating their "first Holy Mass" in the Seminary itself. Similarly a certain exercise of active apostolate or ministry was considered an essential part of their formation, such as the teaching of catechism and helping in the parishes around. As a result, there was regular contact between the seminarians and the neighbouring people whom Fr. Grosjean found to be very open and docile, and so he was hopeful of much fruit among them.

Speaking of these youngsters in the Seminary, Fr. Van der Aa, S.J., who came from Belgium in February, 1895, wrote with esteem and admiration of "These young men of different castes and races serving by turns and reading at table, sitting side by side without any distinction of class or clan, passing on plates and water from one to another without any fear of being sullied, practising the usual penances common in religious houses such as reciting grace before and after meals with arms out stretched, eating on their knees, making their self-accusation in public, etc." They did manual work for one hour on ordinary days; they helped in the sacristy, in gardening, cultivation, book-binding, and other types of work.[7]

The students at first reacted negatively to manual work: "We have come here to study, not to do manual work", they said. But when they were told that the Rector of the Seminary, and the Apostolic Delegate himself would join them in this humble occupation, they relented.

Their habitual dress was white cotton cassock on usual days, but for Holy Mass and other religious ceremonies they wore a blue cassock with red sash, as in the Roman Colleges.

In due time, following the directions of Msgr. Zaleski, more land was acquired, a few kilometres away from the seminary, for a "villa" where the students spent their weekly holidays and the summer vacation. Zaleski had in mind buying another convenient place in the hills for summertime, but such a plan never materialised.

At last, by the end of June 1899, the main building was ready for use. By the end of July it was able to accommodate more than a hundred seminarians representing twenty dioceses. Other buildings were added, as need arose, in the course of the years. Giving his impression of Kandy, in 1893, Msgr. Van Reethe, S.J., Bishop of Galle, could write: "We are here as in an immense botanical garden, surrounded by woods, mountains and fine sunlight..."[8]

The Financial Situation of the Seminary

What about the finances? Well, the financial situation of the house was never, at any time, easy or comfortable. The funds were in the hands of the Delegate, and what he regularly sent to Grosjean was not always sufficient to meet the needs of this young, growing institution, all the more so, that the Rector could never bring himself to limit the number of admissions because of financial difficulties. Instead, in order to remedy the lack of means, he had recourse to begging. Thank God, his friends in Belgium were generous and ever ready to come to his help, and so, too, at times, his superiors there. However, inspite of all his efforts, the situation remained precarious. He wrote to the Provincial: "If you knew what we have, you would be surprised! We have the necessary, it is true, but we have also the practice of poverty... The rooms we occupy are poorer than those of any of our communities in Belgium. We have nothing that is not truly modest... In Bengal I never felt poverty to the extent we are experiencing it here these last months.[9]

Nevertheless, ironically enough, it fell to Grosjean's lotas we said, to be blamed by Rome for a situation that was not of his making. For while he was totally free in all that pertained to the government of the seminary and the formation of his seminarians, he had *no say whatever* in the financial administration of the institution which remained with the Apostolic Delegate. At a certain moment Cardinal Ledochowski came to the decision of writing to the General of the Society, asking him to replace Fr. Grosjean by another man, since the finances of the seminary were in a deplorable state (*omnino perturbata*). Grosjean could not remain insensitive to this misunderstanding in his regard, but a thoroughly supernatural man that he was, he took it in his stride quite peacefully and wrote to his Provincial that Father Adessi, the one chosen to succeed him, was most welcome at any time. The building of the seminary was almost complete, he wrote; as to the finances, Adessi will judge forhimself...

Fr. Thomas Adessi who was at that time Rector of the Jesuit theologate of St. Mary's, left Kurseong, on May 15, 1899. According to Cardinal Ledochowski's letter, he was to take in his hands the administration of "the buildings under construction". Evidently, there was a misunderstanding here. In reality, the construction of the buildings was never at any time Grosjean's responsibility; it was in the hands of the Delegate Apostolic. Adessi received, in Kandy, his decree of appointment from Brusselson June 13, and on 14 he took over the rectorship of the Seminary. Grosjean was transferred to Kurseong. Since he had been Superior at Kandy already for about six years, all thought this was just a normal, routine change of personnel, nothing more.

Fr. Grosjean Transferred

Fr. Grosjean remained in Kandy as a simple member of the community for another two months. The young seminarians whom he had served all these years so generously, without sparing himself, in the least, were distressed to hear about his transfer and gave unmistakeable proofs of their appreciation, love and gratitude to one who had done so much for them. Father Grosjean left Kandy on August 12, 1899. On his way to Calcutta he visited Galle, Madurai, Trichy, Shembaganur, Madras and Bombay. He arrived at Calcutta on September 4 and left the following day for Kurseong, where he took up his work as Professor and Minister of the house.

In an old leaf found in the Seminary Archives, we have the following portrait of the first Rector of the Kandy seminary: "The portrait we have of him (Fr. Grosjean) is excellent, and quite characteristic of him as he was in familiar intercourse. Read his life by Fr. Josson and the idea of him will expand and grow and cause you to wonder and say of him with the Very Reverend Father General

Anderledy: *vir magnis caeptispromptus et audax*: a man ready and bold to launch out into great enterprises.

He was a middle sized man, without an ounce of extra flesh; quick in his walk but steady in his movements and in his gestures if he made any. He was always active but never gave you the impression of hurrying you; he had always time to let you speakand was attentive to any idea you would suggest. His speech was clear, perhaps overmuch articulated, from the need of making a somewhat husky voice carry far. In French they say: to govern is to foresee, and Fr. Grosjean was a master man in planning and foreseeing. The outline of what he planned was vigorous and so was the execution; no difficulty was able to dishearten him." As we see, Zaleski had found the right man for his job.

Notes

1. H. Josson, S.J., Le Pere Sylvain Grosjean, S.J., Museum Lessianum, Louvain, 1935, p. 214.
2. Idem, ibid., p. 222.
3. Mgr. Leo P. Kierkels, C.P., Golden Jubilee of the apostolic Delegation of the East Indies, "Belmont", Bangalore, p. 52.
4. Sylvain Grosjean, S.J., *Historia Fundationis Seminarii Kandyensis* Msspreserved in the Archives of the North Belgian Province, Louvain, p. 18.
5. There seem to be some uncertainty regarding the exact date on which classes were opened at the Kandy Seminary. In his Manuscript History Fr. Grosjean states clearly that the first two seminarians to come to Kandy arrived there at the seminary on 24th April (Swaminather, from Tuticorin, and Joseph Chereath, from Trichur) and the third one, William Smith from Agra, on the 27th of the month. He then adds: Mense Maio, quarta, ut puto, die, coepi docere tres saeculares alumnos cum quinque benedictinis.

   This means that at the time he wrote his "Historia Fundationis" Grosjean seemed to be not quite certain about the exact date of the inauguration of the classes in Kandy, hence the clause "ut puto"; yet there is no such doubt or uncertainty regarding the days of the arrival of the first three students, namely April 24 and 27. In his Lettres de Kandy, Fr. J. B. Van Der Aa, S.J., who was professor in Kandy for several years, tells us quite simply that "the seminary was inaugurated on May 4" (p. 32). It is therefore, strange that H. Josson, S.J., the biographer of Fr. Grosjean, should give May 17 as the date of the arrival at Kandy of Swaminather, the first candidate (op. cit., p. 241). Yes, strange because, from his references one can see that he had in his hands the text of Grosjean's Historia Fundationis where, as we have seen, it is clearly stated that the first three seminarians to come to Kandy arrived there "towards the end of April" sub finem mensis Aprilis 1893 p. 30), two on the 24, one on the 27. Josson, it seems to me, is mistaken here and so, too, the "Silver Jubilee Souvenir and the Souvenir of the "Golden Jubilee Celebrations" (Nov. 30 - Dec. 3, 1946), p. 20. How to account for this confusion of dates? It seems to me that the origin of this mistake may be the following passage in Grosjean's Manuscript where, on p. 66, he writes: "Kandyae per 10 menses a die scilicet 12a. Julii 1892 ad diem 18 am. (ut puto) mensis Maii subsequentis anni habitavi apud Delegatum apostolicum, in domo ad caput amoenissimi lacus Kandyensis sita". That is to say, till May 17 or 18 - even after the classes had started on May 4 - Grosjean continued to stay at the Delegation. He went daily to Westcliffe House to give classes to his three seminarians, and probably spent the day withthem. From 18 May he took up actual residence at the seminary (Westcliffe House), hence I surmise, the discrepancy regarding the date of the inauguration of the Papal Seminary.

6. "The Pontifical Faculties of Kandy were established with this end in view, namely, that the students of the Athenaeum be instructed in the sacred disciplines of catholic doctrine of a higher academic standard and adequately formed in the art of consulting the sources and doing scientific work. Consequently, in tune with the method followed by the Athenaeum, better trained evangelical labourers taken from all over the country will be prepared for the mission of propagating the Christian faith and exercising the sacred ministry in the various regions of India". (*Statuta Facultatum*, Art. 2).
7. H. Josson, S.J., *op. cit.*, p. 273.
8. H. Josson, S.J., *op. cit.*, p. 266.
9. *Idem, ibid.*, p. 286.

Chapter 3

Struggle Towards Growth (1899-1918)

Father Adessi was the second Rector of the Papal Seminary of Kandy. He was well prepared for this post through the experience he had gained as Professor and Rector of the Jesuit Theological Faculty of St. Mary's, Kurseong.

A deeply spiritual man, kind and gentle, quick in assessing the character and qualities of those who came in contact with him, he was also a sure, understanding and encouraging guide to those who sought his advice and came to him with a sincere mind and a generous heart. Even after they had left the seminary, the young priests toiling in the Lord's vineyard had recourse to the advice of their former Rector in the various problems with which they happened to be confronted, in their life as missionaries. His letters to them show something of the depth of his own inner life of prayer and union with God, of total trust and confidence in God's fatherly love for us, his children, as well as of his concern and solicitude for his former seminarians.

An example: To one of his confidants he writes: "Confidence, even boundless confidence in our Lord, and leave everything to him". And he continues: "St. Philip Neri would have preached to my son cheerfulness and confidence. Learn this lesson for later. If a young man has the excess of humility, a certain habitual fright, a continual dissatisfaction with himself, you would do him great harm if you were to mortify him, except in the way in which I used to mortify you: namely, not allowing you the satisfaction of telling all the details of your faults, of reading a paper you had prepared for my inspection, etc. Self-love feeds on that excess of humility in pandering to one's weaknesses, etc. To such as these St. Philip would have given a good box in the ears and nothing else. So, believe me, put away false humility. Take and hold all that brings you joy, all that makes you realize that really Our Lord loves you".

And where is humility?, you ask. In this that Our Lord loves you just because you are miserable, fickle, unfaithful etc. I ask you: "can a son give a greater pleasure to his father than to show that he is convinced of his father's love even after he had offended him time after time?"

To another he wrote: "Every day at Mass I put you under our good Mother's protection. May she find you always a good child of hers. Before answering difficult questions about the spiritual life, I am sure you turn instinctively to Our Lady of Good Counsel for advice."

The finances of the Seminary

As Rector of the Papal Seminary, Fr. Adessi's first concern, in the conditions in which the institution then was, had to be its financial situation which was then at its lowest. The new Rector took decisive steps to remedy the state of things. To begin with, he represented the matter so forcefully to his superiors in Belgium that the Provincial, Fr. Auguste Petit, made up his mind to insist with the Roman authorities and obtained for Kandy an increase of Rs. 500/- per month, and an additional reasonable sum. Secondly, acting on his own, the Rector took the bold decision of limiting the number of admissions to the Seminary in proportion to its resources. Those exceeding that number were asked either to pay for their boarding and lodging, or request their bishops to do so. He gave up the holiday house that had been rented in the hills. He also, for the time being, reduced work for the improvement of the estate to what was strictly necessary. Finally, just like his predecessor, he had recourse to begging. The Indian Bishops and his Jesuit Provincial in Belgium came to his help. Things did improve, yet the financial embarrassments never fully subsided. It is reported that one day, the good Rector came all full of joy to there creation room with this wonderful piece of news: "We have received money today! I can buy a hat for the Brother, and a rain coat for the other". Besides, contrary to the custom followed by Fr. Grosjean, Adessi felt the need of charging those who sought the hospitality of Kandy for a holiday or a period of rest. He also started a farm and a piggery and put Fr. Dasnoy incharge of its management, with the result that both farm and piggery proved a real asset to the Seminary particularly during the difficult years of the First World War. It is said that the Rector one day received a telegram from one of the customers of the farm with the following message: "Piglings no good. Send superior..." Imagine the reaction of the poor superior!

Anyway through such drastic measures, Fr. Adessi brought the situation under control in such a way that his successor had no financial problem to worry about, but "enjoyed - we are told - the most prosperous era of the Seminary's history."[1]

The Seminary - A home

As Superior of this large community of Seminarians, Jesuit Fathers, Brothers and Scholastics, Fr. Adessi sought to continue in the line followed by his worthy predecessor. He endeavoured to keep up at the Papal Seminary the atmosphere of mutual love and charity, cheerfulness, dedication to duty and prayerfulness of which Fr. Grosjean had laid the foundations. In such a family, the professors themselves became, on occasion, the target of innocent fun and mischief on the part of the students, and they gladly lent themselves to it. Everybody felt at home in the Seminary - students, professors, visitors. All were happy and cheerful. As Walter Wickremasinghe, one of the students who was ordained priest in 1907 attested, "Grosjean, Adessi have been tous more than our parents." It was this first generation of Kandyans who erected the old grotto of Our Lady of Lourdes on the Seminary premises as a significant token of their filial devotion to the Blessed Virgin Mary. Years later, on 11 February, 1910 it was replaced, as we shall see, by another, a beautiful one, which stands there still today.

The Apostolic Union

In 1901, thanks to the Rector's zeal, an Apostolic Union was formed among the students of the Seminary, with a simple rule of life intended to promote their fervour and spiritual advance. Informed about the prosperous "Apostolic Union of Secular Priests" founded in France by Msgr. Victor Emmanuel Lebeurier, Fr. Adessi contacted the Founder with the intention of incorporating the Kandy Union with the French one. In one of his letters to a Kandyan priest, Adessi notes down the answer he received from France: "It has been a day of great consolation to me - the fourth day of the Octave of the Sacred Heart - when I received the letter of Msgr. Lebeurier, the General Director, saying that he is willing to affiliate your Union to the general one of which the Holy Father himself is the head; and what is more, Msgr. Lebeurier himself wishes that the Seminary should remain the centre. This Union is pushed by the Holy Father most energetically. What a great blessing it will be for the secular priests in India."[2]

Truly, the Apostolic Union has been a very dynamic and flourishing organization in the Seminary with a definite influence on the life and ministry of our priests, as former Kandyans testify in the letters they write in the official organ of the Union - AUMOL - sharing their experiences in their respective fields of action as pastors. After having been so zealously directed by our regretted Father Robert Criem, it was then in the competent hands of Fr. Lionel Mascarenhas who also edits the "AUMOL".

In 1902 what is known as the "Short Course" was introduced in Theology for the benefit of those of our students who happened to fail in any year and were on that account not entitled to continue their studies in the degree course.

After the year 1902 new members joined the staff: Fathers Verstraeten, Lenuin, Fallon, Dom, Limbourg, Dupont, Berrewaerts and the scholastics Heptia, Dohet, Lambot and L'Hoir. Some of them became true pillars of the institution and spent their entire life at the service of the Kandy Seminary.

The Galle-Trincomalee Mission

This is the place to mention an important development which is linked with the Seminary's history. From the very beginning, when he came to Ceylon with the mission of preparing the way for the establishment of a National Seminary for whole of India, Msgr. Zaleski had another project in mind which he had already discussed in length with Cardinal Simoni, Prefect of Propaganda Fide, and with the General of the Society, Fr. Anderledy, and had the approval of the Holy Father himself.[3] He had taken goodcare not to mention it to anyone in India except Fr. Grosjean, and that too under strict secrecy (*sub secreto pontificio*). It was this: in case the choice of Kandy for the seminary were to be definitively ratified, the Holy See had in mind to detach from the existing dioceses of Colombo and Jaffna a sizable territory and entrust it to the Jesuits as their "Mission", eventually to be erected into a diocese or two. This had already been Msgr. Agliardi's proposal as early as 1886 or 1887, but it was kept secret, and in any case was not to be put into effect during the lifetime of Archbishop Bonjean of Colombo. Thanks to this arrangement the Seminary would no longer be an isolated entity, as it were, all by itself; it would be part of an entire mission territory served by the Jesuits, to which it would be attached and within which it would be functioning.[4]

Archbishop Bonjean, O.M.I., expired on August 3, 1892, and Msgr. Zaleski presided at the funeral service at Colombo. On his return to Kandy, Fr. Grosjean went to receive him at the station. When the two of them were alone in the carriage Zaleski reminded Grosjean of the secret he had confided to him on his arrival in India, and urged him to write immediately to the Provincial of Belgium, pressing him to accept by all means the new Mission-territory the Holy See was bent on entrusting to the Society, in Ceylon. The matter was to be considered as urgent because the Holy See was eager to settle that matter while the See of Colombo was still vacant.[5] Msgr. Zaleski himself wrote to the Cardinal Prefect of Propaganda asking him to hasten the conclusion of the affair.

This new "Mission" was made up of territory taken partly from the Archdiocese of Colombo and partly from that of Jaffna. It was finally erected on August 23, 1893. It is situated in the south and partly in the east coast of the island of Ceylon, and it extends from Galle to Trincomalee, covering a surface of 7000 square miles, or 17000 square kilometres, with a total population of 850,000 inhabitants. Towards the beginning of 1895 Fr. Joseph Van Reethe, who was then the Superior Regular of the Bengal-Ranchi Jesuit Mission, in succession to Fr. Bodson, was appointed Bishop of Galle.[6] He would also temporarily govern Trincomalee till a Bishop was appointed for that part of the Mission. Eventually the Trincomalee Diocese was taken over by the French Jesuits of the Province of Champagne. Bishop Van Reethe landed at Colombo on October 16, 1895. With him came three Fathers and one Brother from Belgium. The Jesuits working today in Ceylon, of whom the vast majority are Ceylonese, form now the one Jesuit Province of Sri Lanka.[7]

Speaking of Kandy and of Msgr. Zaleski, we cannot pass over in silence one particular point that came up for consideration during the rectorship of Fr. Adessi: the question of admitting the recently converted adivasis of Chotanagpur to the Papal Seminary. His Grace the Archbishop of Calcutta, Msgr. Goethals, had requested the Delegate Apostolic to receive in Kandy a few seminarians from Ranchi which at that time was part of the Archdiocese of Calcutta. They were adivasis who had finished humanistic studies, and would be happy to be allowed to begin Philosophy in Kandy. On the other hand, there was no Major Seminary in his Archdiocese, nor had he the men or the means to start one. True, the Delegate had already on an earlier occasion given a negative reply to a similar request, yet Msgr. Goethals now asked him to please reconsider his decision in view of the pressing needs of Ranchi. Zaleski, however, was adamant in his refusal to make any concession in this matter. He was already displeased at the fact that during his absence one *adivasi* candidate had already been admitted to the seminary. During a second longer absence, three more were received. When on his return to India, the Delegate heard about it, he resented it deeply. "If the Archbishop insists on admitting adivasis to the priesthood - he said - let him ordain them himself in his diocese, but I declare positively that not one more should be sent to Kandy. The Kandy Seminary belongs to the Holy See and nobody has the right to impose on Rome such an experiment". And he explained: "You need at least one century of Christianity and of contact with civilization before a community can give true vocations: *Il faut au moins un siècle du christianisme et decontact avec la civilisation pour trouver de vraies vocations*".

This was the clear stand taken by Msgr. Zaleski in this matter. The Delegate might have been influenced by St. Paul's reserve regarding new converts being raised to the sacred orders (cfr. 1 Tim 3:6). He meant well, of course, yet circumstances were not the same here, and history has shown that had the Ranchi Mission adopted the Delegate's policy, the Church particularly in the northern part of India would have suffered a substantial loss.

The Financial Administration

Passing on to another point, up to this time the financial administration of the Seminary had not been fully in the hands of the Jesuits. In 1905, under Pope Pius X, a decree of the Propaganda Fide, of May 31, transferred the financial administration of the institution to the Society. The Bishop of Galle was, for all legal purposes, to act as Proprietor, for the time being. On this occasion, the Delegate Apostolic gave the administrators the following directions: 1. The Seminary should have no less than 80 students free. The Seminary will receive from Propaganda for their maintenance the annual sum of 50,000 Lire; 2. More students could be admitted provided they could be maintained through funds coming from the existing Foundations or other sources; 3. The estate should be cultivated with great care and the Delegate informed about the annual produce of the land; 4. Every year the account of the income and the expenses should be sent to Propaganda, Rome, through the Apostolic Delegate.

Father Adessi completed his term as Rector of the Papal Seminary in 1907. His health had already been impaired by the time he came to Kandy after six years as Rector of St. Mary's, the Jesuit Theologate situated at the extreme north of the country, near the Himalayan range, Kurseong. During his last two years in Kandy he was almost an invalid. So, he went back to Calcutta accompanied by Fr. Lambot. He had the happiness of seeing that by this time the Seminary was well established, enjoying the favour of the Indian Hierarchy. In 1905 the number of the seminarians was 88 from 21 dioceses of India.

Father Julien Meunier

In 1907 Fr. Julien Meunier succeeded Fr. Adessi as Rector. Unlike his immediate predecessor, Fr. Meunier was not prepared for this post by any previous office of superiorship held till then. Besides, he came to Kandy not from a house of priestly formation but from a hill school where young boys of well-to-do families were brought up in learning and discipline, namely St. Joseph's, Darjeeling, right in front of the vast range of Kanchinjunga. It is to his credit that he rose to the challenge and settled down to his new office with ease and grace.

During his rectorship the number of students in the seminary rose to a hundred, and it went on increasing year by year. Being a professor of mathematics and physics, he saw to it that a well equipped physics laboratory was installed at the seminary: so, too, a telescope.

The year 1909 was saddened by a couple of events that were deeply felt by the Seminary population. The first was the departure for Belgium, in August, owing to ill health, of Fr. Van Der Aa, after fifteen years of devoted service in Kandy. Two days after receiving the news of his recall to Belgium, he announced it to the seminarians in the following brief words: "I leave the Seminary tomorrow morning for Belgium. Be good seminarians and good missionaries. Adieu! We shall see one another in heaven". This bit of news came to the students as a bolt from the blue and caused deep sorrow, for Fr. Van Der Aa was a much esteemed and loved member of the community. The following day, August 6, Father said the community Mass. It was the First Friday of the month, so at the end of the Mass he recited the Act of Consecration to the Sacred Heart of Jesus. After Mass, group photos were taken and then he left the house at 10.30. Here mained till the end of his life a great friend of the Seminary which he loved very much, indeed, and he felt extremely happy whenever he received in Belgium the visit of any of his former students who had gone abroad for further studies, and he did all he could to make them feel at home in a place that was new to them.

Father Van Der Aa spent the last years of his life in the novitiate at Tronchiennes, giving himself to prayer and work, and calmly awaiting the hour of death with characteristic peace and serenity of mind. When receiving the Last

Sacraments he saidgently: "This is the most beautiful day of my life!" Then he waited quietly for the Master's call, and just before breathing his last he had still the strength to whisper: "One is really well only near Him..."

The other sad news was the death of Bro. Innaya Galli of the Archdiocese of Madras, which occurred on December 18, 1909, at Phirangipuram, his native place.

Bro. Innaya was a model seminarian, loved by all for his piety and cheerfulness. He was sent home because of the symptoms of a chest disease. A few days before his death, he wrote to Father Rector: "I received Extreme Unction on Sunday evening. That same day in the morning I had received Our Lord in Holy Communion with all fervour. I am now only waiting to be taken to Our Lord andour Mother. I will pray for you there, in return for all the kindness you have shown me. I am happy to die and I am not afraid".

On February 11, 1910, the feast of Our Lady of Lourdes, the new beautiful grotto of Our Lady was duly inaugurated. It was the fruit of the love, devotion and labour of the students who generously gave their time and energy to its construction. Outstanding among them was the Jesuit scholastic Anskar Sevrin who later became Bishop of Ranchi. The young seminarians' devotion to the Blessed Virgin Mary found expression in, and was fostered by, their visits to the grotto which helped them to keep up their familiar relationship with the Mother of God and their Mother - MARY. Hardly any student begins his day's study without first visiting Our Lady's shrine and placing his day's work under her maternal protection.

Also, on the premises of the Seminary a spacious school was built for the children of the neighbourhood. In the course of time it came to be looked upon as one of the best educational institutions in the island. It is a standing tribute to the efforts of Fr. Berrewaerts who collected the necessary funds for its construction. It was blessed by Msgr. Zaleski on the same day of February 2, 1910.

Father Meunier is described to us as "a perfect gentleman", and at the same time "a strict disciplinarian". He placed before the seminarians the high ideal of the Catholic priesthood and of the demands of the priestly life and ministry. Nevertheless, it is during his time that complaints went up to the Apostolic Delegate that Bishops visiting the Seminary were not given the attention and consideration that was their due. In his letter of May 10, 1909, Msgr. Zaleski transmitted to the Rector their sentiments in this regard. They felt that they were treated at Kandy in a rather "summary way". Several said they did not like to visit the seminary because they do not want their seminarians to see them treated with such little respect that, as a result, the seminarians, too, when they return to their dioceses, might feel inclined to make little account of episcopal authority and dignity!

Msgr. Zaleski confirmed these complaints from his own experience. One day, a short time earlier - he said - he was accompanying the Bishop of Galle to the

Seminary. Several students were walking in the corridor, yet none came to wish or greet the bishop. So, on his return from Nuware Eliya that Bishop did not go back to the Seminary. Something similar had happened with the Bishop of Cochin.

The Delegate then went on to inform the Rector that Msgr. Makil would pay a visit to the Seminary within a short time. He should be received with the usual courtesy as in the past, namely: 1. If time permits, all the students of his diocese, and some of the Latin Rite of Malabar - that is Quilon, Verapoly and Cochin - should go and meet the Bishop at the station; 2. The following morning, all the Changanacherry Brothers should present themselves to him at the Delegation where he would be staying; 3. when he comes to the Seminary, he should be received at the entrance by all the seminarians. They should offer him a little séance during which an address should be read; finally, they should invite him to celebrate Holy Mass on the Sunday following, or on any other convenient day, in the Chapel of Ostrobrama, with the attendance of all the seminarians.

The attention of the Rector was called by Rome to the following point, regarding *admission to the Seminary.* Care should be taken not to admit too many students of the same diocese, particularly if that diocese happened to have already a seminary of its own. For instance, there were eleven seminarians in Kandy from Changanacherry alone! Now that diocese had a large number of priests, and a good seminary of its own at Puthenpally. True, at Puthenpally they had to pay for themselves, but this was necessary, else the seminary would not be able to function. Infuture, therefore, the admission policy should be such as to enable dioceses that have no seminary of their own to send students for their higher studies to Kandy.[8]

Another sad event was the death, on June 27, 1911, of the Bishop of Kandy, Msgr. Clement Pagnani, O.S.B. in whom the Seminary lost a true friend and well-wisher. His funeral took place on July 1 with the seminarians doing all the singing inpure gregorian chant. Bishop Pagnani was succeeded a year later by Msgr. Bede Beekmeyer, O.S.B., one of the first students of the Seminary, in 1893.

On December 3, 1911 the Seminary community was happy to witness the episcopal consecration of the first Kandyan to be raised to the episcopal dignity: Mar Augustine Kandathil. His consecration took place in the Cathedral of Kandy. He became the Coadjutor Bishop of Ernakulam Archdiocese with the right of succession. Together with him was also consecrated Msgr. Thomas Kurialacherry, for Changanacherry.

In 1912 the *new Rules* of the Seminary came into force. They were the fruit of the combined work of the seminary authoritie sand Propaganda. They were approved on trial for a period of seven years.

Around this time three new scholastics came to Kandy to teach the preparatory courses: Paul Sanders, J. Phillips, and R. Tanghe. Fr. Lambot came back after completing his studies and began his long career as Professor of

Ontology. Fr. Frutsaert too joined the staff, and two years later, Fr. Griffoy and Bro. Pieters.

On November 26, 1913, Fr. Meunier announced to the community the unexpected news of change of rector! In the farewell séance dedicated to him the students voiced their sentiments of gratitude in an address in which, among othert hings, their spokesman said: "As to your dealings with us, what a really kind, gentle and genial openness was yours that made us thankful for the warnings and exhortations that were necessary be times. And we would particularly mention the trust you placed so largely in us, a trust that put us on our best mettle and madeus feel that we were made to be men who could be relied upon". Early the following morning Fr. Meunier left for Calcutta. That same day, at dinner, Fr. Leonard Vossen was proclaimed the new Rector of the Seminary. This news gladdened the hearts of the students because Fr. Vossen was not a stranger to them: most of them knew him personally, and he knew them. There is no room here, they said, for the embarrassment and the apprehensions of a first meeting with an unknown personality.[9]

Fr. Vossen (1913-1920)

Fr. Vossen's rectorship coincided with the War years and was marred by all the anxieties, uncertainities and preoccupations of wartime. This will be better understood if we keep in mind that Kandy, its life and its destinies were closely linked with the Belgian mission of Bengal, and consequently with the Belgian Province of the Society of Jesus.

We mentioned above how the financial condition of the Papal Seminary had considerably improved under the rectorship of Fr. Adessi. This, of course, is true, but unexpectedly the war came, and it brought new problems in its wake. Belgium, we know, became the first victim of the war. It was invaded, overrun, occupied, laid waste, and therefore rendered unable to go on helping the seminary, run mainly by the sons of Belgium till then. For a time it was feared that the Seminary might have to close down as long as the war situation prevailed. However, Almighty God came to it said in order to prevent such a calamity. A benefactress came unexpectedly to its help and made up for the deficiency. At the same time, Fr. Motha Vaz, a former Kandyan working in Madras, appealed to the generosity of old Kandyans, and this resulted in a very substantial help that to a great extent made up for the lack of funds from abroad.

The year 1914 was the centenary year of the restoration of the Society of Jesus by Pope Pius VII. The Papal Seminary Fathers celebrated this event on 7 August 1914. In keeping with the directions given by Father Ledochowski, it was to be an opportunity for an effort of spiritual renewal and rejoicing rather than of gorgeous external demonstrations. The Fathers of the community had a triduum with a daily special hour of adoration of the Blessed Sacrament. On the last day, there was a solemn High Mass of thanks giving. At 11.00 before noon there was a gathering in the hall at which His Excellency the Apostolic Delegate was present, as well as the Bishop of Kandy and the Father Abbot of the Benedictines, and a few other guests. After the congratulatory address the seminarians staged the operetta "Pady Blake". In the evening a joint meeting of both the Academies (Theologians' and Philosophers') was held. Among the items presented, two were connected with the history of the Society: "The suppression and the restoration" and "India and the Society of Jesus". The two essays were very much appreciated.

Zaleski's Departure

Two years later, Msgr. Zaleski who, as we have seen, was so closely connected with the Papal Seminary from its very foundation, and down the years, came to the Seminary for a farewell visit to this institution that was so dear to his heart. At 4.30 a.m., Fathers and Brothers were all assembled in the Chapel. When His Lordship entered the chapel in procession, the choir sang the "Ecce Sacerdos magnus". The Delegate sat on a fald stool and listened with emotion to the address in Latin read by one of the theologians. At the end he was offered, as a souvenir of Kandy, a sandalwood casket containing a parchment adorned with pen and ink drawings of the Seminary, St. Mary's, the Tooth Temple, the Kandy Lake, and other artistic ornamentations.

In reply, His Excellency read his last circular to the clergy of his delegation (see chapter one), and gave his blessings to all present. A solemn Pontifical Benediction followed and the kissing of the ring. On the day following he made a surprise visit to the Seminary, and for a last time entertained the community for more than one hour with most interesting stories drawn from his own experience. At St. Mary's, on the wall opposite the sacristy door, there is a marble tablet with only the two commandments of love inscribed on it. By Zaleski's express wish, his name was not mentioned. On one of the days following Msgr. Zaleski left Kandy for Colombo by the 2.30 p.m. train. He had forbidden the students to be present at the station lest their presence should make the parting more painful. He bequeathed to the seminary the entire furniture of his house and the beautiful potted garden plants: for about seven days there was a regular carts service between the Delegation and the Seminary to transport these goods to their new destination. From Rome, Archbishop Zaleski sent a telegram on December 17 to congratulate the ordinandi: 17 priests, 4 deacons, 11 subdeacons.

New Delegate Apostolic

Four months later, on May 8, 1917 Kandy had the joy of welcoming the new Delegate Apostolic, His Excellency Archbishop Peter Fumasoni-Biondi. He arrived at the station accompanied by the Bishop of Dacca, at 6.00 p.m. on May 7, and was led to the Cathedral, where the clergy and laity of the town were assembled, together with their Bishop Bede, to give him a hearty welcome. On the following morning both His Excellency and the Bishop of Dacca came to the Seminary which was to be for sometime the Delegate's residence. The Papal colours were flying high up on the central tower, with the Union Jack and the Belgian flag on either side, at a lower level. The seminary orchestra struckup a welcome tune, as the Apostolic Delegate with his cortège was on his way to the reception hall. Here, Father Rector first read the Papal Bull appointing Msgr. Fumasoni-Biondi Titular Archbishop of Dioclea and Delegate Apostolic of the East Indies. He then made a brief speech welcoming the new Delegate in the name of the community and placed the house at his disposal. One of the students read an address on behalf of the seminarians.

His Excellency replied in very affectionate terms, telling the students of the high hopes the Holy Father, Pope Benedict XV, and himself, entertained about them, "the select and youthful sons of the great and noble Indian Empire" whose soil had been watered by the blood of Saint Thomas and the sweat of St. Francis Xavier. He expressed the hope that the students would come to be the honour and glory of the Church and the salt and light of their noble country. He ended his speech by giving his blessing to all present. On June 16, His Excellency left the Seminary for his bungalow situated on the Peradenya Road, Kandy.

During Christmas time 1916 the Seminary received the visit of a learned guest, Fr. Gombert, S.J., of St. Joseph's College, Trichy. He took a special interest in the wild figs growing in the jungle near-by, only from a scientific point of view, we are told. With him came two new arrivals: a pair of canary-birds. Soon they multiplied and threatened to outdo even the piglings in the farm.

The Silver Jubilee of the Seminary

We now come to the year 1918 - the year of the Silver Jubilee of the Papal Seminary. This joyful event was duly celebrated from May 18 to 20. 18 was spent in prayer and recollection. In the morning, the Rector gave an instruction exhorting the members of the community to a deep spirit of thanks giving to God for all the graces He had showered on the Seminary and the priests formed in Kandy, working in the various dioceses of the country. At 7.00 p.m. there was Solemn Benediction. Fr. Rector read out the prayer of Pope Leo XIII and consecrated the Seminary a new to the sacred Heart of Jesus. Consecration to the Blessed Virgin Mary was also renewed.

Given the circumstances of the time the number of old Kandyans present was limited, but all were extremely happy to be back together in the "Home of Love". The first to arrive was the one who had been the very first to land in Kandy twenty-five years earlier: Fr. Swaminather. Besides him, there were only two other old students from India: Fr. J. Ribeira from Quilon and Fr. Jeganather from Trichinopoly. The rest were all from Ceylon itself. It was a truly joy-filled gathering, presided over by His Excellency the Delegate Apostolic and our old student, Bishop Beekmeyer of Kandy.

On May 20 the Delegate celebrated the Pontifical High Mass of thanksgiving. The Mass was followed by the solemn Benediction of the Blessed Sacrament and the Te Deum. In the afternoon there was the unveiling of the Memorial Tablet, - a fine tablet of white marble bearing the following inscription in Latin:

LEONI XIII P. MAX
Qui, Curante Delegato suo L.M. Zaleski,
Hoc Seminarium Pontificium fundavit,
Filii tui, India, administri tibi Salutis
Hanc lapidem posuere
A. D. MCMXVIII
a fundatione XXV.

Immediately after the ceremony of the unveiling of the Memorial Table there was an academic session in the Philosophers' Hall with the following programme:1. Overture: Fantasia, 12th. Mass by Mozart; 2. The Holy Father's Brief; 3. Historical Notes; 4. Rev. Fr. A. Swaminather, first alumnus, recalls the beginnings; 5. "Strike the Harp" Chorus; 6. Rev. Fr. Rebeira speaks about Seminary training; 7. Rev. Fr. A. Jeganather portrays the Catholic Indian Missionary; 8. The absent, present in spirit, send their greetings; 9. H. L. The Bishop of Kandy addresses the students; 10. His Excellency the Delegate Apostolic closes the meeting.

In his speech, Msgr. Fumasoni-Biondi said among other things the following: "We are not alone in the field now. During the last twenty-five years several theological seminaries have been started, and those which already existed have been very much improved; so that today, thank God, every diocese can train its candidates in its own, or in one of the several provincial seminaries. Let us hope, therefore, that the Bishops, when sending students here, will make a selection and choose the brightest, thus facilitating the Superiors' intention to suppress the 'short course', and give all the students an advanced courseand a thorough training".

The second day, too, began with a Pontifical High Mass celebrated this time by Bishop Beekmeyer who belonged to the Kandy Seminary in a two fold sense. He is one of the first batch of students who joined the Seminary in 1893, and he was the present Bishop of Kandy.

The next item at 12.00 noon, was the Jubilee Dinner. There fectory was festively adorned for the occasion and during the meal the Seminary Band enlivened the hearts of all with its select pieces. His Excellency began the series of speeches by exhorting the students to keep up the good reputation the Seminary had earned during the first quarter of its existence. Bishop Beekmeyer, in turn, regaled those present with choice stories and anecdotes connected with the early days of the Seminary. In touching words he remembered Msgr. Zaleski and Fr. Grosjean, and expressed his esteem and appreciation of Fr. Vossen, the present

Rector of the seminary. Fr. Vossen then rose to thank all the guests present and in particular the old students who had taken the trouble of coming all the way to bewith the Kandy community on its family feast day. Brother Massilamany proposed to the health of the "elder brothers". Thanking the community in the name of these last, Fr. Jerome Pereira expressed his joy at being again at the Alma Mater which had such a large place in the hearts of all old Kandyans. A group photo was taken at the end of the dinner.

In the evening, after an early supper, there was a musical and dramatic entertainment, during which the play "For a Crown" was staged. During the intervals of the Five Acts, the Orchestra executed with much taste select musical pieces like Rossini's "Ilbarbiere di Seviglia", Shattuck's "Chiming bells of Long Ago", "Lead Kindly Light" and Sullivan's "The Beleaguered". There was also a Violin Duet: "Vilja Song". The entertainment, we are told, was a grand success, thanks to "the in trinsic merit and lofty character of the drama, the consummate skill of the actors, the beauty of the new dresses, and the brilliancy of many a news cenery on which our artist painters (with Fr. Rector at their head) had spent long hours of painstaking labour."[10]

Before passing on to another chapter it will not be out of place to reproduce here from the Silver Jubilee Souvenir a few data regarding the priests formed in Kandy during the first quarter of century of its existence: Priests formed in Kandy: 191: students who died during their stay in the seminary: 15; students who left to join other seminaries and were ordained priests: 9; or are still awaiting ordination: 3; those who discontinued their studies: 46; total number of inscriptions: 340; present students in 1918: 76.[11]

The end of November 1918 brought the good news of the Armistice marking the end of the World War I. The joyful event was celebrated with a full day's holiday which all the inmates of the Seminary heartily enjoyed. It raised the hope that the signing of the Peace Treaty between the Allies and Germany would soon relieve the financial strain under which the house laboured since the outbreak of the war. Such hopes however failed to materialize due to the unprecedented drop in the rates of exchange, coupled with the rise in the price of almost every article of use. A time came when again the very continuing in existence of the Seminary became a question mark for those incharge of it, but God came to its rescue.

Pope Benedict XV's Letter to the Rector of Kandy

Dilecto Filio
Leonardo Vossen, e Societatis Jesu Pontificii Seminarii Kandiens is Moderatori

BENEDICTUS PP. XV
Dilecte Fili,
Salutem et apostolicam benedictionem

Ad afferendum gentibus, quae divinae redemption is beneficium ignorant, lumen Evangelii, ea velut compendiaria via est, delectos ex ipsis adolescentes rite educare, qui deinceps apud populares suos apostolico munere fungantur. Non enim suspicionemdant, ut alienigenae solent; quin ipso immo, ob ration emsamicitiarum ac necessitudinum, faciles usquequaque habent aditus, atque ipsa sermon is generisque communitas gratiam eis fidemqueconciliat.

Peropportune igitur decessor Noster Fr. Leo XIII, abhincannis XXV, istud Kandiense Seminarium condidit alumnis indis in Indiae salutem instituendis; et praeclare usque adhuc ressuccess it. Scimus enim ex is to pietatis studiorumque optimorumdimicilio non paucos jam prodiisse sacerdotes sacrorumqueantistites aliquot, eosque ad Apostolatum egregie instructos acprorsus Societatis Jesu disciplina dignos. Hisce de fructibussalutaris instituti, Nobis gaudentes vobisque gratulantes, magnas Deo grates agimus: quaesumusque ut tibi tuisque in hac readjutoribus adesse perseveret. Nos certe opus vestrum tuerinunquam desistemus : cui quidem omnes ex India episcopos velimussuffragari, hoc sibi persuadentes, satis se suo satisfacisse officio, cum sanctam cleri indigenae curaverint institutionem. Accaelestium auspicem munerum et peculiar is benevolentiae Nostraetestem, tibi, dilecte Fili, atque omnibus istius Seminarii magistris et alumnis apostolicam benedictionem amantissime in Domino impertimus.

Datum Romae apud S. Petrum, die IV, mensis Martii MCMXVIII., Pontificatus Nostri anno quarto.

BENEDICTUS, PP. XV.

Notes

1. Papal Seminary, Kandy, Ceylon: Golden Jubilee Celebrations (1893-1943), p. 24.
2. Letter of 11 June, 1904 (Letters of Fr. Adessi, S.J., compiled by Fr. B. Baker, Ms.).
3. S. Grosjean, S.J., Historia Fundationis Seminarii Kandiensis, p. 70.
4. H. Josson, S.J., o.c., p. 255-257.
5. *Idem, ibid.*, p. 256.
6. *Idem, ibid.*, p. 262.
7. However, the Pontifical Seminary continued to be under the jurisdiction of the Jesuit Provincial of Belgium. In 1908, it was transferred to Calcutta. From then on, it is the Superior Regular of Calcutta who did the annual visitation of the Seminary (cf. H. Josson, S.J., o.c., p. 263f). It is only twenty years later that it became part of the Jesuit Mission of Galle (*ibid.*).
8. Letter of Msgr. Zaleski to the Rector of the Kandy Seminary, 30 September 1908; Letter of Cardinal Gotti, Prefect of Propaganda, 9 February, 1909.
9. Cf. Aumol, March, 1914, p. 1.2.
10. The Papal Seminary: Silver Jubilee, p. 26.
11. *Ibid.*, p. 32.

Chapter 4

Growth and Consolidation (1919-1943)

A new era began for the Papal Seminary of Kandy with the year 1918. The stage of infancy was now a thing of the past. Also, by now, the Kandy Seminary was fairly well known in the country and enjoyed the favour of the Indian Hierarchy: twenty dioceses or more were represented among the students. It had now to take further strides towards the full realization of the purpose for which Pope Leo XIII wanted it in India. In tracing out its progress we shall follow mainly, as we have done till now, the chronological order of events.

Father L. Vossen continued as Rector of the Seminary till the end of his term - 1920. During his tenure of office, the dairy farm of the Papal Seminary was transferred to a more suitable site, enlarged and placed on a sounder basis. The cows were better housed and so, too, the piggery. Both, as we said before, were an asset to the community particularly during the war and the post-war years, when supplies were difficult to obtain, the prices were high and the institution was left largely to its own resources.

Yet, these were not the only cares of the superiors. In April 1919 the death of Fr. Paul Dom, S.J., inflicted a heavy loss on the Seminary. Fr. Dom had come to Kandy in May 1902. A versatile talent, he taught at different times Dogma, Ethics, and the subject he liked most - Holy Scripture. In addition to this, he gave lessons of French, Greek, Mathematics, and, as if all that were not enough, he was also Minister of the House, Choir Master, Spiritual Director, and what not!

One of Fr. Dom's students evoked his memory in the following terms: "Father Dom's life was a constant sermon on what the higher life of sanctity is and how it can be achieved without prejudice to the discharge of one's other duties. He really saw God in everything... Always modest, retiring and unpretentious, glad to remain in the background, he was nevertheless, in spite of all this, a power in the seminary. To me, he was one of the dearest friends, surely the holiest among them, one to whom I am more indebted than to anyone else in Kandy, for he taught me what a saint must be like, and to have a glimpse of this is a grace, indeed, and leaves impressions that are ineffaceable."[1]

Fr. Dom's parting words, after receiving the Last Sacraments, were: "I have devoted my life to you, my heart is too full to say anything more". He passed away peacefully at 5.00 a.m. on a Sunday, just as the prayers for the dying were concluded and the bell rang for the community to rise.

Among the ordinandi of the year 1919 we find the name of one who was destined to be one day our dear Vice-Patron, after the transfer of the Papal Seminary to Pune: Father Andrew D'Souza. He was ordained priest on December 21, 1919, together with Fr. Ignatius Rodrigues who later became Bishop of Belgaum. On his return to his diocese, after the completion of his priestly studies, Fr. Andrew became the Assistant Parish-Priest of St. Peter's, Bandra, Bombay. Here, much to the delight of his former companions, he took the initiative of publishing a small paper to which he gave the significant title of "The Exile". Its sole purpose - as he stressed in the editorial - was "to keep a lasting and interesting contact with the Alma Mater" (January 1920, no.1). On his side, Fr. Ignatius Rodrigues expressed his sentiments on bidding farewell to Kandy in the following terms: "We had a very pleasant journey right along till Bombay – my heart began to feel the pangs of parting from my lovely home at Kandy. When the train was nearing that little strip of land that forms the farthest part of beloved Ceylon - Talaimannar - I felt that I was leaving that lovely pearl in the ocean where I spent the happiest of my happy days."[2]

Father L'Hoir Rector

At the end of Father Vossen's term Fr. Francis Xavier L'Hoir was appointed to take his place as Rector of the Papal Seminary.

The financial situation of the Seminary was again at a low ebb. Fr. L'Hoir wrote to the Delegate Apostolic, Archbishop Peter Pisani, acquainting him of the state of things. The question was also asked whether the seminarians should be informed of the difficulties the institution was being confronted with. "What ought the students to know of the subject?" The Delegate answered: "The staff may be entitled to be informed about it, but that the Seminarians should feel depressed and doubtful about their very existence in the near future does not seem to me a matter of course. They must breathe and live in a fairly wholesome atmosphere thanking God for the daily bread, spiritual as well as material, they receive the paternal care of their Superiors, unmindful of the trial imposed on their Alma Mater by exceptional circumstances which will be overcome thanks to divine Providence and to the solicitude of the S. Congregation as well as of their beloved Rector. Did the Seminary's very existence not seem imperilled last year on the same ground which underlies our present anxiety? Yet last year's Bilan has proved satisfactory. Let them pray and work out their vocation outside and above any trouble of Bilan and Budgets, at least so far as it may depend on you and your staff". (Letter of August 9, 1922, from Bangalore).

On May 12, 1923, news came from Rome that the S.C. of Propaganda had given its definitive approval to the Seminary Rules. Only a few changes were made. Registering this piece of news, the Apostolic Union Report of 1924 says: "It will please the old Kandyans to know that we will go on being trained in the same good old fashion that made them what they are".

His Lordship the Bishop of Kandy, Dr. Beeckmeyer, O.S.B., celebrated his sacerdotal silver jubilee on June 21, 1924. The Seminary participated joyfully in this celebration. On the June 22 all attended the Pontifical High Mass at the Cathedral. On June 24 there was a reception in honour of this distinguished 'oldboy' in the Seminary itself, with several priests present and one illustrious layman of Colombo, Sir Thomas de Sampayo, lately knighted. Replying to the speeches, His Lordship recalled with gratitude his first years in the Seminary. Solemn Benediction and *Te Deuum* followed. The day ended with an entertainment put up by the seminarians.

July 18, 1925 was kept as a special first class holiday in honour of St. Thomas Aquinas, to mark the sixth century of his canonization.

Early in the month of January of this year, Archbishop, Later Cardinal, Alexis M. Lépicier, the Apostolic Visitor, paid avisit to the Seminary. On the 7 of the month, an "appeal" for the Chapel was launched with a warm recommendation from the Visitor.

Visitors to the Seminary

It was during Fr. L'Hoir's tenure of office as Rector that the Seminary was honoured by the visit of no less a person than King Albert of Belgium, who was accompanied by his wife, Queen Elizabeth. It took place on 23 October 1925. For days together, since the 20th, when the news of the royal visit was announced to the community, the seminarians were seen busy decorating the house for the occasion. The royal couple arrived a little pastten in the morning, preceded and followed by two police cars and accompanied by their suite. It so happened that the Queen arrived first accompanied by the Governor of Ceylon. On seeing her, the seminarians spontaneously cheered in joy, as they had been taught: *Vive le Ro*! The King, however, soon appeared on the scene, and the Belgian Fathers and Brothers paid their homage to their King and Queen, welcoming them to "*ce petit coin de la Belgique*" as the Rector said, expressing their joy at being able to welcome to this distant place "what was noblest and grandest in the soul of Belgium: their own King and Queen!" One of the senior students presented to the King their address beautifully adorned, and enshrined in a silver casket bearing the royal initials engraved on it. The Visitors were then taken to the Library where they inspected some old precious Manuscripts. They admired the lovely view of the Dumbara Valley, and put their signatures to two beautiful photographs of the Seminary. Expressing his joy at this opportunity of meeting the students and his own countrymen in Kandy, King Albert said: "It was difficult to find time for this visit; but I wanted by all means to come, to show our sympathy and our admiration for the work of the Fathers in the Mission", and he added: "Kindly let them know this".

Speaking of the visitors we take this opportunity to record the names of other distinguished personalities who visited the Kandy Seminary during or around this period.

The All Ceylon Catholic Conference or Reading Circles was held in Kandy on April 25, 1926. Those present at the Conference - over 30 persons: ladies, gentlemen and children - paid a visit to the Seminary, accompanied by their President Sir Thomas de Sampayo.

Among other visitors were a Hungarian Abbot and an ex-Prime Minister of Hungary (November 1926), the Delegate Apostolic Msgr. Edward Mooney (1927), the Prince and Princess de Ligne (1927), a group of distinguished persons who were on their way back from the International Eucharistic Congress at Sydney in September 1928: Msgr. Heylen, Bishop of Namur, Abbot Lamy of the Pre monstratension Abbey of Tongerloo, Belgium, Msgr. Prince de Croy, a scion of the princely House of the old Roman Empire of Germany, Father Prince Ghika of the royal family of Romania, Msgr. Caccia-Dominiani, the Pope's Maestro di Camera, Msgr. Respighi, the Papal Master of Ceremonies, Msgr. Michael Curran, Vice-Rector of the Irish College, Rome, Chavalier Chiesarotti.

In 1928 the Seminary welcomed Cardinal Ceretti, the first Cardinal ever to visit Kandy, and Msgr. Lamér and, International Director of the Apostolic Union of Secular Priests.

Another visitor of rank was the ex-king of Saxony. He came with his aide-de-camp, his chaplain and the German Consul in Colombo. He was a devout Catholic who had given his eldest son to the Society of Jesus. His brother, Prince Maximilian, was a priest well known for his authority in matters liturgical. Nor can we forget to mention the name of two Pierres, both Jesuits: Pierre Lhande the famous preacher of Notre Dame, in Paris, and Pierre Charles, the renowned Belgian theologian and missiologist, who was the guest of the Seminary also on two or more previous occasions during his lecture tour in India and beyond.

We may here include one who came to Kandy a few years later, in February 1933: Major Alex Waley, an English convert well known in the world of scouting, Privy Chamberlain to the Pope. He came to Kandy together with his old father-in-law Sir Henry Fielding Dickens, son of Charles Dickens. Though an octogenarian, this robust Englishman did not shrink from climbing right up to the second storey of the main Seminary building, just to have a look at the long row of his father's novels which adorn the shelves of the English Academy Library.

Last, not least, comes the American Jesuit Fr. Wallroth who dropped in at all haste, from nowhere so to say, at 9.00 a.m., and left as hastily at 1.30 p.m. taking with him from the Seminary a set of Breviaries and a black sash. This was because his own were mislaid somewhere during his journey to the Far East. The seminarians recorded this event in the followingverses:

> "Lives of great men all remind us
> We can sail life's troubled sea,
> And departing leave behind us
> Sash and Roman Breviary! (with apologies to Long fellow)"

The Seminary Chapel

Our readers may find it surprising that though existing since the year 1893, the Papal Seminary did not as yet have a Chapel of its own! For thirty years the seminarians made use of two large rooms within the Seminary building itself, one for the philosophers and another for the Theologians, where the Blessed Sacrament was preserved, and where they went for Mass and their Visits to Our Lord. For Sunday Mass, and the more solemn occasions, they availed themselves of the church built by Msgr. Zaleski and dedicated to Our Lady of Ostrobrame which had now become the parish church of the place. It was Fr. L'Hoir's privilege to have the Seminary Chapel built and blessed during his term of office. Till then only the foundation stones were there, laid thirty years earlier, in 1896, and left just like that, for lack of funds.

Things, however, began to take shape when, on March 1, 1925, Bro. Polydore Verbrugge, S.J., who had come to Ceylon thirty years earlier and had never left the island, was sent to Kandy as the engineer and builder of the new chapel. Together with him came another Jesuit, Brother Donven, who was to help him as the master carpenter. With the coming of these two stalwarts the construction of the chapel began in right earnest on March 6, 1925, the first Friday of the month. It began with a brief prayer service attended by the staff and students of the seminary. The chapel was blessed a year later, on March 27, 1926 and solemnly inaugurated in May of the same year, in the presence of Bishop Beeckmeyer of Kandy and the Bishop of Kottayam,[3] both alumni of the Seminary.

The style of the chapel, following the design prepared by Fr. Vossen, was an imitation of the early Romanesque, and its cost was met by funds collected from our former alumni, but mainly from generous donations received on two occasions from Pope Benedict XV and Pope Pius XI.[4]

Pope Pius in particular was deeply interested in the early completion of the chapel and sent a donation of Rs. 27,900/-. On that occasion he expressed his hope that he would before long receive the good news that the work would be pursued with due energy and ardour.[5]

At the same time His Holiness was so considerate as to send for the new chapel a large consignment of altar vestments, chasubles, stoles, maniples, albs, surplices, purificators, palls, lavabos, cinctures, a chalice, paten, a pair of cruets, a small ciborium, and a host of other sacred objects, as a token of his esteem for the Seminary.

The affection and concern of Popes Benedict and Pius for the Papal Seminary is commemorated through a shield or tablet containing the effigy in white marble of the two Supreme Pontiffs. This tablet was placed right above the entrance door of the chapel. It was gifted to the Seminary by the General of the Society, Fr. W. Ledochowki, as an expression of gratitude of the Seminary to its two great benefactors. The chapel was estimated by specialists of the time at two lakhs of rupees.

On April 1and 3, 1926, the Tenebrae and other services of the Holy Week were held for the first time in the new chapel. On Good Friday the new Stations of the Cross were erected. On Easter Sunday, the altars of different saints were placed in the chapel: in the right aisle, St. Peter, St. Paul, St. Thomas Aquinas and the Guardian Angel; in the left, the Immaculate Heart of Mary, St. Ignatius of Loyola, the Curé d'Ars and St. Aloysius. The big statute of St. Francis Xavier filled the niche on the main altar, and those of the Sacred Heart and the Immaculate Virgin were placed at either side, at the entrance of the sanctuary. The paintings of St. Joseph and of St. Thomas the Apostle were put near the side-entrance of the chapel, while from the wall in the back of the chapel hangs a fine portrait of St. Thérése of Lisieux, the Patroness of the Missions, smiling on the future missionaries undergoing their training in the Seminary.

Once the chapel was finished, the Rector hastened to convey the news to the Holy Father expressing his gratitude for the personal interest he had taken in the speedy completion of this place of prayer and worship. The Rector did so by sending His Holiness an album containing the photographs of the external view of the chapel as well as of its principal interior parts. In aletter addressed to the Rector through Cardinal Gasparri, the Pope showed his appreciation of the album and congratulated him "for having completed in so short a time a work of such proportions."[6]

In October 1926, the Rector appeared one day in the students' dining room with a letter in his hand, his face beaming with joy. He conveyed to them a message from Pope Pius XI communicated to him through the Delegate Apostolic. In his letter, the Delegate wrote: "I am deeply pleased to convey to my dear seminary the paternal blessing of His Holiness Pope Pius XI who in an audience granted me yesterday (6 October), deigned to listen with the greatest interest to my report on the situation of the Seminary. Tell them, he said textually, that the Holy Father is extremely keen on the spiritual as well as the material welfare of the seminarians, and that he most heartily blesses the Seminary as well as those who take care of it". His Holiness manifested similar sentiments years later in an audience given to Bishop Roche of Tuticorin, during which he spontaneously inquired about the new chapel of the Kandy Seminary and asked whether it was properly furnished.

This goes together with the news transmitted by the Provincial of Belgium who in a letter to the Rector says: "Let me tell you that the Delegate Apostolic has spoken with praise to the Propaganda authorities of Kandy priests, as much from the point of view of their intellectual attainments as of their sacerdotal formation. He said they are in no way second to the priests formed in Rome".

Another little item of good news to the seminarians was that they could hence forth go to the town in white cassock.

About two years later, Pope Pius sent to the Seminary as his gift a portrait of himself - a fine large painting in oil. It was placed by the side of the portrait of the Founder of the Seminary, Pope Leo XIII, at the centre, in the ground floor corridor.[7] Mention has been made above of Cardinal Ceretti's visit to the Seminary. On his return to Rome the Cardinal took it upon himself to speak to the Holy Father in favour of the Seminary. The result was that Propaganda sent to Kandy a sum of 50 for the installation of electricity in the entire house - a need keenly felt by all in the Seminary. At the same time the Cardinallet the Rector know that both the Pope and Cardinal Van Rossum, the Prefect of Propaganda, were extremely pleased with the report he gave them of his brief stay in Kandy.[8]

Faculty Doctorates Granted

Reference must now be made to an event that took place in 1926 and gave the Seminary its distinctive mark, unique at the time among the existing institutes of priestly formation in India. In response to the petition made by Father Ledochowski, the General of the Society of Jesus, the S. C. of Propaganda Fide was pleased to empower the Kandy Pontifical College to grant the degrees of Licentiate and Doctorate in Philosophy and Theology. The news was soon conveyed to the Rector on St. Ignatius' Day, 1926 in a cablegram worded: "Faculty Doctorates granted Ledochowski". A long and thunderous applause was the seminarians' response to this unexpected piece of news which was read out to them all assembled in the main hall by Fr. Villaert, the Jesuit Visitor who was then in Kandy.

The syllabus of the College was accordingly modified so as to suit its new status as a Faculty. An extra year was added for the doctorate in theology. It was also stipulated that one of the conditions for the doctorate was that the candidate had secured aconstant 2/3 marks all through the curriculum of his studies in all subjects, from the first year of philosophy to the fourth year of theology. Besides, the following were the requisites laid down for doctorate in any of the two Faculties: A written examination of two to five hours. One whose written paper was not found satisfactory was ipso facto excluded from the oral examination. The oral examination lasted for one hour for the doctorate in philosophy, and for two hours for doctorate in theology. For this last, three suffrages with first class marks were required. The written examination could never be repeated, in case of failure. As for the oral examination, it could be repeated in Philosophy provided one had obtained first classmarks and no third class marks in any subject. In

Theology, the oral examination could be repeated only with the permission of one's respective bishop. Another requirement for the doctorate in theology was that the candidate should have previously secured adoctorate in philosophy.[9]

However, Propaganda sanctioned favourably a request made by the authorities of the Kandy Seminary, namely, that, at least for the first four years since the promulgation of the above degree, students of Kandy could be admitted to the Doctorate in theology even though they had not obtained a previous doctorate in philosophy as required by the concession, provided they had done the full course of philosophy in Kandy, and, in addition, had passed an examination for aptitude to the degree of doctorate in philosophy. The reason for this request was that at the end of their philosophy, these students had no opportunity to apply for a doctorate in philosophy. Accordingly, the first Kandy students to obtain the doctorate in theology were Fr. Valerian Gracias (4 Feb. 1927), later Archbishop of Bombay and Cardinal, Fr. Leonard Raymond (12 Feb. 1927), later Archbishop of Nagpur, and Fr. Lawrence Pulithanath, later Monsignor and a very efficient pastor in Cochin. Others followed in the course of the years. (cfr. Appendix).

Then, in 1931, came the Constitution '*Deus Scientiarum Dominus*'. It reflected the mind of Pope Pius XI who was bent on promoting higher standards of scholarship in the Ecclesiastical Faculties. The Professors in Kandy were once again at work trying to upgrade their programme of studies so as to meet the heavy demands of the new Constitution. A total reorganisation of studies was planned in keeping also with the recommendations of Father Ledochowski who urged the Seminary authorities to prepare a new syllabus and apply for official recognition, first for the Faculty of Theology, and then for that of Philosophy. This would naturally require some time, but the Pope himself told Father General that a period of transition could be considered until things took proper shape, in line with the Papal Constitution. For the meantime, the recently created "Congregation of Seminaries and University Studies" (now "Catholic Education") decreed that "in the Faculties run by the Society of Jesus, the application of the existing Statutes containing the power of granting academic degrees in Philosophy and Theology may for the time-being remain in force, subject to the modifications that may be come to be prescribed later, after further examination of the same."[10]

A list annexed to this decree mentioned the colleges of the Society of Jesus to which this power was recognized. The Seminary of Kandy figured in the list.[11] On his side, Father Ledochowski did not cease to urge the Indian Major Superiors to greater zeal in seconding the desires of the Holy See in this important area of the formation of future priests. It would certainly ask for a sacrifice on the part of those missions, he said, but it was closely linked with the common good, and would bring down on them God's more abundant blessings.[12]

He at the same time appointed Fr. Francis Xavier L'Hoir as his delegate empowered to enter into direct contact in his name with the various Jesuit Major Superiors in view of obtaining the necessary personnel for Kandy.

Father L'Hoir was not quite successful in securing the help he needed for Kandy. So, three years later, Father General himself wrote directly to the same Superiors in the same sense. In the meantime Kandy had been transferred from the jurisdiction of the Bengal-Ranchi Mission to the Galle Mission of Ceylon. The Galle Mission, however, Fr. General told his men, would not be able alone to cope with the task of supplying Kandy with the Professors the Faculties needed. On the other hand, there was the danger that if Kandy failed to come up to the expectations of Rome, the privilege it was given might be withdrawn. And this would mean a great loss to souls and to the Church in India. He therefore earnestly exhorted the superiors not to hesitate, even at the cost of great sacrifice, to prepare and send apt professors to the Kandy Faculties, and to begin setting aside gifted young men for Kandy. Moreover, he told them to send him names of eligible Fathers or Scholastics with the necessary information regarding their qualifications, so that he himself might decide what would be best for the greater glory of God and the progress of the Church in India.[13]

Statutes Definitively Approved

The Statutes of the Kandy Faculties were forwarded to the Sacred Congregation of Seminaries and University Studies, and were definitively approved and confirmed by the same Congregation on 11 February 1940 under the title of "Statuta Facultatum Theologiae et Philosophiae Pontificii Athenaei Kandiensis 1940". According to these Statutes the degrees are conferred not by the Seminary, but by the Athenaeum. This is also evident from the Diploma given to successful candidates: no reference at all to the Seminary. This is also explicitly stated by the Statutes, in Art. 1 and Art. 5.

The way was thereby thrown open for Indian students to be engaged in scholarly work in both Philosophy and Theology, and eventually give the lead in these studies as professors of Faculties in our seminaries, and without necessarily having to go abroad in order to earn those degrees. This was precisely the intention of Pope Leo, when he gave the Papal Seminary as its motto "Filli tui, India, administri tibi salutis". By this he meant that the sons of India were called not only to give their countrymen the knowledge of the essential tenets of their faith but also to be their leaders in scholarly investigation and research in the area of the same universal religion. India remains ever grateful to this great Pope for his initiative in this respect.

Language Academies

A word may here be added regarding what among us goes by the name of "Language Academies". The term may perhaps sound somewhat pretentious, but it stands for the various language groups among the seminarians formed for the purpose of fostering the study of the particular language, literature and culture of each respective group. In this way the members of each group not only keep in touch with their native language but prepare themselves for their future missionary work in their home dioceses.

The first language academy was the Malayalam Academy, started in the very first year of the existence of the Seminary - 1893. In the course of the years other similar "Academies" came into existence: Tamil, Singalese, Hindi, Telugu, Marathi, Gujarati, Konkani. They continue still to be part of the life of the Seminary.

Other Events

The centenary of *St. Augustine* was solemnly celebrated in Kandy on August 28, 1930 with a special session of the theologians' Academy. An image of the saint was enthroned, and the following papers were read on the Doctor of Hyppo: 1. The place of St. Augustine in the history of the Church; 2. St. Augustine's speculation on Creation; 3. St. Augustine, the great theologian. Musical items enlivened the session during the intervals.

Another important celebration was the fifteen hundredth anniversary of the definition of the *Divine Maternity* of the Blessed Virgin Mary as an article of faith (28 June 1931). It was called to mind how on this day - 28 June 1431 the Council of Ephesus prolonged its session late into the night till it proclaimed this truth as a dogma of faith, to the great joy of the Ephesians: the Blessed Virgin Mary, Mother of Jesus, is truly by that very fact the Mother of God. The seminarians had Deogratias at dinner and a half holiday in the afternoon. Later in the evening a special Academy was held in the theologians' Library. The Rector presided, and the following programme was conducted: 1. Overture: Largo of Handel by Orchestra; 2. Essay on "The Problem and Victory"; 3. Hymn "Salve Regina" by the choir; 4. Essay: "Nestorius"; 5. Essay: Cyril of Alexandria; 6. "Ave Maria" of Gounod by the Orchestra; 7. Essay: Celestine I; 8. Essay: The Council of Ephesus; 9. Hymn "Mother of Christ" by choir.

The feast of Christ the King served as the occasion for Fr. Rector to offer each of the seminarians the little book of the Rules of the Apostolic Union of the Clergy. In a meeting especially convened for this purpose the Rector explained to the students the purpose of this little publication, namely, to foster their fidelity to the practices of the Apostolic Union and their missionary zeal. The Apostolic Union had been established in the seminary in December 1901. It keeps the seminarians in contact with their elder brothers working in the mission field and encourages them to help them by their prayer, work and sacrifice. In this connection, we may quote here the special word of encouragement received from Msgr. Lamérand, the International Director of the Union, in 1926: "I know of no other seminary where the students live in such close bonds of union with the priests of the Apostolic Union and pray so much for them".

About this time, on April 29, 1932, the seminarians went to St. Anthony's College, in the town, to listen to a song recital by a Dutchman, Dr. A. Bake, who spent several years in India studying Indian music, particularly with Rabindranath Tagore, at Shanti Niketan. He treated his audience to a selection of songs in Bengali, French, Italian, English, Dutch, German and Russian. They came back saying: "It was a linguistic feat as well as awonderful display of soul-stirring musical powers!"

They were also allowed to go to the Empire Theatre in the town, to view Fr. Adrian Le Tellier's Film - the only authenticated one - of the 1931 Exposition of the body of St. Francis Xavier in Old Goa, the deserted city which once countedas many as sixty churches and a good number of religious houses. The Church of "Bom Jesus" and the tomb of St. Francis Xavier were well shown, as well as the crowds of devout pilgrims flocking to old Goa on that occasion. During the intervals, Mrs. Jeanne Armstrong made short explanatory comments. Mrs. Armstrong is a one-time bigoted Protestant lady from Australia who was cured at Goa of a paralysis of the limbs and, more noteworthy still, of her scepticism and religious agnosticism.

Our life on earth is made up of events joyful and sorrowful. One of those events that filled the hearts of Kandyans with deep sadness was the death on April 26, 1935, of Bro. Louis de Vadder, S.J.

Born in Belgium in 1873 Louis joined the Society of Jesus in1897. He came to India in the following year. After a number of years in Kurseong and Calcutta he was transferred to Kandy in1922. During his fourteen years of humble, devoted service to the Papal Seminary as linen-keeper, infirmarian and gardener, he seemed to have no other concern than to be of service to others. He was outstanding in patience and kindness in his relationship with people, and spent all his time in work and prayer: it was atruly edifying sight to watch the good Brother saying his beadsor making the Way of the Cross in the chapel. Not even failing health could diminish his assiduity at the estate dispensary even in the hottest hours of the afternoon. The thought of death did not frighten him. One day, during his last illness one of the students asked him in jest: "Well, Brother, not yet gone!" No, came the reply, with a quiet smile, "What's to be done? No ticket yet: all placed booked..." Acute bronchit is and fits of suffocation finally brought him to the end. He received the Last Sacraments on April 7, 1935. "I am the happiest of men" he declared the following morning to a visitor. On the 26 of the month he told the one who was keeping watch by his bedside "I wish I could die". His wish was fulfilled that very day at three in the afternoon. His body was laid in the chapel where he had spent so many hours in silent communion with the divine Master. Besides the members of the seminary community, lots of people came from all over to pay their respects to one whose selfless charity and dedication they had so often experienced.

Fr. L'Hoir was at the helm of the Papal Seminary since 1920. It was his lot to govern the institution during the years that followed the First World War, when the Seminary had to struggle for its very survival. No help could come from abroad, but Fr. L'Hoir's firm trust in the Sacred Heart of Jesus went a long way to help him not only to hold out but even undertake new enterprises: the building of the Chapel, the reorganization of the curricula of studies in view of the Faculty degrees, the corresponding increase in the number of professors, and new buildings - an extensive suite of rooms with refectory, dormitory and halls for study and recreation. Fr. L'Hoir has been called "the second founder" of the Papal Seminary, after Fr. Grosjean, and he was, indeed, the living embodiment of what came to be known as the "Kandy spirit". The number of letters and telegrams on his desk, on the silver jubilee of his priestly ordination (13 December, 1938) were a tangible sign of the esteem in which he was held by old Kandyans.

Father L'Hoir was succeed by one whom the seminarians had come to know well and for whom they had much respect and love: **Fr. John Ancot**. In his speech on the following Rector's Day (17 July, 1935), Fr. Ancot told his community that he was happier now as Rector because he had the opportunity to cooperate more directly in what had always been the great ambition of his life: the conversion to Christ.

Around this time malaria attacked many people in and around Kandy. The seminarians took it as a call to their generosity, and they rose to the occasion: they promptly went out in service to the poor people and devoted themselves whole heartedly to those in need, visiting them and taking them food and medicines, irrespective of creed or caste. On foot, on bicycle, the goodwork was carried out, far and near, unobtrusively and efficiently.

The Golden Jubilee Celebrations[14]

As we said above, the year 1943 was the Golden Jubilee year of the Seminary. However, due to the Second World War no celebration could be held at that time. It was therefore put off to a later date: November 30 to December 3, 1946, during the rectorship of **Fr. Ignatius Glennie**.

The celebrations began with the welcome given on December 30 to the Chief Guest, His Excellency Archbishop Leo P. Kierkels, C.P., Apostolic Delegate of the Holy See in India. Among other distinguished guests present were Bishop Chulaparambil of Kottayam, Bishop Peter Francis of Kumbakonam, Bishop Laudadio, S.J., of Galle, and Bishop Valerian Gracias, Auxiliary of Bombay.

The celebrations followed a well thought out plan meant to highlight the main features of life in the Seminary, as well as, through personal witnesses from old Kandyans, the fruit of the formation imparted in Kandy.

First came, at 3.00 in the afternoon of November 30, the defence of a doctoral thesis by Robert Falleiro on "The Influx of Christ-Man in His Mystical

Body" - a subject of great actuality and of practical import in the life of every Christian and of the Church.

The First Day: December 1, 1946 was set apart as a Thanksgiving Day. Bishop Peter Francis celebrated the Pontifical High Mass at 8.30 in the morning. At 12.30 noon, during lunch a seminarian made a speech welcoming the guests. Among those present were Sir Gerard Wijeykoon, the Grand Chevalier N.A.D. Silva and the Honourable Mr. George E. De Silva, Minister of Health.

At 5.30 p.m. the "Academic Meeting" was held in the Hall with the following programme:

1. Survey of the Seminary's Fifty Years, by Fr. Rector, Ignatius Glennie.
2. The Material Developments, by Fr. L. Vossen
3. The Spiritual Formation, by Fr. F.X. L'Hoir
4. The Intellectual Training, by Fr. John Ancot
5. The Meeting was Immediately Followed by a Visit to the Chapel, where Msgr. Joseph Fernandez Gave the Benediction of the Bl. Sacrament.

The Second Day: December 2, 1946 - This day was dedicated to a survey of the Kandyans' apostolic labour in the country. It began with a Pontifical Requiem High Mass for the deceased professor sand students, celebrated by Bishop Chulaparambil. Later, at 10.00 a.m., there was, what was called, an Open Forum with a brief exposition on the ministries of Kandyans in the mission field, by the following Fathers: Msgr. Mariadas on "Parish Ministry", Fr. L. Raymond on "Schools", Msgr. Panjikaren on "Charitable and Social Work", Msgr. K. Joseph on "Mission *ad paganos*", Msgr. J. A. Fernandez on "The Apostolate of the Press".

The meeting at tea in the afternoon was brightened by representatives of six successive generations of Kandyans giving short reminiscences of life in Kandy in their time: 1893-1901, 1902-1910, 1911-1919, 1920-1928, 1929-1937, 1938. At 7.00 p.m. the Pontifical Vespers were presided over by Bishop Valerian Gracias who also directed the Holy Hour (*ad libitum*) at 9.30 p.m.

The Third Day: December 3, 1946 - The theme was "dedication of the Seminary to its Ideal".

The day began by our chief guest, the Delegate Apostolic, celebrating the High Mass at 8.30 a.m. A group photograph was then taken. When the Fathers saw Fr. Lambot, though old and weak, struggling to come for the function with the help of a walking stick which he had never used before, their hearts went out to him in a spontaneous out burst of warm applause. This was Father's last appearance in public.

The principal item of the day was the session at which H.E. the Delegate Apostolic presided. In his memorable speech he expressed the gratitude of all for the Seminary's fifty years of fruitful existence, for the priests it has helped to form and prepare for their sacerdotal ministry in the country. Gratitude, he said, "first of all to God whose divine Providence has destined this institution to such an important role in the history of the missions and has hallowed the name of this privileged spot in Ceylon in the annals of the Church; gratitude to the Holy See, who took and takes such particular interest in this pontifical institution, to Archbishop Zaleski, to the Society of Jesus, to Fr. Grosjean and his first helpers, to his successors, to all members of the staff, past and present, who have made Kandy Seminary what it is, to the many benefactors who have helped materially, to the Bishops and clergy and people of Kandy who have ever shown their enlightened appreciation of this institution, and last but not least, to the former pupils, deceased or living, present or absent, whose names and lives honour their Alma Mater in the ranks of the hierarchy and clergy of India, Ceylon, Burma and who are examples of the ideal to which today their Seminary is being re-dedicated". He added – "St. Francis Xavier should be our model and leader. But if we need leaders and models nearer at hand, I may point to the standard bearers of Kandy: the Bishops who are this Seminary's highest credit and glory...In them we hail the highest fulfilment of the Holy See's and Kandy's ideal". Msgr. Kierkels ended his long speech with these words: "This unforgettable Golden Jubilee will ever be, I am sure, one of our happiest memories, and when fifty years hence another generation will celebrate the Seminary's centenary, they too will have reason, I hope, to look back to these days as to a signpost on the road of history, bearing the words: Onward, Kandy forever, *in spemdiututnitatis*!"

Other speakers followed: Bishop Chulaparampil, Bishop Peter Francis and Bishop Gracias. This last began by conveying "the grateful thanks, cordial greetings and good wishes of His Grace the Archbishop of Bombay, Dr. Roberts, for all that Bombay owed to Kandy".

A few of the numerous messages received on this occasion were then read out by the Rector: First came that of the Sovereign Pontiff, which said: SENDING CORDIAL FELICITATIONS JOYOUS OCCASION GOLDEN JUBILEE FOUNDATION SEMINARY HOLY FATHER LOVINGLY IMPARTS SUPERIORS PROFESSORS STUDENTS EX-ALUMNI PLEDGE ABUNDANT SPIRITUAL FRUITS APOSTOLATE. PATERNAL APOSTOLIC BLESSING IMPLORED.

Messages came from the Cardinal Prefect of Propaganda, the Hierarchy of India and Ceylon, the Father General of the Society of Jesus, and the Acting Chief Justice of Ceylon, Sir F. J. Soertsz. Fr. Rector announced that a cablegram was sent to the Holy Father thanking him for his benevolence and generosity to the Seminary.

The Jubilee dinner at 1.30 p.m. was also punctuated with several speeches namely, by Bishop Chulaparampil, the Lord abbot A. Weerasinghe, OSB, Fr. Archibald Mowforth, and the Beadle of the house, Bro. Kurien Vanchipurackal, and finally the Rector.

At 5.30 p.m. all proceeded to the chapel where the Te Deum was sung and Benediction was given by His Excellency the Delegate Apostolic. During the ceremony the consecration to the Sacred Heart of Jesus and the Immaculate Heart of Mary was renewed.

A commemorative marble tablet offered by the alumni of the Kandy Seminary perpetuates the memory of this jubileecelebration.

1893 1943
DEO OPTIMO MAXIMO
QUI Ministerio Societatis Jesu
RECTORUM IMPRIMIS EORUMQUE ADJUTORUM
PONTIFICIUM SEMINARIUM ATHENAEUMQUE KANDIENSE
UBERRIMIS DONIS DITAVIT
HUNC LAPIDEM IN GRATI ANIMI TESTIMONIUM
ALUMNI DEDICAVERUNT
DIE FESTO S.F. XAVERII A.D. MCMXLVI

Extracts from the final speech of the Pope's representative in India are well in place here:

> "We are assembled here to perpetuate the memory of this Golden Jubilee and to convey even to future generations the main sentiment which has inspired our rejoicing: gratitude to God and to His chosen instruments for all the benefits conferred on the Pontifical Seminary of Kandy during the fifty years of its existence".

It is a spontaneous human impulse to give lasting expression to, and place on perennial record, views or facts or sentiments in which we are deeply interested. The vast epigraphical collections in existence well show how universal is the wish expressed already by Job: *quis mihi tribuat ut scribantursermones mei, ut exarentur stylo ferreo et plumbi lamina, velcelte sculpantur in silice* (19:23-24). From bricks to copper plates, from cave walls to obelisks and columns, the most varied materials and objects have been used for all sorts of inscriptions, relating mostly to historical facts or religious matters, all in the endeavour, not only to elude the transit oriness of things and to frustrate the edacity of time, *tempus edax rerum* (Ovid), but also to stress and emphasize the purport of the inscriptions.

That too is the two fold aim of the marble tablet we are unveiling and inaugurating today. In measured and lapidary language the students of Kandy have emphasized, in marble, thoughts and sentiments they wish to be ever lasting. While every detail of the tablet before us offers matter for interesting consideration, from the years marked at the top to the date of the inauguration below, I shall point out only the three main ideas conveyed by the inscription, viz.: 1. gratitude of the students; 2. for the benefits received by the Pontifical Seminary of Kandy; 3. through the instrumentality of the Society of Jesus.

The Fathers of the Society, from Fr. Grosjean to the present Rector and staff, have certainly come up fully to the expectation of the Holy See, of Archbishop

Zaleski, and of the hierarchy. Inpleading with Fr. Grosjean to accept the work, Msgr. Zaleski repeatedly insisted that the Society of Jesus was indispensable to inspire confidence in the Seminary's success, and fifty years of proficiency have more than justified that confidence. When Pope Benedict XV addressed a letter to Fr. Vossen on the occasion of the Seminary's Silver Jubilee, he remarked that a number of priests and some bishops had already gone forth from the institution "*eosque ad apostolatum egregie instructos, ac prorsus Societatis Jesu disciplina dignos*". That aptly expresses orcon notes all the benefits conferred on Kandy through the Society of Jesus.

And by Kandy I mean not only this instrumental seat of piety and learning, but also its entire extra mural sphere of influence, throughout India, Ceylon and Burma. When of old Athens erected acenotaph to Euripides, whose real tomb was elsewhere, they inscribed on it these words: All Greece is the monument of Euripides. So all India, Ceylon and Burma are the monument of Kandy and of the benefits conferred on them through Kandy. Hence in erecting this marble record of perennial gratitude, the students voice not only their own appreciation but that of the entire country, to which they belong and especially of the hierarchy. Benedict XV, in the letter already quoted, made the note worthy statement that the Bishops could consider *satis sesuo officio satisfecisse cum sanctam cleri indigenae cureverint institutionem.* For many Bishops Kandy performed or is performing that duty, and all, I am sure, wish to join the students inproclaiming their undying gratitude through this marble tablet. It has been said that also ".... marble and recording brass decay, and like the graver's memory, pass away" (Cowper).

Even if that were to happen to this tablet, the dynamism of Kandy will always inspire the Church in these lands and "*aereperennius*" more enduringly than brass, the sentiments expressed in this memorial will live on forever.

With that confidence we now entrust this tablet to history and posterity who no doubt echo our words: Forever!"

The session ended with the singing of "God bless the Pope" and the Seminary Anthem, after which Bishop Gracias called for three "hearty cheers for Kandy" to which all responded with at hunderous applause. Deo gratias.

The Apostolic Delegate's Letter to Fr. Ignatius Glennie, S. J., Rector

Colombo, December 6, 1946

Very Reverend Dear Father,

With the impression of the Golden Jubilee still fresh in my mind I wish to assure you once more of my great satisfaction with the most successful celebrations. While it must have been a period of unforgettable days for the present and former Kandyans, it was a very impressive, informative and edifying experience for me, and a permanent initiation into the Kandyan atmosphere and spirit. It has confirmed my conviction that Kandy fully justifies Pope Leo XIII's far seeing intention and hopes, and that the Pontifical Seminary and Athenaeum worthily hold their own among the best institutions of ecclesiastical training and formation.

Please convey to all the Reverend Fathers and the students the assurance of my happiest impressions and my ever greater interest in the welfare and prosperity of the Seminary.

Accept for yourself my heartiest thanks for your attentions and kindness.

With cordial greetings and blessing to all, I remain,

Yours devotedly,
+ P. Kierkels, C.P.
Apostolic Delegate

Very Rev. Ignatius Glennie, S.J.
Rector, the Papal Seminary, Kandy

Notes

1. V. L., Apostolic Union Report, 1919, p. 80-81.
2. Apostolic Union Report, 1920, p. 59.
3. Apostolic Union Bulletin, 1925.
4. Apostolic Union Report, 1925-26, pp. 3, 15.
5. Letter of 12 March, 1925.
6. Letter of 16 July, 1926.
7. Letter of Fr. Rector to the Holy Father Pope Pius XI, 30 March, 1928.
8. Letter from Rome, 15 February, 1929.
9. Decree of S.C. of Propaganda Fide, 27 July, 1926. H.
10. Letter of Cardinal Cajetan Bisletti, 8 September, 1932.
11. *Acta Romana*, 1932, pp. 62-63.
12. From Tusculum, letter of 21 July, 1931 (cfr. *Acta Romana* VI, pp. 550)
13. Letter of 6 January, 1933 (*Acta Romana*, VII, pp. 550-552).
14. See Papal Seminary, Kandy, Ceylon: "Golden Jubilee Celebrations".

Chapter 5

Unto Wider Horizons (1943-1955)
The Transfer to Pune

In spite of the advantages of Kandy many felt that a General Seminary for the whole of India situated at the extreme south of the country, almost, as it were, out of its boundaries, seemed, at least in principle, an incongruity, out of touch with the reality. On the other hand, Kandy was somehow close enough to the most catholic part of India, the South. Besides, given the mildness of the climate, the exquisite beauty of the scenery around, the peace and quiet that were so conducive to prayer, study and recollection and finally the fine set of priests it produced in the course of time, Kandy came to be accepted and was taken for granted. But then came the proclamation of India as an independent country, separated from Ceylon which also obtain edits independence in 1948. This momentous event brought matters to a head: a general, or central seminary for the whole of India outside its own boundaries was an anomaly. A way had therefore to be found to remedy the situation by transferring the Seminary to India.

An Old Idea

Actually, the idea of an eventual transfer of the Papal Seminary to the Indian mainland was not something new and unfamiliar: it had been playing in the mind of the superiors forquite some time, long before the actual transfer was decided upon. In his address at the inauguration of the seminary Church in Pune, and its solemn blessing, Archbishop Thomas Poothecamury said: "The idea of the transfer of the Papal Seminary to India was first suggested to me in May 1945 by Fr. Ignatius Glennie, the Rector of the Seminary, later Bishop of Trincomalee. It came then to me as a rude shock. I was startled by the novelty of the proposal. We, old students of Kandy, were so deeply attached to its hallowed precincts. But the trend of events rendered the change imperative. At the Catholic Bishops' Conference of India held in Bangalore in October 1949, it was I who introduced the question of the transfer. The reasons adduced were: 1. Radical changes in India and Ceylon, following Independence. 2. Difficulties of obtaining passports; 3. Cost of living in Kandy already high; 4. Money could not be sent from India to Ceylon; 5. Too long a stay in a foreign country would deprive students of contact with their own homeland since most of the students were Indians. The subject of the transfer was discussed in the Plenary Council, in January, 1950. A few suitable centres were proposed, and all the members unanimously favoured Bangalore. When I went to Rome in June 1950, both Cardinal Fumasoni-Biondi and the Secretary of the Sacred Congregation of Propaganda, Archbishop Celso Costantini told me that the Papal Seminary would be transferred to Bangalore. A few days later they told me that it would be transferred to Poona."[1]

The earliest reference in the Seminary Archives to the transfer of the Seminary from Ceylon is found in a letter of Fr. F. X. L'Hoir dated March 17, 1921, to the Apostolic Delegate, Msgr. Peter Pisani. In that "strictly confidential" letter, the then rector of the seminary discusses the pros and cons of a shift of the institution from Kandy to Bangalore. Pune was not then in the picture.

He first states the reasons for a change to Bangalore: 1. Cheaper cost of living, but how long will this last?; 2. Bangalore is easier of access, yes, but this wouldn't make much of a difference to the students in Kandy: they rarely travel outside the place. Besides, it might have the inconvenience of visits too frequently from friends and relatives; 3. The new Seminary could be built along more practical lines.

Fr. L'Hoir then goes on to enumerate the reasons for the Seminary continuing in Kandy: 1. The fait accompli: the immense capital that had gone into the buying of the estate and the plantations; 2. The difficulty of finding one who would be interested in acquiring the entire estate, together with the various buildings that had come up there in the course of the years, viz. the seminary, the chapel or church, the chapel of Msgr. Zaleski, the two schools, the farm, the other houses on the estate, the cemeteries, etc. 3. A very suitable climate, with no danger of an epidemic; 4. The admirable position of the seminary on the top of a hill with its quiet and solitude, sufficiently away from the noise of the town, and yet close enough, the pure air, the pleasant surroundings, the beautiful scenery; 5. Isolation from India, conducive to a perfect fusion of races and castes among the students; also a certain distance from the political ferment agitating India at that time; 6. The great advantages coming from the farm and the vegetable garden; 7. Finally, the traditions of 27 years of life in Kandy...

Fr. L'Hoir's conclusion was this: even granted that, all things considered, Kandy was not the best choice for a General Seminary for India, now that it was there and had been running smoothly for 27 years, a change seemed hardly possible or advisable without heavy odds, not compensated by possible advantages.

For the time being, then, the matter seemed to have been shelved. In reality, however, it continued to be a matter of preoccupation to those responsible for the future of Christianity in India. Bishop F. Perier, S. J., then Auxiliary of Calcutta, mentioned explicitly in a letter to Fr. Ancot that the Delegate Apostolic had spoken to him about it and had not put it aside. Indeed, the Delegate himself wrote to Fr. L'Hoir saying: "Keep all that we have privately discussed on the matter as absolutely confidential. I have not yet submitted the question to Rome nor do I think I will do so, not at least in the near future" (Letter of August 10, 1923).

About twenty years passed by, and the topic came up again explicitly in 1942 in several letters exchanged between Jesuit Superiors in India. For instance, Fr. J. Moyersoen, S. J., the Delegate of the General of the Society in India during the war years, writing in 1942 to the Superior Regular of Calcutta underwhose jurisdiction the Kandy Seminary had been till recently, says: "We must foresee the possibility of the Kandy Seminary having to come over to India". He added: "As the Seminary has so much to do with the S.C. of Propaganda, I have asked the Delegate Apostolic's opinion on the subject". He concluded: "I have already informed the local authorities to make use of their initiative, should any emergency arise". By "local authorities" he meant evidently the Rector of Kandy and the Jesuit Superior Regular of Galle, under whom Kandy came, since 1941.

The War Years

In the same strain, Fr. Ancot, the then Rector of the seminary, says in one of his letters, in February, 1942: "I have started enquiring about the advisability of shifting. As I was told by a government official, evacuation would become very difficult if not impossible in time of danger, but this seems to be rather far off. We trust in God and keep our confidence, going ahead with our intellectual activities".

These were war years, and the inmates of the Seminary had already, as we have mentioned earlier in this History, begun to experience the implications of this reality. The Second World War broke out on September 30, 1939. As a result, when Belgium, Holland and France were occupied, all material help coming from the "Opus Sancti Petri" of these countries came inevitably to a stop. Communications with Italy, too, ceased. Providentially, however, the "Opus Sancti Petri" of the United States and Canada took over the charitable task. So, too, generous help came from the Catholic laity who came to be acquainted with the criticalsituation which the inmates of the Seminary were facing - Catholic laity, I say, from India and still more from Ceylon.

With the fall of Singapore in 1941, the danger of a Japanese invasion of our country began to be more threatening than ever before. For instance, the Seminary authorities were informed that in the eventuality of the Kandy hospital being damaged, or becoming unable to cope with the number of causalities, the Seminary buildings might be requisitioned for the purpose. Consequently, the reasons for shifting the institution to the mainland became ever more pressing.

Nevertheless, "trusting in the Divine Providence, Fr. Ancot took the courageous risk of remaining in the island."[2]

At the same time, on the advice of the Superior Regular of Trincomalee, Ancot asked all the students to give him in writing a statement as to whether they preferred to remain in Ceylon, or return to the mainland. Out of the 130, only eleven chose to return to India. Out of these, eight were deacons, almost at the end of their priestly studies in Kandy. As things turned out, the Japanese invasion never took place, nor were the Seminary buildings ever requisitioned by the military authorities.

Transfer to Pune

However, after an exchange of views between Propaganda, the Jesuit General, the Indian Hierarchy and the Jesuit Superiors in India, it was finally decided that the Papal Seminary should move to Poona (presently called Pune), where the Jesuits had their theologate - De Nobili College.

Reacting to this news, Fr. Ancot, who in the mean time had been transferred to Kurseong as Rector of the Jesuit Theologate there, wrote on 5 October 1950: "The news you give me about the transfer was not expected; I still hoped that the seminary would be left where it is. Providence has his own views, and now that *alea jacta est* we must, it seems to me, do all we can to make the transfer and the future Seminary a success".

Little did Ancot then suspect that this task of "making the change a success" would fall to a large extent on his own shoulders. He was then, as we said, Rector of St. Mary's, Kurseong, but he would soon be transferred back to Kandy as Rector once more and as such would have to bear the burden of effecting the move to Pune. However, between the decision about the transfer and the actual shift, six years had still to elapse.

In this connection, it is strange that even as late as January 1954 - little over a year before the shift to Pune - nobody in Kandy seemed to know who was to succeed the Jesuits at Ampitya, to whom they had to hand over the estate, or what was the destination of the entire Kandy property. It was necessary for them to know this, also because of the poor, needy people who in the course of the years, had on their own, occupied bits of the land in the periphery of the big seminary estate. They had been implicitly allowed to do so, because of the fact that they were poor people who had no home of their own. If the Fathers knew who would be taking over they could acquaint them with the situation of these indigent people and come to some settlement in their favour.[3]

It is alluding to these and other problems of the sort, that Fr. Ancot wrote to Fr. Hans Staffner, S.J., who was Rector in Pune: "Problems which no one could solve in a satisfactory manner for the last thirty years are expected to be solved properly *hicet nunc* by myself and Fr. Pou. He is certainly good for administration" (letter of October 28, 1952). And again: "This business cannot be simply hurried through; too much of a capital is involved which belongs partly to the Society and partly to the Seminary, and we are now at the eleventh hour asked to find out exactly which is which... The result is that both Father Superior (of Galle Mission) and myself are preparing a 'memorandum' before we ask Rome what exactly is to be done with regard to the various properties, movable and immovable" (letter to Fr. Conget, February 23, 1953).

Be that as it may, what was certain was that the Jesuits in Kandy had at any rate to begin preparing the shift of the Seminary to India. This is easily said, but the whole business of this transfer to India gave both Ancot and his right-hand man, Fr. Pou Montfort a lot of headaches.

At long last, word came from the Vatican as to the future of "Kandy": a letter from Cardinal Fumasoni-Biondi, the Prefect of Propaganda, announcing that a Regional Seminary for Ceylon was to be established at Ampitya under the management of the Oblates of Mary Immaculate. The entire estate with all its belongings would continue to be the property of the Holy See but the income from the estate would accrue to the new Regional Seminary, as it had till then to the Pontifical Seminary.[4]

So, that was that. One thing was now certain: the Papal Seminary was to go to Pune. The Oblates of Mary Immaculate would take over directly from the Jesuits. The estate would not for a single moment be left without a master on the spot. Besides, it was also suggested that in order to avoid multiplication of the staff, the three institutions should function in the same locality: the Papal Seminary, the Pontifical Athenaeum comprising the Faculties of Philosophy and Theology, and the Jesuit scholasticate of Pune - De Nobili College. Father Conget wrote on February 23, 1951: "I am inclined to think that the decision concerning the place comes from Propaganda. Father General would very much like to have the three together (in order to save professors). He knows by experience how difficult it is to get professors for the '*opera communia*'. Nevertheless, the General was prepared, in case Propaganda were to choose some other place, to shift De Nobili College to that place".

However, the Kandy community had no knowledge of the arrangements that were being made for them in Pune. Their only source of information seems to have been Fr. Josef Neuner, Professor of Dogma in De Nobili College, Pune, who kindly let them know from time to time what buildings were coming up there, one after another: the lecture block first, then the seminary building itself, and so on... Yet, they had no clear idea as to what things they had to carry with them to the new place from what was part of their movable property in Kandy.

A letter from the Superior of Pune Jesuit Mission, Fr. Pius Geisel, throws some light on this question. On April 16, 1955 he wrote from Pune that the front wing of the Fathers' block was just getting the roof. The students' quarters were ready. He adds: "It looks to me that what was given *intuitu communitatis* should go to the community. You will need a villa here, just as much, or rather more than in Kandy. So, sell the villa and bring the funds to buy another here".

Father Geisel also informed Fr. Ancot that in Pune the portable altars were ready but they had still to get the altar-linen and other pertinent articles. He took it for granted that they would bring from Kandy the necessary objects for ordinary use, or else he asked Ancot to give him the required information, so that he might provide. Also they should bring with them some 75 to 100 bedsteads. The rest-mattresses, mosquito-nets, and bed-sheets-would be supplied in Pune.

Anyway, after consultation with the Oblate Fathers, and in keeping with directives from Rome, the following sets of articles were taken to Pune, so as to make sure that they had the necessary things for their use, as soon as they landed there: some chalices, Mass vestments, a certain number of iron bedsteads from the dormitories, a piano, the harmonium from the chapel and the music room, napkins and table clothes; statues and images of Jesuit saints or those more particularly connected with the Pontifical Seminary.

They left behind for their successors: the furniture of the chapel and of the house, namely altars, benches, about six hundred seats, tables etc., priests' vestments (four sets), the entire furniture of the kitchen, refectory and bakery, a large part of the furniture of the dormitories (50 iron and wooden beds), pictures and images for the adornment of the house, the carpentry, farm and cattle with their equipment, pumps and engines, etc. - all amounting to some hundred thousand rupees.

No compensation was envisaged, evidently, for all this. As Fr. Ancot remarked, it would be like Propaganda paying Propaganda! The entire Seminary with its large estate of over 200 acres was Propaganda's gift to the Church in India and Ceylon. So, too, the land and the new buildings in Pune: the Athenaeum, the Library building, the Seminary block. However, writing to the Jesuit Regional Superior of Ceylon, Father Fortin, O.M.I., told him: "Rev. Fr. Ancot handed over to me some time ago a list of things he wished to take with him to India. I submitted the matter to Propaganda. I am glad to say that he may take with him whatever he likes."[5]

The question of the *Library* is a distinct item. The main library was entirely built up with the Society's funds and as Jesuit property. It was transferred en bloc to Pune and it forms the basis of the present Jnana-Deepa Vidyapeeth Library containing over a lakh of books. At present it receives over 500 reviews from different parts of the world. All those using the library for their study, research and information are heavily indebted to the Librarian, Fr. Aloysius Schlegel, S. J. Over and above his task of keeping the library up-to-date, he is always available to both members of the staff and students for whatever help they may be in need of in the use of the books existing in the library, or acquiring new ones. After over forty years of exemplary service as librarian and competent adviser in these matters, he continued to help in the library, together with Fr. Josef Lombart, S.J., the then Librarian and Fr. Douglas Dias SJ, who succeeded Fr. Antonio Sabino as Assistant Librarian.

We may here ask the question: How did the community of Fathers and brothers in Kandy react to the proposed transfer of the Seminary to India? Fr. Ancot tells us something about this. He writes: "The news of the probable shifting of the seminary to India has caused dismay to all those who are connected with Kandy, with very few exceptions, I believe. Some will call it sentiment, may be, but the fact is that it will be the end of what makes Kandy loved by its students. The facts that have swayed the Bishops in their decision were, I think, the difficulty of sending students to Ceylon and the high cost of living. As to the first reason, it was very acute then, when conditions were very upset, there is no difficulty at all now; as to the second, the expenses here compare favourably with the fees charged in our Scholasticates in India. The Bishops, in fact, are keen in sending their students here; they have to pay in the Indian seminaries (Rs. 70/- in Mangalore, Rs. 35/- in Trichy) while here they pay nothing..."

"The Bishops pay nothing for their students in Kandy". This statement calls for an overall exposé of the financial situation of the Kandy Seminary from the time of its foundation down to the time of its transfer to Pune.

Finances Again

The original donation of Mr. Wodehouse was never used directly for the maintenance of the seminary. It was kept in Rome as a sort of reserve fund, for any emergency situation. The ordinary expenses of the seminary were met by the *Opus Sancti Petri Apostoli* founded by two magnanimous French ladies, Madame Bigard and her daughter, and it contributed 140 dollars per year for each seminarian. In addition to this, the Seminary received Rs. 37,000 annually from the Opere Pontificie di Propaganda Fide. Further help came from the produce of the estate and the farm, and from donations received from benefactors in Ceylon, India, Belgium and elsewhere, plus the income from the burses established in the Seminary, yielding on the whole about Rs. 7000.

As the financial situation continued to remain most of the time precarious, Pope Leo went so far as to write an Encyclical Letter appealing to the entire catholic world for funds in favour of the Pontifical Seminary of Kandy: the Encyclical *Ad extremas Orientis gentes*. He put Cardinal Ledochowski, Prefect of Propaganda, in charge of the task of collecting funds for Kandy. The Jesuit Provincial of Galicia, too, helped by distributing a brochure in favour of Kandy, signed by Cardinal Ledochowski and Archbishop Zaleski.

In the year 1913, Cardinal Gotti, successor of Cardinal Ledochowski as Prefect of Propaganda, suggested to the Rector, Fr. Meunier, to reduce the admission of the seminarians to the possibilities of maintaining them through the ordinary income of the seminary - a thing which Fr. Grosjean had consistently refrained from doing. Meunier was also told to avoid making new plantations except after all the necessary expenses of the seminary had been gone through.

In July of the same year, Fr. General Ledochowski suggested to Propaganda that the Bishops whose students are maintained in Kandy could be asked to contribute the sum of Rs. 50/- per year for each of their candidates. The Secretary of Propaganda answered saying that the bishops could be "invited" to make such a contribution freely, if they felt like doing so. Later, however, Cardinal Gotti let the Rector of Kandy know that such a contribution was contrary to the intention of the Founder, hence, that he would not sanction such a move (October 11, 1913). Seeing, however, that it was extremely difficult for those in charge of Kandy to make ends meet, Fr. Veys, Superior Regular of the Bengal-Ranchi Jesuit Mission, made Propaganda understand that the Society would stand by the terms of the bilateral contract by which it consented to undertake the direction of the Kandy Seminary, on the understanding that it would be entirely financed by the Sacred Congregation of Propaganda Fide. It was there foreup to Propaganda to do its part of the contract (Letter to Archbishop Pisani, March 27, 1922).

In 1920 Pope Benedict XV was pleased to come to the rescue of the seminary with a personal donation of 50,000 Lire – a striking proof of his love and concern for the Seminary and for the formation of the native clergy in India. This was in addition to the 125,000 Lire sent the previous year for the construction of the chapel. Unfortunately, on account of the low rate of exchange of the Lire at that time, the two donations fetched only Rs. 8,000 and 20,000 respectively. At a certain moment during the rectorship of Fr. L'Hoir, the rate of exchange was so low that for about two years or more Kandy simply stopped withdrawing any money from Italy, but preferred to leave it pending in Rome, in expectation of a more favourable time. In the meantime, the superiors in Kandy had to borrow money for their more urgent needs. The Rectors, Fr. Vossen and L'Hoir obtained full permission from the Delegate Apostolic for making debts if necessary.[6] Nevertheless, the financial condition of the institution was becoming increasingly difficult, hence, appeals for donations: appeals to the Hierarchy, to old students, to people in general.

In his letter to the Rector of the seminary dated April 30, 1940, Archbishop Kierkels informed him that the Cardinal Prefect of Propaganda expressed his disappointment at the fact that so far India had not been able to endow the seminary with sufficient means to make it self-sufficient, independent of assistance from outside. He asked: "Was it ever made clear that the Holy See expects the Seminary to be endowed by local funds, and was there not an understanding that the Holy See through the Pontifical Associations was to provide at least in a substantial way or degree for the maintenance of the Seminary?" From all we have seen, yes, there was such an understanding, but the personnel connected with the various institutions changes, and commitments can be forgotten with the passing of time.

Delegate Pisani seems to have expressed the hope that the Society of Jesus would come to the rescue of the Seminary in its financial difficulties. Fr. L'Hoir set things right in his letter to His Excellency, of May 3, 1922: "Your Excellency's tenacious hope that the Society will come to our rescue is, I am sure, a wrong assumption. The Society gives us means to have holidays; but this is a small thing, and meant to save the Fathers from suffering too long and too seriously from the effect of Propaganda's inadequate support : the seminary already owes Rs. 10,000 to the Society". By the middle of 1922 the situation had become almost desperate. Around the year 1945 the debt had reached the sum of Rs. 20,000 and it increased every year by Rs. 6,000. On October 1, 1948 the Rector wrote to the Delegate Apostolic asking for his intervention with Propaganda on behalf of Kandy.

However, gradually things began to improve, so that by September 1950, Fr. Ancot, the Rector, could inform Fr. Conget that "the debt of the Seminary which had risen high, has now been completely covered" (Letter of September 29, 1950). Deogratias!

Kandyans on Kandy

Before passing on to Pune, we would like to include in this chapter a few extracts from the letters or oral testimonies of Kandyans, which express their sentiments and their attitude to their Alma Mater during their stay in Kandy, or after they had left the Seminary as priests and were working in their respective dioceses.

I shall begin by stating that going through the old Archives of the Seminary I have found there not a single negative remark on the part of the students regarding the Seminary, either during their stay in Kandy or later as full-fledged priests and pastors. On the contrary, it is a pleasure to see how all felt happy in Kandy. The relations between the Brothers and Fathers were open and cordial; so too, among the seminarians themselves, though they came from different parts of the country, with different backgrounds. They appreciated the guided freedom they enjoyed in the community, the opportunity they had to work at their spiritual progress, through the time set apart for prayer and the spiritual exercises, the spiritual direction, the holiday each week at the villa as well as the longer holidays at the end of the scholastic year. (We should remember that in Kandy the seminarians, once they joined for philosophy [or a year or two earlier, for the humanities], never returned home except after seven or eight years, that is, after their priestly ordination and First Holy Mass. This was the rule then. Exceptions to this rule were very rare, due to very special circumstances). The few extracts we now reproduce here bear testimony to what we have stated. We take them at random.

Msgr. Joseph A. E. Fernandez, Rector of St. Thomas Seminary of Tanjavur, wrote in 1942: "The dawning year is the *Annus Jubilaris* of the Seminary and I cannot help feeling the exultation of the Jubilee. Will you give us all the opportunity of being there once more in the loved surroundings?" (January 29,

1942). A few years earlier the same old pupil of Kandy told his younger brothers studying in Kandy: "The more one thinks of Kandy the more one feels how much the great work of the Church in India is bound up with it. Pardon me, you would not now feel how much Kandy is doing and can do, as we feel it out here, in the actual work that has to be tackled" (Letter of November 11, 1935).

Writing to Fr. Ancot, in answer to his letter, another Kandyan, Fr. Ronald D'Souza, says in July 1953: "It was such a pleasure to get your little note with its scent of the happy atmosphere that is for ever linked with Kandy". Incidentally, Fr. Ronald raises the following point: "What will be the nature of our relations with the Seminary-to-be in Poona? Step-mother? Anyway I am extremely glad to know that you will be the first Rector and I hope you will be nominated Rector perpetuus".

Now comes a Jesuit scholastic who for reasons of health had to do his theology at Kandy, Fr. H. Hosten: "Seventeen years more have since gone by; many are those of ours who have succeeded one another at Ampitya; many too are the generations of students that have followed one another, and now the old Kandyans, both among ours and among the students are to be found everywhere, and not one but speaks of the old place as of one which, in God's Providence, it was a signal privilege to have lived in. I believe, for myself, that the six years I spent in the Seminary have had, in spite of myself, an elevating influence on my later life... I cannot but dwell with special fondness on the memory of those who have gone to their reward already. Chief among them stands Fr. Grosjean, a saintly, zealous Jesuit...' (Silver Jubilee, p.18).

Sharing his reminiscences during one of the sessions of the Golden Jubilee Celebrations in 1946, Msgr. D. Swaminather, the first student to arrive at Kandy in 1893, said: "It is with mingled feelings of joy, pride and gratitude that I rise to speak today... When I consider the eminent and distinguished prelates and priests turned out by the Kandy Seminary, when I call to mind the works achieved by the alumni of Kandy, which Kandyan priest's heart will not overflow with happiness and legitimate pride at having been one of the pioneers and corner-stone of so great an Alma Mater?... If we are to judge a tree by its fruit, then from the excellent spiritual force and energy generated in this spiritual 'Power House', it can be said in all truth that the formation given here is solid..."[7]

Last, here is one from Fr. Valerian Gracias writing on May 10, 1927, from Bandra, where on his return from Kandy as a newly ordained priest, he was posted as Assistant Parish Priest: "It is only when one leaves the Seminary for good that he realizes how much the good Belgian Fathers have done for him. During my course it often appeared to me that the explanations of my professors were much too theoretical, that they were over-particular about enunciating principles, rather than giving practical hints; and I often wondered whether all that would be of practical service tome in the Missions. But I have been sadly mistaken. And now I see that those good professors of mine, shut up as they are in their sanctum, know enough and more of this world. One of them was never tired of telling us in class that the best means to convert the educated non-Christian is to fortify the Catholic layman. And to do this every priest must be a thorough master of his theology, dogmatic and moral".

About thirty years later, he visited his Alma Mater, after his return from Rome as a Cardinal. On the Visitors' Book, he wrote: "25/5/53 to 29/5/53. This visit of mine has been an act of the deepest gratitude for all that I have received from my Alma Mater. The three days, though they have been full, have given me the opportunity to recall the happy memories of the four years I was privileged to spend at Kandy. May the spirit of the institution endure and flourish whatever and wherever its local habitat be". + Valerian Cardinal Gracias.

The Exodus

The exodus from Kandy was fixed for May 23, 1955. According to the original plan, it was to be a journey by boat from Colombo to Bombay, and then by train from Bombay to Pune. The students had accordingly planned their deck entertainment programmes. That plan, however, had to be dropped in favour of a journey by train from Madras to Pune.

In Kandy the school year opened in January and ended with the examinations in November. During the fourth year of theology the students were ordained priests on December 3, the feast of St. Francis Xavier, Patron of the Seminary. Then the Major Holidays started. In Pune classes begin in June and the year ends in March, with April and May as holidays. The programme for the Kandy seminarians coming to Pune had therefore to be adapted to the circumstances. It was done in the following way, after a long exchange of letters between Fr. Josef Neuner, the Prefect of Studies in Pune, and Fr. Ancot: The newly ordained priests left Kandy for good and proceeded straight to their respective dioceses. The students who had finished their philosophy, they, too were back in their dioceses. They would remain there till the end of May, at the disposal of their bishops, helping as best they could in the parishes and other institutions. In June they were to join their older companions in Pune for theology. As for those who had completed their first, second and third year of theology in Kandy in November, they would go to Pune to continue their theology there in June. What were they to do in the meantime, that is between November 1954 and June 1955?

After a period of rest and holiday, they were given some helpful courses in keeping with their needs or their preference: Greek, Latin, Hindi or Sanskrit, French, German, Italian. For those who had finished their ordinary courses, special "Economy"or "Indian Philosophy" classes were foreseen. Due provision was similarly made for Philosophers due to go to Pune in May. In addition to this, a good deal of their time was spent in packing up the things they would have to take to Pune.[8]

The "handing-over" was to take place on May 21, 22, and 23. No special ceremonies are needed - wrote Fr. Ancot to Fr. Fortin, O.M.I. "Let us do it all very simply, without drum or trumpet: *Faisons cela tout simplement, sans tambour ni trompette"* - and so it was done.

The community left Kandy on May 23: some 120 ecclesiastical students from India and Ceylon clad in their traditional blue cassock and red sash and the following members of the staff accompanying them: Fr. J. Ancot who was the "Rector Magnificus" of the Athenaeum, Fr. Peter Pou Montfort, the Minister of the House and professor, and Fathers R. Criem and N. Tornese. Other members of the staff took different routes: Fr. Grasso, G. Jannaccone, G. Koelman, Puthota Rayanna, C. Starace, N. Uricchio. Those who travelled by land boarded the train at Madras on May 26 night and reached Pune on 28 night, after five hot days since they had left Kandy, covering a distance of 1275 miles. In Pune they received a warm and hearty welcome from the De Nobili College Scholastics, Brothers and Fathers. On the 29, after supper, the Jesuit scholastics of De Nobili College put up in honour of the newcomers a variety entertainment that was greatly appreciated by everybody. Immediately before the entertainment, they had their night meal in their new refectory. Here is how one of them registered his impressions: Here, you are greeted by the smiling faces of the Rectors (the photos up onthe wall), who are of the past and the Pillars of the Seminary. The Word of God comes to you through the mike. Then 'Deo Gratias'. The din of youthful voices that respond heartily, not only drown the clatter of crockery but also all doubts and misgivings, worries and troubles and, in the flush of an instant, you realise: This is still the Home of Love."[9] The end of the Exodus!

Notes

1. A Souvenir of the Inauguration and Solemn blessing of the Papal Seminary Church, 1957, p. 37. It is interesting to see what a learned and experienced Jesuit priest, well versed in the history of the Church in Sri Lanka has to say in this regard: In an article on "Papal Seminary of Kandy" he says: "When I did my theology in Kandy... I felt that the situation of the staff was anomalous. The choice of Kandy at the beginning had been a real blessing: away from India, away from the strict caste system in India; in a very congenial healthy climate. But now to me this situation looked anomalous. Here, was a staff dedicated to teach mostly Indian students in Sri Lanka. The professors could take full interest neither in India nor in Ceylon. Going through the documents I find that Fr. Taymans had experienced the same, for he wrote thus in 1934: "The greatest obstacle to the intellectual progress of the Seminary is its isolation. When one asks the professors why they do not write anything whatsoever, they reply that they see nothing and know nothing. And it is true..." Hence it is, very soon steps began to be taken to choose a site in India, and finally, in spite of all the attachment shown by several professors and students, Poona was chosen as a suitable site and the Papal Seminary was shifted there, and there it now flourishes". ("Papal Seminary of Kandy" by Fr. V. Perniola, S.J., p. 4).
2. Papal Seminary, Kandy: Golden Jubilee Celebrations (1893-1943), p. 33.
3. Cfr. Letter of Fr. Pou-Montfort, S.J., to the Superior of the Galle Mission, 19 January, 1954.
4. From the Vatican City, 18 May, 1954. Here, we give the Italian original:

Questo Sacro Dicasterio ha creduto opportuno di affidare agli Oblati di Maria Immacolata la direzione di quello che sara il Seminario Regionale per le diocesi di Ceylon ed essi hanno accettato, in linea di massima, l'incarico loro commesso intera proprieta dell'attuale Pontificio Seminario di Kandy restera intestata alla Santa Sede, anche quando ditto Pontificio seminario sara transformato in Seminario Regionale. Le rendite che si percepiscono di tutto l'immobile andranno naturalmente a favore del Seminario regionale, come ora vanno a beneficio del Pontificio Seminario di Kandi.

5. Fr. Ancot had the following to say in this regard, in his letter to the Superior of the Pune Jesuit Mission, Fr. Pius Geisel: "The OMI Fathers are expecting the furniture to remain. I told them about beds. They don't mind our taking some provided they know in time what they have to prepare. I wrote to Rome asking for more directions. As the Secretary of Propaganda died some time ago, things move slowly... The best for us is to come to an agreement with the OMI and ask Propaganda to sanction it... Propaganda has undertaken to help both Kandy and Poona with OSP (Opus Sancti Petri) burses, and they may also be willing to help financially the initial settlement expenses, but to what extent?... I understand that Propaganda paid for the building in Pune, but does this include the furniture?..." As we see from what has been said above, there was a certain amount of communication gap between Rome and Kandy, so that those in Kandy did not know for certain what would be at their disposal in Pune, and what they had to take with themselves from Kandy. Hence, doubts in the mind of those in Kandy whether they should ask for some compensation for the things they left behind in Kandy, enabling them to eventually purchase the things they would need in the new place... As things turned out everything that was needed was placed at the disposal of the newcomers on their arrival in Pune. The pity is that the latter had no clear idea about all this in Kandy, hence the uncertainty and confusion – a thing that would have been avoided, if there had been a little foresight and better mutual dialogue between Rome, Pune and Kandy.
6. Letter of Msgr. Pisani to Fr. Vossen, from Wellington, 18 May, 1920.
7. The Papal Seminary, Kandy: Golden Jubilee, 1893-1943, p. 76.
8. The seminarian Mervyn Coelho gives us the following details: "... On March 20, 55, "The big job" was begun, the packing of all library books into large wooden boxes. It was a laborious task calling for infinite patience; but Fr. Stephen Gak, adept in bookish affairs, in his characteristic slow and methodical manner proved his mettle and merited the title of "Doctor Librorum".

   The libraries were finally squeezed into 173 boxes (2.8 ft. by 2.2 ft by 1.8 ft in size). The other house possessions totalled 185 packages, all of immense size, while personal trunks were 100 in number, the grand total then being 458 boxes. On 15 May, '55 large sized lorries arrived and the loading commenced. We worked well into the night to send off 18 lorry loads to Colombo... The wagons left Tuticorin on May 30, '55. On 12 June the first wagon arrived at Poona and luckily it contained all our personal trunks. By 21 of the same month, the last wagon arrived. Even the damage and breakage were comparatively small". (Souvenir of the Inauguration and the solemn blessing of the Papal Seminary Church, 1957, pp. 23-24).
9. "Come and see the Seminary in Poona" by Vanigasooriyar, in Souvenir of the Inauguration and the solemn blessing of the Papal Seminary Church, p. 29.

Chapter 6

Developments in Pune (1955-1967)

"The Home of Love". This is the experience the newcomers from Kandy treasured in their hearts and brought with them as they crossed the threshold of the newly built large edifice that was to be their dwelling place in Pune all through the remaining years of their preparation for the priesthood. The weather here was rather warm then, but soon monsoon rains would come to soften the summer's heat. Unlike Kandy, there were no trees, no greenery around the place: it would be their task in the coming months, under the dynamic leadership of their Father Minister, Fr. Peter Pou-Montfort, to plant trees and water them, till two beautiful gardens rose as form nowhere to delight the eyes of one who crossed the portals of the Seminary.[1]

Their main impression, as they entered the house and made themselves familiar with their new surroundings, so, different from their beloved Ampitya, was that of freshness, novelty. They, too, were young men, open to the new and the unforeseen, and so, although their hearts were understandably so full of Kandy, and somewhat "homesick", they entered into their new life and their new surroundings with characteristic zest, relishing to the full the good things they found in Ramwadi. Nothing was, in fact, lacking of what could go to make their stay in Pune an enjoyable and fruitful experience, and their youthful hearts were lifted up in praise and thanks giving as they settled down in their newrooms for prayer, study and rest.[2] They arrived at Pune on 28 May, as we have said. Very fittingly, it was the eve of Pentecost, the great feast of Love, the mystery of the One who makes all things new (Rev. 21:5).

Pune is the headquarters of the district of Pune, in Maharashtra. Situated 1850 ft. above sea-level, 192 kms southeast of Bombay, it was the monsoon capital of the Bombay Presidency during the British Raj. It is called "The Queen of Deccan", because of its historical associations, its importance as a cultural, educational and political centre, with the beautiful scenery around. Pune is the seat of a University founded in 1948 with over fourteen central departments and a fairly large number of constituent and affiliated colleges: arts, science, medicine, commerce, agriculture, engineering. The College of Military Engineering and the Armed Forces Medical College are likewise situated in Pune, which is also known for its Artificial Limb Centre, one of the best of its kind in the whole of Asia.

It is therefore not surprising that when Jesuit Major Superiors had to select a place for a second theologate in India, the thought of Pune should have occurred to them as the most suitable place for their purpose. They bought from the diocese a large estate and started building there. However, as soon as the building was ready, it was requisitioned by the military, with the result that the new theologate itself ("De Nobili College" as it was christened), consisting of some twenty scholastics, a small number of professors and the Rector, had to be temporarily transferred to the Jesuit residence attached to St. Vincent's High School, situated in the area of Pune Cantonment. It had only a short stay there, for owing to the insufficient number of students it had to be closed down in March 1946, to be opened again in 1948, this time in buildings of its own, now free from the military occupation. It is situated along the Nagar Road, at Ramwadi. In June 1952, once all the buildings were completed, in keeping with the original plan of the Jesuit Superiors, the Philosophate was added. In 1955, as we have seen, the Papal Seminary and Athenaeum came to Pune. "The whole institution now received the official title of the Pontifical Athenaeum of Poona, comprising two faculties and possessing the right of conferring the degrees of Baccalaureate, Licentiate and Doctorate both in Philosophy and Theology."[3]

Soon, in addition to the seminarians and the Jesuit scholastics, scholastics of other religious institutes, too, were admitted to the Athenaeum as regular students: the Fransalians, the O.I.Cs, the S.V.Ds. The C.M.Is were already sending their students of theology to De Nobili College since many years earlier. Years later, religious Sisters too would join the Athenaeum as its students, as well as some laymen/women.

Kandy in Pune

The Kandy seminarians, arrived in Pune well in time for their annual retreat, before beginning the new scholastic year (1955-56). Father Geisel, the Jesuit Superior Regular of Poona who had been put in charge of preparing the buildings of the Athenaeum, had very wisely warned the Kandy authorities against their sending the students to Pune earlier, for holidays. "It would be extremely inconvenient to have the students here for one and a half months doing nothing and the installations still going on..." he wrote to Kandy. "For the students the hottest season of the year with no scenery for such a long time would be very bad indeed."[4] After discussing matters with those concerned, he proposed that the students could be sent home and told to come to Poona only at the end of May. But a small party of handy and willing brothers could however come to Pune in

April to help putthings up. The material goods could be sent in April, but "the students for their happiness on no account. There is nothing worse than to have to sit about in the heat and have nothing to do".

This advice of an experienced man was duly followed. Several students did go home. Other arrangements were made for the rest of them in Kandy itself. All were in Pune before the commencement of the new school year. The *schola brevis* had to be held in two sessions, since the Aula Magna was not yet built, and not even the largest of the class rooms available could accommodate more than just one half of the student body. All felt, nevertheless, that the shift to a city of colleges like Pune would contribute significantly towards the improvement of their own intellectual and cultural life. As the buildings were not yet fully completed, the "official" inauguration of the Pontifical Athenaeum was deferred to a later date as we shall see. In the meantime students were pursued with fresh ardour and enthusiasm. In addition to the professors who came from Kandy, they benefitted by the presence on the campus of the members of the De Nobili College staff: Frs. Hans Staffner, Josef Neuner, Felix Clausen, Lionel Mascarenhas, Joseph Miranda, Richard De Smet, Jean de Marneffe, Thomas Dorairaj, Peter Savarimuthu, Joseph Edamaram, Fidelis Buck, Edouard Hambye, Ignatius Errazquin, Paul Kheres, James McGinley, Theodore Bowling.

Studies

Priestly formation entails, besides the help given towards progress in the spiritual life, a thorough acquaintance with those disciplines that are necessary for priests to exercise their ministry fruitfully: Holy Scripture, Systematic and Moral Theology, Liturgy, Spiritual Theology, Canon Law, Church History, Patristics and several other relevant subjects. It is preceded by two or three years of philosophy, during which the young candidates to the priesthood follow regular courses in scholastic and modern philosophy, sociology and psychology, Introduction to Hinduism, Buddhism and other religions, etc. However, the order and the actual time or stage in which the various subjects or treatises were given were not the same in Kandy and in Pune. Besides, the scholastic year began in Kandy in January, while in Pune it was in June. All these factors evidently called for acertain amount of adjustment in the disposition of the various courses in Pune, to the benefit of both communities. This matter was minutely discussed between the Rector of the Kandy Seminary, Fr. J. Ancot and the Dean of Theology in Pune, Fr. J. Neuner, as we can see from the exchange of letters between the two of them. In the Appendix we give one or two of those letters which go to bring out the seriousness and the thoroughness with which the points were trashed out. What struck me very particularly when going through those letters is the seriousness and the thoroughness with which the various points at stake were thrashed out as well as the attitude of frankness and mutual esteem, respect and courtesy with which the discussion was conducted. The following few extracts will bring this out:

On December 17, 1952, Fr. Neuner writes to Fr. Ancot regarding the assignment of a subject to a certain professor from Kandy: "I may mention that it is in no way our intention to force a man into a line which he does not like. We had to make proposals according to the facts which personal knowledge of all the people concerned... Remember us in your memento, and that with all these buildings of stone, we may not forget the spirit with which they have to be filled". Then again in 1954: "I feel like the man in the Gospel who did not give up worrying his neighbour. I hope you see that it is not for the sake of worrying you, but to solve our problems. Will it be possible to let us have an answer before March 26, so that we know our position when the superiors come here" (March 8, 1954). "Let us hope that, once our staff are combined, such problems will belong to the amusing remembrances of the past, but for the time-being we cannot help being pressed by them... I hope you enjoy these last months in Kandy" (January 13, 1966). A last quotation taken from Fr. Neuner's letter of 27 April, 1955: "All good wishes for the weeks to come - it will be a busy and troublesome time, but in the end things will come out alright... I hope the Fathers in Kandy have not the impression that with these timetables, etc. we want to boss over them. Somehow we cannot help making plans and I really try to take into consideration (all points of view)".

The Seminary Church

As we have seen, in Kandy the student community had no proper chapel for over thirty years: the Blessed Sacrament was reserved in two large rooms which functioned temporarily as chapels, one for the philosophers and the other for the theologians. In Pune, the chapel (or church) was completed only in 1957, about a year and a half since the arrival of the seminarians from Kandy. Before that date the large hall, between the philosophers' and the theologians' wing served as a temporary chapel for the theologians' community. Below it, a similar hall functioned as the philosophers' chapel till 1957. Later, the large hall above was partitioned: one part of it was converted into a "domestic chapel", and the other into the recreation room of the theologians. Concelebrations had not yet become a common practice in the Latin Church; so "private Masses" were celebrated on small, temporary altars put up on the third storey of the big library building which was then empty and free.

The Official Inauguration of the Seminary in Pune

The present big chapel or church came only in 1957 and its solemn blessing was made use of for the solemn "official inauguration" of the Papal Seminary. As the then Rector of the Seminary, Fr. Lawrence Fernandes, S.J., wrote in the Foreword of the Souvenir published on that occasion, "The Papal Seminary is now established in India, so that the sons of India might be trained in her own soil."[5]

The official inauguration of the Seminary in Pune took place on December 2, 1957. It began with the blessing of the Church and Consecration of the Altar by the Most Reverend J. R. Knox, the Papal Internuncio in India. His Excellency arrived from Bombay at 11.00 a.m. on that day, bringing with him a very precious gift from Rome: the casket containing the hallowed remains of Archbishop Ladislaus Michael Zaleski who, as we have said, desired to be buried in the Papal Seminary grounds.

The ceremonies of the blessing of the Church and the consecration of the Altar began at 5.00 p.m. in the presence of three Archbishops (Their Graces Joseph Fernandes of Delhi, Thomas Poothecamury of Bangalore, and Mar Gregorios of Trivandrum), nine Bishops, five Domestic Prelates and thirty-six invited members of the diocesan clergy, all of them old Kandyans. All the professors of the Athenaeum as well as the students and their respective Superiors or Rectors were present together with the clergy of Pune, representatives of the various Religious Houses of men and women in the town, delegates, too, of the Catholic associations, and the Christian faithful in general, including those who had participated in the building up of these various edifices. All in all there were around 800 persons present.

Father Lawrence Fernandes, the Rector of the Seminary, welcomed all with kind words of appreciation and gratitude, and asked them to feel quite at home in their midst. A family atmosphere was thereby established which characterized their mutual relationships during those three days. His Excellency then began the long ceremony of the blessing of the Church and the consecration of the Altar. All the students participated in the singing. The first Holy Mass at the new altar was celebrated later in the evening by the youngest of the Bishops present, Msgr. Arulsamy of Kumbakonam.

December 3 began with the solemn Pontifical High Mass celebrated by the Internuncio, with the choir, made up of seminarians and Jesuit scholastics, singing a Palestrina Mass. The Church was packed to capacity, with invited guests, the clergy and the rest of the faithful: the distribution of communion alone took full ten minutes. The solemn ceremony ended with the granting of a plenary indulgence announced by Fr. Robert Criem, the MC, and the Papal Blessing given by the Internuncio. At the dinner that followed, three Jesuit Provincials joined us: those of Bombay, Madurai and Belgaum-Pune, the superiors of the Houses on the campus, the professors of the Athenaeum and priests of the town: over 250 persons in all.

At 4.30 p.m. the next great event of the celebrations tookplace, namely, the inauguration of the Hall - the *Aula Magna*—or the Auditorium, again under the presidency of the Internuncio, and in the presence not only of the seminarians, but also of many guests and several workers, in all about 600. The session began by the Rector reading the telegram sent by the sovereign Pontiff Pope Pius XII conveying his good wishes and his apostolic Blessing. He then went on to read the congratulatory letters of Cardinal Fumasoni-Biondi, Prefect of Propaganda, Cardinal Pizzardo, Prefect of the Congregation of Seminaries and University Studies, of Archbishop Sigismondi and of the General of the Society, Fr. John Baptist Janssens.

In a short speech Fr. Pius Geisel, who was in charge of the buildings, mentioned that the decision to shift the Seminary to India was taken in 1950. Pune was chosen in the following year as the site for the Seminary, and the locality was selected by the Apostolic Delegate Msgr. Kierkels. After three designs were set aside, a fourth one presented by the Italian architect Silvio Galizio was approved in the year 1953. That same year the foundation stone was laid and blessed by the Internuncio Archbishop Martin Lucas, SVD. Fr. Geisel ended by expressing his thanks first to the Divine Providence, then to the Sacred Congregation of the Propaganda that had placed at his disposal the large sum of money required for the purpose, to the three Jesuit Brothers who for four years had put themselves whole heartedly into the work of raising up the vast buildings: Brothers Pfiffner, Herbert and Widmar, and finally to the group of energetic workmen who by their labour and sweat had succeeded in making this project a reality.

The second day of the celebrations was a *Thanksgiving day*. His Grace, the Archbishop of Delhi-Simla, Dr. Joseph Fernandes, offered a solemn Pontifical Mass for all the benefactors living and dead, chief among whom was Archbishop Zaleski whose remains had now fittingly been placed in a tomb in front of the main altar of the church. The Internuncio and all the Bishops and prelates were present together with the seminarians and past students. Later at 10.45 a.m. there was the meeting of the Apostolic Union for Secular Priests presided over by the Internuncio, who spoke briefly on the importance of the spirit of prayer for priests. At 4.30 in the evening, the representatives of the civil and military authorities of the town were gathered together in the seminary dining room for tea. Finally at 6.00 p.m. Tirso Molina's play "Damned or Predestined" was staged before an audience of some 800 people. Concluding the celebrations, Father Rector expressed once again his gratitude to all who had contributed to the success of the festive commemorations. Archbishop Angelo Fernandes, of Delhi, the oldest person present from among the former students of the Papal Seminary, was the last one to speak, thus bringing the celebrations to an end. All expressed their disappointment at the fact that due to illness such a dear and worthy personality from among the Papal Seminary's alumni as Cardinal Valerian Gracias could not be personally present. He was represented by his Vicar General, Msgr. V. Dyer, also an ex-Kandyan.

These celebrations of the official inauguration of the Seminary and the Athenaeum in Pune was a boost to the "new comers from Kandy": they made them feel more at home in their new surroundings, though a certain complex lingered on affecting somewhat adversely the mutual relationship between the members of the two communities of Papal Seminary and De Nobili College.

The Name: Jnana-Deepa Vidyapeeth

Regarding the name to be given to the Athenaeum now transferred to its new place, suggestions were put forward by some, of a Latin name like "Leopianum."[6] We should be grateful to Fr. Josef Neuner who intervened in time with the following judicious letter which had its effect. Writing to Fr. Ancot on March 11, 1955, he said: "As to the name, we must by all means get an Indian name. Your proposal sounds all right in Rome, and to such Catholics who are familiar with these names. But we do not need the name for Propaganda purposes in Europe, but to introduce an institution to our Indian surroundings. Reverend Father Rector (that is, Fr. Conget) will make proposals of an Indian name in a few days, and send them to Rev. Fr. Assistant. I hope it will be possible to wait for a decision a few days. (I could add a number of good jokes of what people did with our name "De Nobili"). Not a soul here among our people can make any sense of it, except such people who have made special studies or have received laborious explanations. De Nobili gave up his European name when he took up his work in India - why should an institution which is meant to follow his ideals keep his European name?... For our College it may be too late now - we were on the point of changing the name, but were stopped from doing so. However, for the general name of the institution we are still free, and we must find something which expresses the idea of the institution to an Indian". Eventually, the name chosen and approved was "Jnana-Deepa Vidyapeeth".

The Cemetery

The last part of the buildings planned for the Papal Seminary in Pune was the cemetery. It was completed in 1959. Its need was felt already in the very first year after the transfer of the Seminary to Pune, when a young seminarian died all of a sudden in 1955: Brother Xavier Kappil. He was a nineteen year old seminarian of the Syro-Malankara Rite, just beginning his third year of philosophy. Soon after the retreat, early in June, he was learning cycling, and practising it in the hot afternoon, when he got a sun-stroke, fell from the cycle and died on the spot, of brain haemorrhage, at about 3 p.m. The sudden death of this saintly and lovable brother was deeply mourned by all who knew him. He was buried in the Christian cemetery at Hadapsar. After our cemetery was built and completed, his remains were brought to the Seminary Cemetery and preserved there.

Father Peter Pou-Montfort

Bro. Kappil, however, was not the first to be buried in our cemetery. He was preceded thereby another who came from Kandy and was much involved in the preparation of the Seminary's transfer to Pune and its proper settlement here: the active, devoted and resourceful Minister of the Seminary, Fr. Peter Pou-Montfort, S.J., whom the Kandyans knew well and sincerely loved. Born at Fonollosa, near Barcelona, in 1902, Peter joined the Society of Jesus in 1927. He landed in India in February 1932 and was ordained priest in Kurseong on 21 November 1937. Besides Latin and Greek, he learned English, Gujarati, Sinhalese and Marathi. After working for eight years in the Missions he was sent to the Papal Seminary, Kandy, in 1946. He was a successful professor of Dialectics and Metaphysics for seven years. In February 1947 he was put in charge of the supervision of the Seminary properties and was appointed Vice-Rector in August of the same year, when the Rector, Fr. Glennie, became Bishop of Trincomalee. In 1950 he became Minister of the house - the post he held till his death.

When the transfer of the seminary to Pune was sanctioned, it was Fr. Pou who had to attend to the technical and legal transactions connected with it. He was thorough in all that he had to undertake for the well-being of his community. In Pune he explored the surroundings and acquired the land for the Seminary villa at Vitthalwadi. He was an "outsider" and the men on the spot were Brothers Pfiffner, Herbert and Widmer. Understandably at the beginning there was some tension in his dealings with them. On Christmas day, 1956, Fr. Pou invited the Fathers and brothers of De Nobili to a "high tea" with the seminary staff, and this friendly gesture of his fostered mutual fellowship. His health, however, began to decline till eventually his ailment was diagnosed as cancer of the stomach. Yet it was only in April 1960 that he asked to be replaced by someone else. He awaited the end with characteristic serenity and good humour. He often visited the cemetery and blessed his own grave. On May 16, 1959, he asked every priest who visited him to give him a general absolution. He would have liked to expire on Pentecost day, literally with a song on his lips, but the call of the Lord came to him a day later: he passed away on May 18, at 11.35 a.m. "Fr. Pou's life-conviction - which he taught by word and example - was that everyone should put heart and soul into whatever assignment is given him" (Obituary Notice, Seminary Catalogue 1959-60, p.49.) R.I.P.

On February 4, 1959, Fr. Hans Staffner was appointed Rector of the Seminary, succeeding Fr. Lawrence Fernandes who was made Provincial of Madurai. He was given a Vice-Rector in the person of Fr. Lionel Mascarenhas, Professor of Ecclesiology. Consequently, both of them till then residing in De Nobili College now shifted to the Seminary. In December 1964 Fathers Felix Clausen and Guy Archambeaud followed them also from De Nobili.

On December 8, 1959, the Seminary Sodality celebrated the Lourdes centenary with a solemn session during which two papers were read: "The Titles of Our Lady in the Little Office of the Immaculate Conception", by Fr. Vaz, and "Lourdes, God's Messenger for our times" by Fr. E. Zeitler, SVD. The Lourdes centenary was also commemorated by St. Mary's Cultural Academy of the Seminary with an open session to which all were invited, and two papers were read: "Lourdes, a challenge to our age", and "Mary and Islam".

Our Visitors

On July 27 a Reception and Concert of Indian Music were held in honour of the distinguished singer and musician Pandit V.R. Patwardhan, on the occasion of his sixtieth birthday.

On October 13, 1960, Fr. Fuchs, SVD, gave a number of lectures on anthropology, his speciality, to both philosophers and theologians. To the philosophers he spoke on the social relationship among primitive human beings: property, family, marriage and the primitive form of the State (10 lectures). The five lectures he gave to the theologians dealt with facts about the primitive people: first in the stage of food-seekers, then hunters and finally cultivators: their religions, their ethics and social life.

Among the distinguished visitors to the Seminary in 1959 we must mention the world-renowned Fr. Joseph Cardijn, apostle of the working classes and founder of JOC (Young Catholic Workers). He spent a few hours among us together with Mr. Romeo Maione, the International YCW President. Their talks on the activity of YCW were listened to with great interest and attention.

On January 6, 1960 we had the honour and pleasure of welcoming in our midst no other person than the famous Abbé Pierre, apostle of charity and founder of the Emmaus Communities now spread all over the world. He spoke with much feeling about his house schemes for the homeless and the rag-pickers. They are absolutely poor, but Jesus Christ identifies himself with them. The burden of his message which touched the hearts of his listeners was that "where there is true love and charity God is there".

Still another well-known personality to favour us with his visit was Group Captain L. Cheshire. He gave us an account of the history of his "homes" for the unwanted, the disabled, the incurables. His account of his own conversion from Protestantism to the Catholic Church, brought about through his contact with one of his patients, a non-practising Catholic, was most instructive (February, 1961).

Fr. George Vadakken, also a social worker, a convert from Communism, made us aware of the strength of Communism and of the most urgent social problems of India, particularly of Kerala.

During the school year 1960-61 we had the opportunity of meeting a few leading figures from among our non-Christian brethren. Prof. D. A. Vadekar, M.A., head of the Philosophical Department of Fergusson College, spoke to us on "The Gita and its Interpretation"; Mr. S. V. Dandekar on "The Bhagavata Sampradaya", an important Bhakti movement in Maharashtra.

Among our Visitors this year we had the privilege of Cardinal Gracias's first visit to this Athenaeum as a "Prince of the Church". At a meeting held in the Auditorium at 9.30 a.m. Fr. Rector welcomed His Eminence as our elder brother, recalling the years he spent in Kandy where he distinguished himself as "the best student in his class, being at the same time a goods portsman, a fine actor and a cheerful companion". In his reply, Cardinal Gracias recalled the years he spent in Kandy. Though now in new surroundings - he said - the institution still breathed the same spirit. He exhorted the students to be fully Catholic and Roman, faithful to the Church and to its Head, the Pope. It was for the first time, he confessed, in the history of the Church that an Indian had taken part in the election of the Pope. The Indian Church had now a say in the government of the Catholic Church. In conclusion, "it is our privilege - he remarked – to live in dangerous times. We have a duty to be heroes. We have no right to be mediocre".

Another Cardinal who was pleased to visit our Seminary and Athenaeum was Cardinal Gregory Peter Agagianian, Prefect of the S.C. of the Propagation of the Faith. He stayed with us for a day and a half. On October 4, 1961 he ordained our thirty deacons: 21 seminarians, 3 OICs, 4 SVDs. Five other Prelates were present at the function: the Internuncio, the Archbishops of Calcutta and Changanacherry, the Bishops of Quilon and Sambalpur.

Archbishop Thomas Roberts, SJ, former Archbishop of Bombay, too, paid, us a visit and gave a lecture on "The Moral Implications of Atomic Warfare" (October 15). Earlier, in August, we had in our midst an outstanding Catholic leader, Chevalier M. Rathanaswami, KCSG (Bar-at-law), Vice-Chancellor of the Annamalai University, founder of the Catholic Union of India, and member of the Legislative Assembly both in Madras and Delhi. "The priests in India will have to live in danger - he told us - they will be considered strangers in their country, leaders of a minority, representatives of a foreign culture. They will have to learn to speak to their Hindu brethren in the philosophical terms of the great culture of India".

We were also fortunate to meet a few Catholic writers and scholars of international repute such as Fr. Jean Yves Calvez, S.J., the editor of *L'Action Populaire* and author of a thought-provoking book *La Pensée de Karl Marx*; Fr. Quiles, S.J., professor of the Catholic University of Buenos-Aires, who introduced us to his new way of understanding and exposing philosophy which he calls "Insistentialism"; the Very Reverend Archmandrite Oreste Kerame, Lebanese by birth and member of the Greek Catholic Patriarchate of Antioch. He spoke to us on our relations with the Eastern Orthodox Churches. These Churches, he said, have been preaching Christianity in the East and North and have remained faithful in spite of persecution. In the beginning there was unity between Rome and the East, and even today they venerate the Pope who for them is more than just the Bishop of Rome. On August 17 he celebrated Mass in the Seminary Church in the Byzantine Rite.

Mother Teresa visited us on February 24, 1961. Our Hall was filled to capacity to welcome her. "We are working for somebody, and this Somebody is the small and unwanted Jesus, the naked Jesus, the hungry Jesus, the dying Jesus..." she said. The Missionaries of Charity live in modest homes, like the poor whom they serve. A chapel, refectory and dormitory is all they haveand they spend most of their time out working for the poor. A cheerful temperament and the ability to learn are the two main qualities Mother Teresa expects to find in those wishing to join her.

We must also mention among our visitors two other names: First Dr. J. Pieper, an outstanding Catholic layman well versed in Medieval Philosophy, Professor of Anthropological Philosophy at the University of Muenster (West Germany). He spoke on "The Truth of Things (Ontological Truth) and its implications" (September 18, 1963).

Dr. Parulekar, Editor of "Sakal", the largest Marathi daily in Maharashtra, spoke on "Civic Rights and Duties". Before the end of the year, Sri Patwardhan and his troupe were also kind enough to entertain us this year, too, with a fine recital of Hindustani music, introducing us into the technique and meaning of the various expressions that are unique to Indian singing (December 13).

Something very different but extremely enjoyable and instructive were the scenes from Shakespeare's "The Merchant of Venice", "Macbeth", and "Twelfth Night", staged for us by Mr. George Mendall and his dramatic group. God bless them.

Among our guests during the school year 1964-65, we would like to single out Mr. M. M. Thomas, Director of the "Christian Institute for the Study of Religion and Society". He explained to us the aim of this Institute, namely, bringing together Christians and Hindus to find a common cultural ethos from which, it is hoped, a greater mutual understanding will follow.

Fr. P. Duprey, W. F., Under-Secretary of the Secretariat for Christian Unity, gave us on August 4, 1964, an informal report of his visit to the non-catholic communities in India. He was received most cordially everywhere. He met the leaders of the Jacobites, the Marthomites, and the Church of South India. They expected the Council to clarify the doctrine on the position of bishops in the Church, and on the sources of Revelation.

The well-known Professor of Indology at the University of Paris, Olivier Lacombe gave us a lecture on the "Dynamism of Indian Spirituality". The interior search of the soul for God has led a good many Indians to a natural mystical experience of God, he said. We may not a priori exclude the possibility of cases of even a supernatural mystical experience. Each case would have to be carefully studied and properly assessed.

Centenaries and Jubilees

The year 1959 was the centenary of St. John Mary Vianney's death. We had a special session in honour of the saint with two essays on him: "The Vocation of a saint" by Br. J. Francis, and "St. John M. Vianney, Model of pastors of souls" by Fr. M. Chempothinal. A dramatic play "God among us" by Bro. Mervyn Carapiet brought vividly before our eyes the severe temptation Vianney had to face of running away from his parish life for a life of solitude, prayer and penance. He overcame the temptation with the words: "I have no permission from my Bishop to leave the parish".

On October 8, 1962 the centenary of Rabindranath Tagore was celebrated with a solemn academy. In a few words Fr. Lionel Mascarenhas introduced us to the poetry and music of Tagore. The poetry of Tagore cannot be separated from his music, he stated, and his music bears the traces of a triple influence: the Indian classical music, popular religious music, and western music. Tagore's way of thinking - Fr. Lionel stressed - was influenced greatly by Ramanuja and Chaitanya who taught him to see God present in the whole of the Universe, "the Universe being the song of the Creator".

A song composed by Tagore himself was sung and then Fr. Jean de Marneffe spoke on Tagore's religious outlook. Born in a religious family, Rabindranath was religious in his outlook, and his practice of religion was enriched by his familiarity with the Upanishads and his belief in a personal God. Tagore confesses that in his eighteenth year he experienced that he was not alone, there was Another who wished to work with him. Later on, he passed through a sense of separation between him and his Lord. "I live in the hope of meeting Him", he confesses in his Gitanjali. "He loves me, but does not force my love". However, as one goes on reading Tagore one gets the feeling that he personalizes his own sensitivity. In his lectures, *The Religion of Man* (1931) he presents a sort of synthesis of his thought, in which it appears that the experience of freedom suggested to him an idea of a greater reality, a sense of the whole of humanity which is real and divine, beyond which, however, there is still something greater and more real, of which humanity is only a "character". Tagore was always convinced that beauty and art were paths leading people to God. As an interlude we heard another vocal composition of Tagore: "Gram Chara" (Out of the village).

Principal Damle, the last speaker of the day, presented Tagore and Gandhiji as the two men who were largely responsible for the formation of modern India. Tagore was a man of original creative ideas which he communicated to his people through poetry and music. Gandhi was a strict moralist. Both were deeply religious-minded, complementing each other. The session ended with the chanting of 'Vande Materam'.

A month and a half later, another centenary was celebrated - that of the birth of another great son of India, the well known Christian convert and poet of Maharashtra - *Narayan Vaman Tilak*. The function was presided over by the poet's own son, Sri D. N. Tilak.

Fr. Simplicio Rocha, MSFS, gave us a sketch of Tilak's life. Born in a Brahmin family, Tilak was moved by his desire to search for the truth to make a personal study of the Vedanta, then of the Buddhist Three Pitaka and finally of the Gospel. In this last he found the answer to his quest in the Person of Jesus Christ. He was baptized on 10 February 1895, was ordained an Anglicanminister on August 31, 1904; his wife and children followed him in 1900. From then on, his one overruling desire was close union with Christ. He lived a simple life given to the practice of charity. He died as a Christian sanyasi on April 9, 1919. At the interlude, we listened to two impressive songs in Marathi - words and music by Tilak: "To God" and "Attachment to Christ".

Fr. Velinkar, SJ, took for his theme Tilak, the Poet. Tilak's mother was a poetess and it is she who initiated her son already in his childhood days into poetry. At 17 he was writing verses and at 25 he began to translate western poets into Marathi. He found inspiration in the wonderful book of nature, children and other human beings. In Christ he found the answer to his deep longing for a personal attachment. It was his fervent prayer never to be separated from Christ, and that those who came into contact with him might find in him Jesus Christ who was the One object of his love. The religious hymns he composed are still sung in Christian communities in their prayer services. Sri D. N. Tilak, the poet's son, who was present, expressed his joy at the fact that we had opened the centenary year celebration with our function in honour of his father.

Other Events

A noteworthy event at the very beginning of the year 1963 was the publication of the first issue of the Pontifical Athenaeum Students' Magazine: *Paths-Marg.* It is the fruit of the private research and amateurish attempts of the Athenaeum students, aiming at placing before their readers "the vistas of India's rich heritage of the past and the present". The articles published illustrate this intention quite well: "Kabir's Way of Love" by P. Van Nuffel; "Tukaram - a Bhakta Poet" by Francis da Gama, SJ; "The Tragedy of Tukaram" by V. D. Punolkar, SJ; "Tilak - A Christian Poet" by J. Velinkar, SJ; "Salvation through Self-Transcendence" by A. Vellamthadathil, a seminarian; "Our Missions: the Present Situation" by Joseph, a seminarian; "New Missionary Methods" (according to Bishop Lash) by Sebastian Kannekattil, SJ; "Paths" continued its publication until the year 1970.

Since we are in the academic year 1962-63, we cannot fail to mention an event that affected Pune deeply - the breakdown on July 12, 1962 of Panshet and Khadakwasla Dams, with the result that half the city was under six feet of water and the entire town remained without light and water supply. The water receded by 6.30 a.m. leaving the city streets covered knee-deep with muddy water and dirt, and thousands of fallen houses. The estimate was 4000 houses deeply damaged or fully destroyed, 84,000 people left homeless, over 500 dead! The total financial loss was estimated at roughly Rs. 12 crores.

Our students joined many other Pune students with spades, pickaxes and shovels in hand, in rendering whatever help they possibly could. They made their way through wrecked slums and broken houses full of stench, to unearth cooking utensils and other household goods buried under the debris, salvage whatever could be saved and to clear the badly damaged places so as to make it possible to rebuild them as could best be done. July 17 and July 18 were declared holidays for this purpose.

We have mentioned several times in this chapter the name of Fr. Ancot. He came to Pune with the seminarians from Kandy and continued in Pune as Rector of the Pontifical Athenaeum. He relinquished this office in May 1963 and left for Ranchi, his Province. On May 24 the Seminary had a farewell party in the honour of one who had spent a whole life-time at the service of this institution as professor, rector and spiritual father. He taught almost all the subjects in the Philosophy curriculum. For many Kandyans, Kandy was identified with Ancot. As a speaker on this occasion said, "Fr. Ancot distinguished himself by remaining always young at heart, by his kindness and friendliness to all, and his great interest in each and every member of the seminary, even after they had left its portals for their ministry". Very true.

In May 1963 the Papal Seminary completed 70 years since its foundation in Kandy in the year 1893. It so happened that just a month earlier it received the Hammond organ, which was installedon April 30. It is a gift from His Eminence Cardinal Gracias who on the 33rd anniversary of his priestly ordination donated to the seminary the sum of Rs. 24,000/- for the purpose. The organ will remain an abiding memorial of this eminent alumnus' generosity to his Alma Mater.

The July 3, 1963, feast of St. Thomas, was celebrated with an academy with the following programme which had been prepared by the Professor of Oriental Theology, Fr. Ancot: A hymn to the Holy Virgin in Slave; "The Russian Orthodox Church", a paper in which the SVD scholastic Gnanprakash Luiz, made a historical survey of the church in Russia up to its present state under Soviet Rule; a "Qolo" hymn from the Malankara Liturgy; a conference on "Oriental Churches in America" by Fr. John Waldo, S.J., dealing with the immigration of the various groups of Orthodox Christians to the United States, their present organization and their attitude to the Roman Catholic Church. The Chaldean choir next sang "Rhahamme Shukkana", an invocation from the Syrian Liturgy. Bro. Mathew Chandrankunnel finally introduced us to a modern "Moses" of the Ukrainians, A. Szeptyckyj.

July 31, 1963, feast of St. Ignatius of Loyola, was the day chosen by our new Rector, Fr. John Cyril Pereira, SJ, to assume office. At 10.30 a.m. the Athenaeum held an official reception in his honour. In his speech welcoming Fr. Cyril to his new house, Fr. Lionel Mascarenhas referred to the responsible posts he had held in his Province (Karnataka) as Professor and Rector of the Major Seminary of Mangalore, Rector of the Jesuit Novitiate and Juniorate: all of these had prepared Fr. Cyril admirably for his present post of Rector in Pune. Pointing to his new family, Fr. Lionel told Fr. Cyril that it was made up of young candidates to the priesthood coming from some 61 provincesor dioceses, staff and students of eighteen different nationalities.

An epoch-making event that took place during this period is undoubtedly the Second Vatican Council. October 10, 1962, was the eve of its opening in Rome. On that day we had a biblical vigil of prayer for God's blessing on this event of such importance in the life of the Church. On the opening day itself we had a solemn High Mass in the Seminary Church. The Blessed Sacrament was then exposed for adoration and intercession: from 9.30 a.m. to 5.30 p.m. The seminarians kept an hour's vigil each, for this intention, class by class. At 5.30 p.m. solemn benediction was given, for which the entire Athenaeum was present.

The Athenaeum was privileged to be represented at the second session of the Council by Fr. Josef Neuner, who went there asperitus. After the sessions of the Council were over, Fr. Neuner remained in Rome for a time as councillor in the Commission for Seminaries and Universities.

Extra-Curricular Activities of Professors

We now go on to place on record some of the extra curricular activities of the members of our staff during the period covered in this chapter.

In the year 1962, Fr. Gaspar Koelman, Professor of Philosophy at the Athenaeum, gave a series of lectures to Hindu intellectuals on various religious topics, in Bombay, as well as a conference on "The Sources of Hinduism" to the members of the Newman Association of Pune.

Fr. Hans Staffner took part in the International Academic Congress on "Cult and the Modern Man" at the University of Munich (July 30 - August 3, 1961) in which he read a paper on "Cultand Hinduism". The "Catechetical Centre" under the direction of Fr. Staffner published the following books "The Way and the Life" by Fr. Desmond D'Abreo. This book went through three editions and was adopted by Herder as their Junior Catechism. It has already appeared in Germany, and a different edition has been published in England, by Burns and Oates. Other translations are Japanese, Shona (Rhodesia), Tamil, Hindi, Chinese, Indonesian, Malayalam, Marathi and Konkani. Fr. Staffner's "The Art ofTeaching Catechism" has similarly been translated into Chinese, Japanese, Shona and Indonesian. More recently, Fr. Staffner published an inspiring small life of Fr. Rupert Meyer, S.J.

The "Catechetical Centre" published "Our Catholic Boy", a survey of the religious attitude of our catholic boys in their last three years in the High School, by Fr. Gregory Naik, S.J. In this book the answers of 534 boys from six Catholic Schools to a socio-religious enquiry were assessed.

Fr. M. Zinser translated and published the Gospel of St. Luke in Marathi, under the title of Dayasagar (Ocean of Mercy). He also prepared for publication and provided with footnotes the Marathi translation of St. John's Gospel made by Fr. Vinas and Barranco, SJ.

Fr. Anthony D'Costa, Professor of Church History and Patrology, left us for Bombay on February 8, 1963, to continue there his work of historical investigation. During the three years he spent in Pune he was highly esteemed for his erudition and the clarity of his teaching, his hard work and exemplary religious life.

Father Emile Gathier SJ, and Bro. Joseph Pfiffner SJ

We cannot close this chapter without paying our homage to two men to whom the Seminary-Athenaeum is indebted in more ways than one: Fr. Emile Gathier and Bro. Joseph Pfiffner, both of whom were called to their eternal reward in the course of the year1963.

Fr. Gathier is remembered with gratitude and affection by generations of Jesuit students whom he taught Epistemology, Indian Philosophy and other subjects at Sacred Heart College, Shembaganur. He was also on the staff of the Papal Seminary in Kandy from 1945 to 1947, teaching subjects connected with Indian Philosophy. During his stay at the Indian Social Institute, in Pune, he joined the staff of De Nobili College as Professor of Indian Philosophy and Religion (1952-55). He was transferred to the Gregorian University in Rome in 1955, but he remained deeply attached to India and his many friends here in India. He died all of a sudden due to pulmonary thrombosis on May 9, 1963. Indian ecclesiastical students many of whom had known him as their professor made it a point to carry his coffin on their shoulders from the church where the funeral Mass was celebrated to his grave. RIP.

Fr. Gathier died in distant Rome. Closer by, Bro. Pfiffner was called to his reward on October 18, 1963. The Seminary and the Athenaeum are deeply indebted to the man, of whom the Jesuit Superior of the Mission, Fr. P. Geisel rightly said: "Everycorner in De Nobili College, the entire Papal Seminary and the Athenaeum -all this is his work". Truly, it is Bro. Pfiffner who, together with Bros. Herbert and Widmar, brought up the Athenaeum: the Lecture Halls, the Library, the Auditorium, the Church, the entire Seminary.

Bro. Pfiffner came from a deeply Christian Swiss family that gave to the Church several of its members: two of his brothers are Benedictine priests, and one sister a nun. He joined the Society of Jesus on March 10, 1934. In 1938 he was already in India, and from 1941 he devoted all his time, his talents and energy in planning and putting up imposing buildings for the service of God and the Church, such as De Nobili College in Pune, the Novitiate and Juniorate of the Bombay Jesuit Province (Vinayalaya), the modern Chapel of St. Catherine's Home, Bombay, the hostel for St. Xavier's High School, at Jaipur. He then spent four years at Sangamner, renovating the Sisters' Convent and planning the building of the Dnyanamata High School. From 1959 on he was busy renovating the Fathers' Residence of St. Vincent's, Pune, and building the chapel of St. Luke's Hospital at Srirampur. Finally, from 1961 till 1962 he directed the pulling down of the old building of St. Vincent's High School and completed half of the present St. Vincent's, in Pune.

Bro. Pfiffner was a good mathematician, an experienced architect and a tireless worker. In connection with the Papal Seminary's Church, we read the following remark in his Obituary Notice: "Many a reputed engineers balked at the prospect of raising that mass of hundreds of tons of concrete and steel and balancing it upon a few slender pillars, with a base of hardly six inches each of diameter". Bro. Pfiffner did it. He was kind and gentle with the people who worked under him. They knew that he loved them and they, in turn, had a great esteem and veneration for this religious Brother whose life of austerity and hard work was a silent object lesson for all. May his soul rest in peace.

Notes

1. Actually, it is in view of this that writing to Fr. Ancot, already in February, 1953, Fr. Conget, Rector of De Nobili College, requested the Rector of the Papal Seminary to please send as early as possible Fr. Montfort-Pou to Pune to prepare the place for the Seminary: "We have to try and find a farm or grounds or land where to put it, whose produce may supply the needs of the house, and later on, of the Papal Seminary".

   One of the things most urgently needed here in this dry and barren place is the planting of trees and looking after them, and the taking care of the grounds fit for cultivation; a thing that though so urgent and important has not been done in any constant and methodical manner. This is of some consequence for the Papal Seminary. With Fr. Pou here to look after trees and the garden, I think we would be able to arrange a nice place, so that when you come over, there will be some greenery about the house, playgrounds, etc. In my honest opinion, looking to the future, you will be the gainers by sending here now Fr. Pou (19 Feb. 1953).
2. In Kandy the seminarians had no individual rooms. Even theologians lived in big halls divided by partitions. Similarly, too, they had common study halls.
3. Rui de Menezes, S.J., Silver Jubilee of De Nobili College, in "Paths-Marg", 1963, p. 9.
4. Letter of Fr. Geisel to Fr. Ancot, 23 January, 1955.
5. Souvenir of the Inauguration of the Papal Seminary (in India), 1957. Foreword, p. 1.i
6. In Galle Jesuits News Letter of May 1955 we read on p. 2: "Feverish preparations are in course for the "exitus" for Poona (India). Some of the professors and students will leave early in May and the rest by the end of April. The newly built and majestic Seminary of Poona will be named "*ATHENAEUM LEOPIANUM*", in honour of Pope Leo XIII, Patron of the Kandy Seminary and of Pope Pius XII, Patron of the one of Poona".

Chapter 7

Priests and the Laity in India Today (1968-1980)

The year 1968! Mentioning it in his "Homely Letter" to the members of the Apostolic Union of Priests, Fr. Robert Criem, SJ, its National Director, wrote: "Once more a new year is opening. This one will be another of those memorable ones in the annals of the Papal Seminary: the Diamond Jubilee" (AUMOL, January 1968, p. 2). We shall speak of the Jubilee Celebrations in the course of this chapter.

To Ajanta-Ellora Caves

For the moment we would like to mention an item that belongs to the school year 1967-68. It has its place in this History, because it is a description of one of those "outings" that form part of the seminarians' life. Our brothers had heard a lot about Aurangabad, the historical city situated not too far from Pune - just about a hundred and fifty miles away. It is in the vicinity of Aurangabad that the famous Ajanta-Ellora caves are situated, so our students hailing from all over the country, were understandably eager to pay a visit to those world-famous caves. Their wish was fulfilled on 1 November 1967. That morning they took the bus at 7.00 a.m. accompanied by an SVD and a Jesuit priest. They reached the "Holiday Camp" in Aurangabad at 12.30 p.m.

Aurangabad is about 1900 feet above the sea-level and has a population of more than 90,000 inhabitants. It is placed in the valley of the Dudhna river and is surrounded by the hills belonging to the Lahenwara range. The climate is bracing and healthy.

Their first visit on arrival, after a little rest and tea, was to Bibi ka Mukbara known as the Deccan Taj Mahal, constructed by the Emperor Aurangzeb in the year 1660 on the model of the Taj. Their next stop was Panchakki or Water Mill, built near the tomb of Baba Shah Musafir, the spiritual director of the emperor. One's attention is here immediately drawn to the artificial waterfall close by, at the centre of which is a big fountain and a water mill. Water comes from a distance of four miles, collected through artificial earthen pipes into a reservoir, and then directed by siphon to the top of a pillar from where it is made to fall down into the cistern below. At a corner there is a huge water mill driven entirely by water power. In olden times the mill was used to grind corn for the entire army. It is a wonderful sight to watch the innumerable fishes move about in the cistern - fishes of all sizes, small, big, huge ones. Also the scenery around is truly impressive.

After supper, our seminarians were graciously invited to the Aurangabad Hotel for a cultural programme at 9.30 p.m. It was part of the International Tourist Fair that was then being held at Aurangabad. They witnessed various Indian cultural dances, especially the "Gujarati Garhba"; they, in turn, were requested to contribute their own items, and they felt happy to oblige by singing Konkani and English songs from their repertoire.

The following morning they were ready at 5.30 to proceed to Ajanta, 75 miles further away. Those rock-cut caves seem to cover a space of time that extends from the second century BC to the seventh century AD. There are in all about 33 such caves decorated with sculptures and frescoes expressing the outlook and cultural life of the Buddhists who made them: scenes of their daily life, processions, hunting scenes, elephant fights, men and women singing, dancing, playing on musical instruments, - all most gracefully depicted. About those paintings, Mr. Havell writes: "Very rarely in the world's history has there come together that true symphony of these arts, painting, sculpture and architectonic designs, creating the most perfect architecture, which are so beautifully harmonized at Ajanta".

On November 3 morning, after concelebrated Mass and breakfast, the seminarians proceeded to Daulatabad fort. It is encircled by a moat 100 ft. deep. Whoever got hold of this fort was acknowledged as the master of the entire Deccan plateau. From Daulatabad, passing through Khuldabad where the mortal remains of Aurangazeb rest in a very simple tomb, they went to Ellora, famous for its rock-hewn cave temples. There are three distinct groups of cave temples, Buddhist, Brahmanical and Jain - all in all 34 caves. The most beautiful one is no.16 - a real wonder ofthe world. It is 164 ft. long, 109 ft. broad and 96 ft. high, lavishly covered with life size sculptures of animals and images of gods and goddesses. Their last visit was to Grushneshwar Jyotirlinga, a temple dedicated to God Shiva, built of solid redstone.

The Papal Seminary and JDV

Proceeding with our own history, since August 1967 we have had a change in the highest office of the Seminary and the Athenaeum. Till 1967 we had one and the same person holding the office of both Seminary Rector and Rector of the Athenaeum, and he was appointed by Propaganda. According to the new system, we have two rectors - one for the Seminary, appointed by Propaganda, and another for the Athenaeum, appointed by the Superior General of the Society of Jesus who is the Chancellor of JDV after obtaining the consent of the Congregation for Catholic Education. Fr. Julien Bayart was appointed Rector of the Athenaeum while Fr. Lionel Mascarenhas continued to be the Rector of the Papal Seminary, the post he had been holding since the year 1962. Just as these two offices are distinct, the two institutions too – the Seminary and the Athenaeum - are distinct, though they continue to remain attached, the latter belonging to the former.

This change - as Fr. Staffner, the outgoing Rector of the Athenaeum, explained in his speech welcoming Fr. Bayart, - is in keeping with the Apostolic Constitution "*Deus Scientiarum Dominus*" which determines that "If a University or Faculty is joined to a clerical Seminary, the statutes should clearly and efficaciously provide that the academical direction be properly distinguished from its life and discipline."[1]

The principle underlying this new system is that distinct offices ought to be conferred on distinct persons, so that one and the same person does not accumulate offices to which he is not able to do justice personally, but instead has to appoint another person with delegated power to do the work. Such an arrangement is now strongly discouraged, and rightly so.

In the spirit of these instructions of the Church, the Jesuit *Normae Generales de Studiis* determine that "In each college of superior studies, whether they be ecclesiastical faculties or not, the academic regimen must be distinct from the religious regimen, and therefore as far as possible, the persons should also be distinct, so that the Rector of the college has only the direction of the religious house, and to the Pareses of the institution is entrusted the academic regimen, and in this office he depends immediately on the Provincial". In the case of Pune, this would mean, as we have said, that while the Athenaeum remains attached to the Seminary, and cannot be separated from it, its Pareses or Rector is distinct from the Rector of the Seminary and is not accountable to the latter in whatever regards the government of the academic institution as such.

Fr. Julien Bayart took charge of his office on December 13, 1967. In his speech welcoming Bayart to Pune, Fr. H. Staffner, said: "In you the students of the Athenaeum have a Rector who is really free for them, whom they can consult and who can direct them in their studies. I can say without any flattery that we are very fortunate in having you as the Rector of the Athenaeum. Not only because you are singularly versed in all questions of ecclesiastical studies, not only because you have been teaching for nearly 30 years, but are also specialized inquestions on Hinduism; for years also you have been prefect of studies and by attending the two international commissions on ecclesiastical studies in Rome you are fully acquainted with the present day trends. The staff, more than the students, will be able to profit by your experience."[2]

On January 11 of this year (1968) a strange phenomenon woke the inmates of the seminary violently out of their sleep. At about 4.20 a.m. a strong tremor shook not only the ground but even the beds and the rest of the furniture in the rooms. The inmates, particularly those on the top floor, where the tremor was more strongly felt, ran out of their rooms, not knowing what to do: for some time there was confusion everywhere... It was an earthquake! Happily there were no casualties anywhere in the town, but lighter tremors continued to be felt during the days that followed.

Four days later, on January 15, we received the visit of the Pope's representative in India, His Eminence Archbishop Joseph Caprio, Pro-Nuncio. We had a special session in his honour in the Hall. In his speech, the Pro-Nuncio said: "If there is any institution in India that I can call mine, it is the Papal Seminary with the Athenaeum. All the other religious houses are our honoured guests and benefit from the Faculties in the Seminary". Then, speaking about himself, he confessed in passing in his own gentle, humorous way, "there is not a single letter in my life that has not received a reply!" This certainly is admirable and merited our whole-hearted praise and admiration.

The year 1968 is our Jubilee Year. Well, a tradition of 75 years was broken when one day Fr. Lionel, the Rector, unexpectedly and to the surprise - and joy - of everyone, announced that the Seminary would be closed down from the last week of March to the end of May: all students would leave Pune and go to their respective dioceses, at the disposal of their bishops; all would have to be back in the Seminary on June 1, for their retreat and the new school year. This was something unprecedented for till then the students never left the seminary except at the end of theology, after being ordained priests. They spent part of their major holidays (April-May) at the Villa expressly set up for that purpose. Here in Pune, it is at Vitthalwadi.

During the month of march we received the sad news of the death of our Brother Louis Fernandes SJ, which occurred on March 11 night, in the Holy Spirit Hospital at Andheri, Bombay. The Papal Seminary is very specially indebted to this humble, cheerful, hard-working Brother who looked after our kitchen department for several years and won the hearts of all - seminarians, the Jesuit personnel, the servants and people in general - by his kind manners, his humility, his readiness to oblige, his cheerfulness and thoroughness in the fulfilment of his duties. He fell sick in Pune and was taken to Srirampur due to kidney trouble. He spent the last months of his life at Vinayalaya, Bombay, edifying everyone by his patience and cheerfulness. A verbal report reproduced in "Aumol", May-June 1968, has the following to say about Bro. Luis. "Shortly before the end, he asked to go to the chapel and he spent there more than an hour praying. He had to be told to return to the room, but after some time he asked to be allowed to go back to the chapel, but this was not deemed prudent. So, he remained sitting up in his bed, as he was unableto lie down. He kept looking at his crucifix and suddenly collapsed".

On September 17, 1968 the main Altar of the Seminary Church was demolished. A new Altar was set up more at the centre of the sanctuary, facing the people. The Tabernacle was placed on the top of a pillar, right at the back of the sanctuary, in keeping with the design made by the Ranchi Province architect, Fr. Joseph M. Stevens.

The Priest in India Today

The year 1968, as we said, was the jubilee year of the Seminary. A three-day All-India Seminar was held in this connection from December 1-4. The main topic of the seminar was "The Priest in India Today".

The Seminar began with an inaugural session on November 30 in the evening. Fr. Lionel Mascarenhas welcomed the 240 delegates in a brief speech, after which all proceeded to the Main Hall where Fr. Neuner, the President of the seminar, explained to those present the programme of the seminar, the procedure to be followed, and a few other technical points. The inauguration session ended with a well prepared para-liturgical service in Indian style on the theme: "Christ, the Divine Guru".

On the first day, Fr. Vallamattam read a paper on "The Priest according to Vatican II and modern theology". The paper gave rise to a lively debate and exchange of ideas. These were pursued during the workshops.

During the general session of the second day, Fr. Samuel Rayan SJ read a paper on "The Priest in India's spiritual traditions". He was followed by Fr. Stephen Fernandes, of Calcutta, whose theme was "The Priest in the present setting in India". As the papers were rather long there was not much time left for questions and answers. At noon, the four units of each workshop met to put together their conclusions and draw up a consolidated report of the resolutions and conclusions of each workshop.

The third day-December 3, feast of the Patron of the Seminary, St. Francis Xavier-was the jubilee day proper. There were no common sessions or workshops, but the secretaries and leaders of each workshop met together in several sessions in order to sum up the final conclusions of the seminar.

On the fourth, the last day of the seminar, there was a panel discussion during which Fr. Aloysius Fernandes spoke on "The Human Personality of the Priest", Fr. Valerian D'Souza, (now Bishop Emeritus of Poona), on "The Community of Priests" and Archbishop Angelo Fernandes on "The Priest with Christ". Each of these talks was followed by an exchange of questions and answers. The concluding session of the seminar was presided over by Cardinal Valerian Gracias who gave the final discourse. Dear Fr. Gak was in charge of bringing out, with the help of Julius Lipner, a printed souvenir of the seminar. Unfortunately, his unexpected death, the result of an accident, prevented the fulfilment of this project. Fr. Gak passed away, leaving behind him the exampleof a devoted professor and committed religious.

The life of the students of the Seminary and the Athenaeumis oriented to future pastoral activity in the various dioceses of our country. In view of this,

Archbishop Angelo Fernandes of Delhi, gave our theologians a dozen lectures on this important theme: The pastoral life of priests. They were very inspiring and instructive and not devoid of humour. "The three important things which we Catholics on the whole are very badly in need of, he said, are vision, decision, action. People care only when they share - he added. We have the most precious treasure of our faith. Why do we cover it up in our cup-boards to gather dust?"- he wondered.

At the invitation of one of our companions, five members of "Alcoholic Anonymous" of the town shared with us their experience. One of them said: "I am Mr........ I am an alcoholic. I am sober today by God's grace and due to A.A.". Another said: "My life was unmanageable until I came to believe that a power above could change my life". And a third one: "I approach God in the morning as an alcoholic and beg Him to get me out of this rut". Then the president of the Union made this request to priests and future priests: "Please don't shout at an alcoholic.It will only help him to go back to hell". They began every session with the well known "serenityprayer":

"Lord, give me the serenity to change the things I can,
The courage to accept the things I cannot change,
And the wisdom to know the difference".

Till the year 1969 India was represented in the College of Cardinals of the Roman Catholic Church by only one man. Another name was added to the list on April 30 of that year when Archbishop Joseph Parecattil of Ernakulam received the Cardinal's Hat. Fr. George Arakapadavil, also a former pupil of the Seminary, was present at the ceremony. He informed us that shortly after, that is, on May 3, His Eminence ordained three of our Propaganda Seminarians to the priesthood. After the ordination, the Indian Community in Rome gathered together to greet and congratulate the new Cardinal. In his speech, Cardinal Gracias who was present said that the new Cardinal and himself had this in common, namely, both were trained in the Kandy Papal Seminary. Both of them spoke highly of their Alma Mater. Cardinal Parecattil stated that the training he had received in Kandy had always stood him in good stead; he felt deeply grateful to the Seminary and the Fathers who had helped him in his formation.

Characteristically enough, on his return to India, Cardinal Parecattil made it a point to pay a special visit to the Papal Seminary, now transferred to Pune. We were extremely happy to welcome such a distinguished and dear "old boy" in our midst and gave him a hearty welcome. All were much edified by his total simplicity and his friendly, unassuming ways. The Keralites on the campus had a special "hour" with the Cardinal. "I can do something which no other Cardinal not even the Pope can do"– he told them. "What could it be?" they began to wonder. "I can speak Malayalam!"

In Contact with the Non-Christian World

Fr. Robert Antoine, a Belgian Jesuit working in Calcutta, was perfectly at home both in Sanskrit and Bengali. From June 6, he gave a two-week intensive course on "Ramayana" with special stress on Rawana, the incarnation of evil. Fr. Antoine, who lived in an Ashram in an entirely Hindu area in Calcutta, showed a deep grasp of his subject. One evening he gave us a recital of many of Rabindranath Tagore's musical poems, and other Bengali songs. With his strong, harmonious voice, Fr. Antoine did justice to the eminent poet's compositions. "Without Tagore", Antoine remarked, "Bengali would not be what it is".

Another well known Belgian scholar spoke to us on his favourite subject, again the "Ramayana". It is Fr. Camille Bulcke, S.J., also from the Bengal Vice-Province of the Society. He is the author of a Hindi Dictionary and he gave us an enlightening talk on the various versions of "Ramayana", dwelling particularly on the Valmiki version. Fr. Bulcke was of the opinion that the study of "Ramayana" can be very helpful for our work in India.

On September 16 of this year (1969), a German Benedictine nun, Sister Shradananda, who with permission from the Holy See became an inmate of the Brahma Vidya Mandir, gave us an insight into the life of the community founded by Vinoba Bhave as a living experiment, an attempt of a new way of spiritual life incommon. The main inspiration and strength for their life must come from love. They have no "rules" as such, but only a certain number of "principles", what they call "eleven vows", drawn from the observances kept up by the members of Mahatma Gandhi's ashram at Sevagram. They follow two other principles: Karma Yoga, that is, every kind of work, physical labour, prayers, study of spiritual books which is necessary to achieve purity of mind; and Samahik Sadhana which is a collective striving after Brahma Vidya, namely, the experience of God.

October 2 is Gandhi Jayanti. The year 1969 was the centenary of Mahatma Gandhi's birthday. The Athenaeum celebrated this event with a prayer service in Indian style, in the Hall. It began with due homage to Christ, the Light of the World, the Way, truth and Life. The lamp was lit, and in a few words Father Rector spoke as the prophet and apostle of peace. A passage from Gandhiji's favourite book, the Bhagavad Gita was read, followed by a bhajan and the reading of a passage from the Sermon on the Mount, which had impressed the Mahatma so deeply. Our seminarians then gave a commentary on the passage read, and then various intentions were suggested for prayer. Fittingly enough, the session ended with St. Francis of Assisi's inspiring prayer "Lord, make me an instrument of your peace".

Two weeks later, on October 14, a Parsi High Priest Dr. Mirza gave us three lectures on Zoroastrianism. The Parsis came to India during the Arab persecution, in the seventh century. Their sacred book is Avesta. God is the Creator of all things. Nature works in accordance with God's plan. Man is responsible for his actions. There is no theory to explain the existence of evil. Heaven and hell are conditions of the soul. In the evening we had a joint prayer service. Dr. Mirza spoke of the hidden potentialities in man that need to be developed. Dr. William Gomes, our Bishop, called attention to the contribution of both Parsis and Catholics towards the progress of India.

Like the Parsis, the Jews too belong to the minority class in Pune. It is not often therefore that we meet them in our premises. On 14 February, however, we were pleased to have a Jewish artist with us, Mr. Japheth. He spoke with zest on the topic "Is God alive today?" According to Mr. Japheth, our faith in God and our love for Him must be shown by our love and concern for our fellow human beings. He illustrated his statements with apt examples taken from contemporary history.

Our Laity

As we know well, our laity are beginning to feel, that, at last, justice is being done to them, and that their particular, indispensable role in the Church and the world is being given due recognition. We wanted to know from them what their expectations were regarding their priests. So, we invited three select lay Catholics of Pune, to share with us their thoughts or feelings in this regard. Of the three, only two came: Miss Nalini Vaz and Dr. Freddy Mendonca.

Nalini is connected with several youth associations in the diocese. She felt that priests ought to help and guide young people, but without too much interference in the management of their affairs.

Dr. Freddy Mendonca, a Papal Knight, and a former Head of the Sassoon Hospital and of the Medical Training College of Pune, shared with us some of his ideas in a familiar chat, seasoned with a lot of humour. Priests, he said, must work with the laypeople, but without being one of them. They must be kind-hearted, considerate and understanding towards people. In his younger day she had experienced at times the undue rigour and high-handedness of some priests. Once he became a surgeon (and he was a firstclass one) he took his revenge-he said-whenever he had an opportunity to put priests at the end of his knife!

Should priests wear a cassock? Doctor felt they should not. They should wear a dress suited to the climate, but bearing a sign by which they could be recognized as priests. Some, he added, seem to go in mufti in order to be able to go to pictures without being identified as priests.

He advised priests to be acquainted with business management and personnel management: they must know how to deal with various kinds of persons. They must be able to adapt themselves to the society in which they live and work, avoid both radicalism as well as excessive conservatism, and not make changes too often.

What about having a married clergy? Both speakers were rather cautious and reserved in this matter. People are not quite ready for it - they agreed. "If I say 'Yes' - Doctor Mendonca added, looking at the lady by his side, -"I am afraid, this young lady might get too many proposals!..."

As essential feature of the Church of Christ is its contemplative dimension. The Indian Cultural Academy of the Athenaeum therefore thought it opportune to organize a two-dayseminar on "Contemplative life and the Indian Church". What is the role and relevance of the contemplative life in the task of developing a genuine Indian Church and Indian theology? The main speakers were Sister Sara Grant, RSCJ, and Miss Indu Tikekar (Sarvodaya worker), Fr. Bede Griffiths, OSB, Msgr. Theophilus, a Marthomite, Fr. C. Desrochers, CSC, and Fr. M. Lederle SJ.

About four hundred people participated in the Seminar and a hundred and ten took an active part in the workshop discussions. It was generally admitted that contemplation is a dimension of the Christian life to which all are called in one way or the other. It supposes an awareness of God's all-embracing Presence, openness to the Spirit dwelling in our hearts, and docility to His guidance, and the readiness to embrace the asceticism, self-denial and interior silence that the contemplative life demands. Contemplative life is not reduced only to the time allotted to formal prayer, it penetrates our entire day and supports the soul in its work among people, its fulfilment of its daily duties, helping it "to find God in all things". We thereby tend gradually to become "contemplatives in action". The entire Christian community and its leaders should be helped to become aware of this oft-forgotten aspect of the Christian life, and grow in it.

A Requiem Mass was offered on June 30, 1971, for the repose of the soul of Fr. John Chettupuzha, who expired in a hospital at Bombay. He had been our Minister for several years and served the Seminary generously. His body was brought to Pune and the funeral service was held in our Church, under the presidency of our Bishop Dr. William Gomes. He lies buried in our cemetery.

Passing on to more down-to-earth realities, our Seminary kitchen has a new look since December 1970. Why? For the first time we have now three religious Sisters in charge of our kitchen department: Sisters Loreta, Renita and Candida. They belong to the Congregation of the Holy Cross of Chavanod, France, and are members of their North Indian Province of Amravati. The Papal Seminary is grateful to them, and to those who succeeded them in the course of the years, - the Fatima Sisters, for their generous, self-sacrificing spirit, and the service they rendered to our community. God bless them.

Our new Minister, Fr. Aelred D'Silva, made his presence felt in a tangible way through a number of improvements he brought about both in the grounds outside and within the house itself. One of them is the swimming pool.

"Murder in the Cathedral!" - a name familiar to us: the title of one of T.S. Eliot's famous plays, perhaps the best of them all. Our readers may be surprised to know that on 9 September 1971 we saw the play staged in the Seminary Church itself! But what better place for such a play, depicting the martyrdom of a bishop of the Roman Catholic Church, than a Christian Church, its natural setting? Let us remember that it was written way back in 1935 to be staged in a church, in Canterbury Cathedral, for the Canterbury festival. We had the Blessed Sacrament transferred to our domestic chapel, before the play. Anyway, our audience reacted very positively to the explanation given to them, and participated in the play with more relevance - so the editor of AUMOL tells us - than is seen in many churches during the Passion play on Good Friday (November 1971, p. 283).

Our Visitors

All in India know, or have heard of Raj Mohan Gandhi, the dynamic grandson of Mahatma Gandhi, and a zealous promoter of Moral Rearmament Movement (M.R.A.). He gave us an inspiring talk on his favourite subject. The four absolutes for which they standare: Honesty, Purity, Unselfishness and Love. With these they hope to bring about a radical change in the lives of people. He gave us concrete examples of persons who under the influence of M.R.A. gave a wholly new turn to their life. We cannot but wish those involved in M.R.A. all success in their noble endeavour.

Mr. Hushing, M.A., L.L.M., Professor of Hindu Law spoke to us on "The Implications of conversion to Christianity" (August 17).

A month later Prof. R. Honap, of the Pune Law College, enlightened us on "The Implications of the Constitution Amendment Bill" (27 September).

On September 24, 1971, a group of seventy-six made up of students, seven Professors and the Principal of "Gandhi Shikshan Bhavan", B.Ed. College of Bombay University, paid us a friendly visit. Their purpose was to get to know something of the training given to future Catholic priests. They were rapidly introduced to the various aspects of our formation programme, and then we sat for a get-together. On the day following we had a prayer service planned by those B.Ed. students. Almost all of them were non-Catholics. They were also present at our community Mass in the church. The meaning of our liturgy was explained to them by one of the seminarians. Later, in his speech, the Principal of the College, Prof. Vajubhai Patel expressed his happiness on this - their first visit to a training college of future Catholic priests. "It helps us - he said - to know each other better and respect other religions".

Dr. Egg-Benes is a Swiss lady who had devoted more than thirty-five years of her life to the care of different able children. Fr. Malin, an SVD priest, who runs an institution for such children in Bangalore, introduced to us this deeply religious Protestant lady. The child, as a rule - Dr. Egg-Benes told us - is in need of religion, and retarded children are no exception to this rule. They will believe what they are taught. The Bible stores have a deep hold on them. The teacher should explain to them the Bible text, adapting it to their capacity but taking care not to turn those Bible stores into fairy tales. The children, she stressed, need not only intellectual doctrine but religion of love. They must be taught how to pray and converse with God, and they love to do so. They can learn the common Christian prayers. Forty percent of the so-called retarded children can be helped to become like other normal people. The secret of finding a way to their hearts is to love them, love them just as they are. A lesson to remember.

Two of our Brothers who had gone to help in the refugee campsin the North returned from there on August 24, 1971, after another two went to replace them there. These were refugees from what was then called East Pakistan. The description they gave us of life in the camp was appalling. There was no arrangement about the distribution of food: several refugees had not a bite for day on end. There was dirt, confusion everywhere. Corpses is it lying buried. In such conditions many died, several committed suicide. Little by little things went on improving: good, substantial bread was given, but the queues were so long that the day did not suffice for distributing the ration to all! Very few refugees wanted to return to their homeland. They knew they were not welcome there. They had lost everything they had. Even the title deeds of their lands had been destroyed! In the camp, a small hospital started by "Caritas" took care of the sick, but it was totally inadequate for the immense needs of the campus. While these brothers were out on their charitable mission, those at home followed them with their prayers for their welfare and for their intentions. They also deprived themselves of dessert on Sundays and Thursdays in order to be able to send the refugees some little financial help of their own.

The new academic year 1971-72 began on June 14 with the Mass of the Holy Spirit presided over by Fr. Pramananda Divarkar, the new Vice-Chancellor of Jnana-Deepa Vidyapeeth. After Mass we went to the Aula Magna. Here the Vice-Chancellor gave a formal welcome to Fr. Herbert Alphonso, the newly appointed Rector of the Papal Athenaeum. Fr. Herbert (or Fr. Herbie as we usually call him) is a former student of the Athenaeum. He was novice-master in the Bombay Jesuit Province, and Rector of the Jesuit Theologate of Kurseong, St. Mary's. Truly, "it would be difficult to find one better qualified for the post; he combines in fact youthfulness in age and spirit with experience."[3]

Before reading the official document of the appointment of Fr. Alphonso as Rector by Father General of the Society, the Chancellor of the Athenaeum, Fr. Paramananda, expressed in words full of praise and appreciation our gratitude to Fr. Julien Bayart, who for reasons of health had found himself obliged to ask to be relieved from the office. A cable had been received from Fr. Bayart, from Belgium, welcoming the new Rector.

The "Ecumenical Week" comes every year to remind us of our duty to contribute what each one of us can to the great cause of the reunion of all Christians into one single body underone Head. We had an ecumenical service in our Church. Bishop William Gomes presided and Rev. MacCloed gave a homily. The service was conducted by Fr. Herbert Alphonso.

Some time later Professor Wadekar, former Head of Department of Philosophy at the Pune University and Editor of the Marathi Encyclopedia, was kind enough to come and give us a conference on "The Relevance of Gita today". All found it instructive and thought-provoking.

The month of June 1972 ushered in a new scholastic year. On June 14 Lionel Mascarenhas who had been Rector of the Seminary since 1967 gave his place to his successor Fr. Thomas Mannumel. Fr. Mannumel came from Shembaganur (Madurai Jesuit Province) where he held the responsible office of Rector of Sacred Heart College, the well known Jesuit Philosophate, Alma Mater of generations of Jesuit scholastics. He was given a warm welcome. The Seminary is immensely grateful to Fr. Lionel for his kind and devoted service to the Seminary and to each one of its inmates, during his tenure of office.

The December 14, 1972 was our Community Day - the first under the new Rector. Immediately after Holy Mass all the students assembled outside the church to greet the Fathers. They garlanded Fr. Rector and offered each of the members of the staff a bouquet of flowers. Breakfast followed, and at 8.45 sports at the seminary playground. At 7.30 p.m. the entire community of the seminary gathered together in the main Hall for dinner animated by an enjoyable programme of speeches, songs and other items. It went on till 10.40 p.m.

In 1972, the popular feast of Diwali fell on November 6. The celebrations, organized by the Hindi Academy, began with the morning Eucharist in orthodox Indian style. In the evening there was a variety entertainment attended by a number of guests invited for the occasion. After the lighting of the lamp, appropriate texts were read followed by short plays, songs and local dances contributed by the various houses on the campus. The decoration of the hall was simple but artistic and the lamps on the cornices of the building and the verandahs produced a real Divali light effect.

Diwali is the feast of light and joy, but what does it mean to a vast number of our brothers and sisters living in the slums not far from our houses. Sr. Gladys D'Souza, RSCJ, of Sophia College, Bombay, gave us a lecture on poverty and in justice in the world. Speaking of India alone, a high percentage of the income – she told us - is in the hands of a few, while a high percentage of the population lives below poverty line. The housing for the poor is miserable: no facilities for water, no lavatories, no privacy. In big cities there are more than 200 slums. Unemployment creates terrible problems: in Bombay alone 40% of the unemployed make out a living by selling their blood!

Several of our seminarians are engaged in "social work" in our neighbourhood, under the leadership of Frs. Felix Clausen and Subhash Anand. They pay regular visits to the poor and try to understand their situation, helping them through tuitions, non-formal education, some kind of seminars, etc. Some go to the Remand Home (junior jail) to spend time with the inmates and offer them their friendship and understanding. Some also organize cultural programmes for the less fortunate in our vicinity and elsewhere (e.g., for a leper colony).

In June 1973, at the beginning of the new scholastic year, the question of registering the Seminary and the Athenaeum as separate Trusts came up for consideration. In trying to do so, those concerned had before their eyes the directives given by the Second Vatican Council according to which ecclesiastical faculties were to enjoy a certain autonomy or freedom from other institutions, in line with the autonomy claimed by secular universities that were formerly dependent on bodies like Town Councils, and so on. Having these norms in mind, Fr. Paramananda Divarkar, then the Major Superior for the Pune Seminary and Athenaeum, after due consultation, took effective measures to have two separate Trusts registered, one for the Papal Seminary and the other for the Pontifical Athenaeum. In two or three sessions the Rector, Fr. Mannumel, explained to both Philosophers and Theologians the significance of this move which in no way detracted from the basic connection of the Athenaeum with the Seminary: that connection remains intact. This was a good occasion for a name of its own to be given to the Seminary. The matter was proposed to the students, but it gave rise to undue misunderstandings, and so the proposal was dropped.

It was about this time that opportunity began to be offered to those among the seminarians who chose to do so, to make the Thirty Day Ignatian Spiritual Exercises. This practice has continued up to now and the director of this retreat till now - one much appreciated by the retreatants each time - has been Fr. Josef Neuner, of De Nobili College. It has generally been held during the summer vacation, at Sacred Heart College, the former Jesuit scholasticate in Shembaganur, near Kodaikanal, except for one year, when it was made in Khandala. The pre-philsophers have during the first term, a fifteen day special programme at the Seminary villa at Vitthalwadi, consisting of an eight-day retreat and a week of "orientation programme".

It is known that the Second Vatican Council called for a renewal in the Church. It is true, however, that this word "renewal" is subject to different interpretations, not all of them valid or acceptable. We were therefore fortunate to have with us for a short time a Roman Professor of the Gregorian University, Fr. Edward Malatesta SJ. In his conference on "Spiritual attitudes in the work of Renewal" he pointed out some of the norms that ought to guide us in the challenging task of implementing Vatican II in the Church today. We are grateful to the learned Professor for his lucid lecture.

Saint Thérése of the Child Jesus is both a modern popular saint and an accredited mistress of the spiritual life. On her feast day, this year, October 3, 1973, we had a symposium on her teaching. Fr. Neuner, S J, Fr. Ittoop, SVD, and Sr. Gonsalez spoke on some of the aspects of her spiritual doctrine. This session was followed by a concelebrated Mass in the Seminary church.

On October 18, the energetic leader of the Socialist Party, Mr. George Fernandes gave a talk on "Trade Union Movements in India", at 10.15 a.m. In the evening we had a panel on "Trade Unions and the priest's role in them".

The great majority of the students living in the Seminary are candidates for the diocesan priesthood, coming from the various dioceses in the country. Exceptionally, however, we do have a few scholastics from one or other religious institute living with us, and so we were privileged to have among us for a short time - just about a year or so - a small group of Don Bosco Salesian scholastics. They left us on June 26, 1975. Entering this piece of news in the Seminarians' Diary, the Beadle of the theologians, Sebastian Puthenpura, made this remark: "The community felt strongly about their departure, as the group of salesians who have been with us have endeared themselves to the community". This is literally true, for these Brothers, cheerful, talented, devoted to their duty and friendly to everyone, had really become part of us, and so it was indeed painful for us all to bid them farewell. May our heavenly Father, and Mary Help of Christians whom they love so well, be with them all through their life's journey.

Celibacy is under fire now-a-days for various quarters. However, Fr. Angelo D'Agostino's talk on "Priestly Celibacy and Modern Psychology" confirmed us in our attitude to this much discussed problem touching priests so closely. Fr. D'Agostino, S.J., is the Director of the Centre of Religion and Psychiatry, in Washington.

On October 20 our minor holidays began. Eight of our Brothers left for Khanapur, a village in the Pune District of Maharashtra, in order to help villagers in the construction of a common building for the village people.

In the course of the year 1977 we had a number of sessions of Staff-Students Dialogue, during which relevant themes were discussed like, for instance, The Purpose of the Seminary; The type of formation imparted in the Seminary; Freedom and Discipline; Active Participation in the Liturgy, etc.

A two-credit course on Yoga - theory and practice - given by Swami Amaladass began on July 10, 1977.

Of the unscheduled talks given at the Athenaeum, the following were among those the seminarians appreciated most: "The Church and the socio-political trends in Asia" by Fr. Houtart SJ; "Healing" by Dr. Trevor D'Netto, a much esteemed Professor of Psychiatry in the Armed Forces Medical College of Pune; "Human Sexuality" by Dr. Eustace J. de Souza, Head of the Department of Anatomy, of Topiwala College, Bombay; "The New Thinking regarding the Church's Marriage Law" by Fr. Peter Huizing, SJ, former Professor of the Gregorian University, Rome, and Consultor of the Commission for the revision of the Church Law on Marriage; "The changing face of Indian economy" by Prof. V. M. Dandekar, Director of Gokhale Institute; "Para-Psychology" by Fr. Henry Pauli, an eminent psychologist from Argentina; "Formation for Evangelisation" by Bishop George V. Saupin SJ of Daltonganj.

Bishop Valerian D'Souza

The solemn episcopal consecration of Msgr. Valerian D'Souza as Bishop of Poona on September 25, 1977 brought together a certain number of our Indian Bishops who came to take part in the ceremony, with His Eminence Cardinal Valerian Gracias at their head. On the evening of the same day the Seminary took the opportunity to offer a special reception to its most distinguished old alumnus, Cardinal Gracias. We had, at dinner, together with His Eminence, the following Prelates: Archbishop Eugene D'Souza of Bhopal, Archbishop Simon Pimenta, Coadjutor of Bombay, Bishops Ignatius Pinto of Belgaum, Abraham V. of Khandwa, Joe Rosario of Amaravati, Joe Rodrigues of Jamshedpur, William D'Mello of Karwar, George Anathil of Indore, Ambrose Edanapally of Bellary and Charles Gomes of Ahmedabad. Patriarch Raul Gonsalves of Goa could not be present, but he did pay us a visit on the following day and joined us for lunch. Msgr. Francesco Denettis, Charge d'affaires of the Nunciature at Delhi, and our Vice-Chancellor, Fr. Andre Bruylants were also present. Father Rector said a few words welcoming His Eminence and Their Lordships to the Seminary. Then, Professor Fr. Thomas Dabre greeted in the name of the community each of the Prelates present. A special Goan "Mando" prepared for the occasion and dedicated to the Cardinal was sung by the Konkani Choir. Cardinal Gracias then rose to express his joy at being in the Seminary and thanked the students for the fine programme they put up for the occasion.

A couple of days later we had the happiness of welcoming in our midst our new Bishop Valerian D'Souza. His Lordship celebrated the 6.30 a.m. Mass. At 10.30 the Athenaeum gave His Lordship an official reception. Lunch followed at 12.30. A little girl of Ramwadi performed a dance in his honour. Bro. Donald D'Souza greeted the Bishop in the name of the community. Bishop Vally spoke last recalling with gratitude the years he spent in the Seminary and the training he received here. He concluded with a beautiful song which we all liked very much. On the following morning His Lordship conferred the ministry of "Readers" on 32 theologians and that of "Acolytes" on 36 of them.

On the November 4, 1977 Cardinal Trevor Picachy of Calcutta was the main celebrant at our community Mass. He was returning from Rome after the Synod of Bishops. We had His Eminence with us for supper, as well as Archbishop Padiyara of Changanacherry, together with a group of lay leaders from Kerala. Seminarian George Pattery welcomed our guests. After supper, Cardinal Picachy, who did his philosophy at Shembaganur and theology in Kurseong together with some members of our staff, gave us an informal talk on the Synod.

In Aid of Andhra

From November 27, at the initiative of the Students' Council, the Brothers met in different sessions to discuss the ways and means of helping the victims of the recent cyclone in Andhra and Tamil Nadu: there were thousands of them. One of the concrete decisions taken was to forgo a meal once a week, and do without desert on Sundays and Thursdays. Similarly, to drop all prizes that would normally be given to the respective winners during the Sports Day the following month, and send the amount thus saved to Andhra, together with the money they would be able to collect for the same purpose from other sources.

The situation in Andhra was extremely grave. Returning from Andhra, after a visit to the places affected by the cyclone, Fr. Ambrose D'Mello SJ, our Vice-Chancellor, asked for volunteers from the Athenaeum to go and help personally the people suffering from the effects of the cyclone. Forty-five volunteered from the Seminary. So, after a few days, Fr. Jean de Marneffe, who had succeeded Fr. Herbert Alphonso as the Rector of the Athenaeum, announced that four volunteers would go from the Seminary, five from De Nobili College, two from the SVD community, and one from each of the remaining houses on the campus. The four volunteers from the Papal Seminary were Brothers Xavier Paul, Prakash Mallavarapu, Joji Reddy and Thomas Pulian. They left for Andhra on December 1, together with the other eleven brothers from the campus.

We had heard a lot about the famous Taizé Community in France. On February 3, 1978, Taize came to us in the person of one of its members, Bro. Guiom. We had a first brief meeting with him after lunch. At 8.30 p.m., after supper, Brother Guiom gave us a talk on the life and activities of Taize. All were inspired by his absolute simplicity and the conviction with which he spoke about their work. The talk was followed by half an hour of prayer.

Around this time Bishop George Saupin of Daltonganj gave us a truly enriching talk about "Formation for evangelization".

During the month of July 1978 we received the news that soon the Papal Seminary was going to have a new Rector: Fr. Theo deSales. He took over from Fr. Thomas Mannumel. On the eleventh of the month we bade farewell to dear Fr. Tom. The programme was as follows: Mass at 6.30 a.m. at which the main celebrant was Fr. Mannumel, who also gave the homily. Special items were presented during lunch in his honour. After a "High Tea" with the Staff, and a Football match between the Seminary and DNC, the day ended with a buffet supper of farewell followed by a seance in the Hall. Father was taken to the hall seated on an arm chair. Bro. Prakash gave expression to the sentiments of the seminarians and Fr. de Marneffe spoke on behalf of the staff. The new Rector, Fr. Theo, too, added a few words of his own. Fr. Mannumel left for Madurai the following morning.

On September 11, 1978 we received the sad news of the death of Cardinal Valerian Gracias. We had Mass for the repose of his soul the following day. Fr. Carl Fonseca gave the homily. In the afternoon, Father Minister, Fr. de Marneffe, Fr. Lionel and Fr. Dabre left for Bombay for the funeral.

Father Anthony Sabino, our much esteemed Professor of Epistemology, celebrated his Golden Jubilee in the Society of Jesus on July 22, 1979. He was the main celebrant at Mass. In the evening there was a function in his honour in which beautiful things were said about him by our students who have a very special regard and affection for him. Not to make this write-up too long, we shall only give here extracts from the speech given on that occasion by Fr. Lionel Mascarenhas, the then Rector of the Athenaeum.

"Lest I repeat what has been said and written at various times these days, let me confine myself to: Fr. Sabino and JDV. Fr. Sabino started his intellectual career as a student of philosophy in Shembaganur. His companions soon realised that, beneath his simple and humorous exterior lay a sharp mind and he was easily the first in his class. He returned to Italy for his Theological studies, and then did his doctorate at the Gregorian University, Rome. The fruit of his studies was a brilliant and penetrating thesis on "The Metaphysics of Spiritualism". The prestigious Roman periodical *Civilta Cattolica* several times asked to be allowed to publish extracts of his thesis but, perfectionist that he was, he stubbornly refused.

He came out to Kandy in 1948 when he began his long association with the Athenaeum there and later in Pune. Thirty long years of devoted and fruitful intellectual service, during which he served also as librarian of JDV. He began in Kandy by teaching Theology for a year or two to fill a gap, but then switched over to his real field, Philosophy, in which he has taught the History of Philosophy and his own special subject, Epistemology. His colleagues on the staff and his former students alike often remarked on the depth and keenness and extensiveness of his knowledge, revealed in the outstanding quality of his notes. He has always been a voracious reader who, in his younger days, devoured the folio volumes of the great Scholastics and everything that related to his subject. His intellectual appetite continues unabated and its scope is, if anything enlarged. His intellectual ability and versatility showed itself more than once during the public "Disputationes" which were customary in the pre-Vatican era...Through the years Fr. Sabino has been an example of intellectual alertness and independence combined with a loyalty to Christian tradition; of astuteness joined to a winning childlike simplicity; of intelligence at the service of love...

Fr. Lionel ended by wishing Fr. Sabino "many more years in which to share with future generations of JDV the light of his knowledge, the warmth of his overwhelming humaneness and the spice and charm of his inimitable personality".

For quite a number of years our Chapel and sacristy were looked after by Mr. Anthony. He came to Pune from Tamil Nadu several years ago and carried on his duty here at the Seminary with exemplary fidelity, care and perfection. He edified us all by his silent devotion to his work and his readiness to serve and oblige. His death on July 2, 1979, at the age of 62 was a real loss to the Seminary. May Our Lord whom he served so faithfully be his reward exceedingly great. After the funeral service in the evening, his body was taken to the Hadapsar cemetery, accompanied by members of the staff and students. A special community Mass was celebrated for the repose of his soul on July 6.

September 23 was **Fr. Gaspar Koelman's** Golden Jubilee in the Society of Jesus. At Mass Fr. Rector said a few words of introduction, but Fr. Koelman was the main celebrant. At the end of the service, Father was garlanded, and souvenirs of the event were distributed. In the evening the football match was in his honour. Frs. Ambrose D'Mello and Bruylants were present. Dinner was at 7.30 p.m. Bro. Jose Payapilly gave expression to the sentiments of the community. Fr. Rector read the congratulatory letter sent on the occasion to Fr. Koelman by Fr. General, Pedro Arrupe. Fr. Koelman concluded the meeting with a speech.

Three days later, we celebrated another jubilee. On September 26, **Fr. Robert Criem** completed 60 years in the Society. He was the main celebrant at Mass. The day's special items were dedicated to the jubilarian: the badminton match, the special issue of "Home Herald", the festive lunch with the usual speeches and felicitations. After lunch, Fr. Criem blessed the new Prarthanalaya. In the evening he gave the Benediction of the Blessed Sacrament.

As in the previous chapter, we now go on to mention briefly some of the extra-curricular activities of the members of the Papal Seminary Staff. The list is far from complete.

Fr. Francis Pereira participated in the Conference of the Society for Biblical Studies held at Leonard Theological College, Jabalpur, and presented a paper on "The Galatian controversy in the light of the targums", a paper later published in a special issue of the Indian Journal of Theology, Serampore. He also read a paper on "The Scriptural Foundations of the Theology of Vocation" at the Vocation Seminar in De Nobili College, in May 1971.

Fr. Felix Clausen organized ten meetings of the "Joint Study Group" of Catholic, Protestant and Orthodox theologians to study Mariology, and took part in an Ecumenical Seminar in Bangalore.

Fr. Jean de Marneffe attended the fourth session of the Indian Philosophical Congress held in Pune in November 1971 and read a paper on "Structural Analysis". Together with the Reception Committee he arranged for a visit of the members of the congress to the Pontifical Athenaeum. In December 1972 he participated as an Associate Member in the International Seminar on World Philosophy held for ten days at the Centre of Advanced Studies of Philosophy in the University of Madras. In February 1971 he gave in the same University the Sri L.D. Swamikannu Pillai Endowment Lectures on "Contemporary Christian Philosophy". At the end of February, at the invitation of the Linguistic Society of India Club, Deccan College, he spoke on "Structuralism" to an audience of professors and research scholars of the same college. In June 1971 he attended, at the Pune University, the 21st Session of the Indian Philosophical Association in which the main theme of discussion was the philosophy of Bertrand Russell.

A special mention must here be made of Fr. Kurien Kunnumpuram's commendable study on the salvific meaning of non-Christian Religions, entitled "Ways of Salvation". It is his doctoral thesis written at Innsbruck under the direction of the well known Belgian theologian Fr. P. Fransen, SJ. It is a careful inquiry into the value and role of non-Christian religions in the salvation of good non-Christians. The many positive values these religions contain can well be looked upon as a sort of secret presence of God in them: they are like the seeds of the Word and the fruits of the Spirit, and can therefore be instrumental in leading those who follow them to salvation.

In the year 1970 Fr. Carlos de Melo participated as member of the Central Committee, in the International Congress of Jesuit Coadjutor Brothers held in Rome, at Villa Cavaletti, from May 20 to 30. He presented a paper on "The mind of St. Ignatius on the special role of the Coadjutor Brothers in the Society of Jesus" (cf. *Congreso Internacional de Hermanos*, CIS, Roma 1971.)

Notes

1. Acta Apostolicae Sedis, XXIII, p. 241-62.
2. *Aumol*, Vol. XIV, p.
3. *Aumol*, Vol. XXIII, August 1971, p. 117.

Chapter 8

Towards a Century (1980-1993) and More (1993-99)

In the previous chapter we gave an account of the Diamond Jubilee celebration of the Kandy-Pune Seminary in the year 1968. We begin this new chapter of our history with the description of another memorable date in the life of the Seminary, namely, the commemoration of the 25th anniversary of its transfer from Kandy to Pune, in other words, the Silver Jubilee of the Pontifical Seminary in Pune, Maharashtra.

This event was celebrated from December 2 to 4, 1980, under the rectorship of Fr. Theo de Sales, himself a Punite and an "old boy" of the Seminary in Pune. It was animated by the joyful participation of some hundred priests formed in Kandy and/or Pune. The most distinguished among them were eight Bishops and one Cardinal Archbishop. The bishops present were Archbishop Arulappa of Hyderabad, Bishops Denzil D'Souza of Silchar, Valerian D'Souza of Pune, Patrick Nair of Meerut, George Anathil of Indore, James Pazhayattil of Irinjalakuda, Paulinus Jeerakath of Jagdalpur, Alan de Lastic, Auxiliary of Calcutta, and at the head of them all Joseph Cardinal Cordeiro of Karachi, who took the trouble of coming all the way from Pakistan to be with us on this auspicious occasion.

The celebrations began with a solemn Mass presided over by the Bishop of Pune, Right Reverend Dr. Valerian D'Souza, with no less than 200 priests from the campus and from various parts of the country con celebrating with him. The choir was made up of brothers from the seminary and the several houses on the campus.

The following day, December 3, was the feast of our Patron, St. Francis Xavier, whose statue placed high up at the very entrance of the Seminary buildings, proclaims without words the very aim and purpose of his own life, and the purpose also of all that happens within the seminary walls, namely, evangelization: "Go into all the world and preach the gospel to every creature" (Mk 16:15).

The main celebrant at Mass was Cardinal Joseph Cordeiro who also delivered the homily. Among the Prelates concelebrating with him, three had been ordained priests sixty years earlier, five fifty years earlier, and ten twenty-five years earlier. In tribute to the past, although the Mass was in English, some of its parts were chanted in Latin. On December 4, a touch of inculturation was lent to the celebrations by the Masses being celebrated in several regional languages: Tamil, Malayalam, Hindi, Marathiand Konkani. In the same spirit of inculturation our dear guests coming from the different corners of India were given a taste of the rich diversity of the Indian culture through the songs and dances peculiar to the various regions of this subcontinent, all climaxing in the artistic execution of Bharat Natyam by one of our ex-students, the world famous exponent of gospel themes through Indian dance, Father Francis Barboza, SVD.

This much for the strictly "spiritual" items of the Jubilee celebrations, but the cultural aspect of the event was not forgotten. That same night the seminarians staged Jean Anouilh's play "Becket" in its English version. As Fr. Theo de Sales put it, it provided "three hours of dramatic scenes and sensitive acting by a cast of forty, recapturing the past with an exist entialist glow for the present-day world". Nor was the local import of the event left aside. Two distinguished representatives of the local civil authorities were kind enough to accept our invitation and grace our celebrations with their presence. More, they earned our gratitude by taking the occasion to pay tribute to the active part taken by the Christian community and their clergy in the cause of education and in the struggle against poverty in the country.

A particularly appreciated number of the jubilee programme were the sharings in which all - young and old - participated whole heartedly. On the first day, the panel was formed by Bishop Denzil, of Silchar, and Fathers J. X. Fernando, Merwin Carapiet and John Vallamattam. Their expositions and the exchanges between the panelists and the audience were focused particularly on the apostolate among the youth. On the second day, the sharings turned around the various regions in the country and elicited a lively response from those present. The theme of the sharings on the third day was "Seminary Formation". Fr. George Lobo was the moderator and the two Rectors, namely of the Seminary and of the Athenaeum, Frs. Theo de Sales and Herbert Alphoso were the panelists, together with Fr. Kurien Kunnumpuram and Bro. Thomas Kulangara, a first year theologian from the Archdiocese of Trivandrum (Malankara).

Apart from these formal occasions, what everyone seems to have enjoyed in a deep, personal way, and carried home with himself, was the remembrance of the free intervals, during which old friends and companions, some of whom had never met since they had left the portals of the Alma Mater, mingled joyfully with one another and with their younger brethren in the Lord's vineyard. They recalled the old care free days of their youth or shared their experiences in the mission field, learning from one another. Truly, a joy-filled experience! *Quam bonum et jucundum habitare fratres in unum!*

By now catholics in our country have heard about the so-called "Focolare Movement". It was started fifty years ago by an Italian young lady Chiara Lubich in Turin. Gradually it became well known and spread to several countries of the world. It came to India in September 1980, and has its main centres, one for men and another for women, in Bombay. Their official name is "Opus Mariae". They had their first assembly in India –"Mariapolis" as they love to call it - at the Papal Seminary, here in Pune, in June 1-3, 1981. Bishop Rosario of Amaravati, and Bishop Valerian of Pune were present. Many priests, married couples, religious women and men, and young people from various parts of India participated in the Mariapolis, among them a group of young seminarians. All were deeply impressed by the spirit of mutual union and charity promoted by the movement byword and deed, inspired by a living faith in the Presence of Jesus in our midst: Gesù in mezzo. The Focolarini had another meeting at the Papal Seminary later on the theme "Priestly Unity".

Father Arrupe in Pune

In the past, the Generals of the Society of Jesus seldom, if ever, left their headquarters in Rome, unless, of course, obliged by unavoidable circumstances to do so. This tradition was definitively set aside by Father Pedro Arrupe, the 28th successor of Ignatius of Loyola, who took charge of his office on May 22, 1965. A Basque by birth, like Ignatius, Arrupe, who was just completing his studies in Medicine, joined the Society of Jesus, in the Province of Loyola, in Spain, on January 15, 1927. Early in life he volunteered for the Missions and in 1938 was assigned to the Jesuit Mission of Japan. In the course of time he became the Master of novices and the Rector of the Novitiate in Japan and later Vice-Provincial (1954-1958) and Provincial (1958). It is in this capacity that he took part in the 31st General Congregation that was to elect him General of the Society on May 22, 1965.

Become the head of a large Religious Order that counted as many as 36,000 priests and brothers, Arrupe realized that in the present time it was advisable for him to get into a more direct contact with his men labouring for the preservation and spread of the faith in the five continents of the world, rather than govern the Society from distant Rome alone. Hence the new policy head opted of visiting his brother Jesuits and seeing them at work in the various fields of their apostolate, north and south, east and west, in the old as well as in the new world to which he himself belonged by his ascription to the Japanese Province. By the way, this is also the policy that is being assiduously followed by his successor, Fr. Peter-Hans Kolven bach.

It is thanks to this change of policy that the five hundred odd students of the Papal Athenaeum of Pune, together with the members of the staff, had the opportunity to welcome Fr. Arrupein their midst in January 1980. His congenial personality, his simplicity, cheerfulness and cordiality won all hearts. We, of the Seminary, had him for supper after the JDV Mass celebrated in the Seminary Church at 6.30 p.m. In his address to us he stressed the importance of serious study in preparation for our priestly ministry in India, and of inculturation. After supper, the domestic personnel of the house was introduced to him. Father General then stopped to chat informally with the seminarians for a short while outside the dining room, before proceeding to the staff recreation room. This was not his first visit to us; he had been to Pune some years earlier, leaving always behind him an impression of a man of God who is deeply human and spiritual, humble, open, optimistic, warm and amiable.

Fr. Robert Criem, SJ

The name of Fr. Robert Criem has often been mentioned in the pages of this historical sketch of the Papal Seminary. No wonder, for Fr. Criem spent the whole of his life as a priest at the service of future ministers of the Church in Kandy and Pune. He was Professor of Moral Theology for about forty years. In addition to this he was all the time spiritual director of the seminarians, Master of Ceremonies, Professor of Liturgy, National Director of the Apostolic Union of Secular Priests and Editor of its magazine "Aumol", Scout Master, etc.

Fr. Criem was a man of hard work, but his work proceeded from a heart overflowing with love of God and of his neighbour. He was truly a man of God, witnessing to Him by his life of prayer, deep humility, availability to all who went to him for help or advice, his habitual cheerfulness and gentleness, his charity, practice of self denial and penance, and devotion to duty. He used to rise early, around 3.00 or 3.30 a.m., and prepare himself for Mass by an hour of prayer and the Way of the Cross.

In September 1982 he had to be taken to Jehangir Nursing Home, where he was operated upon on September 6, 1982 for perforation of the duodenum. A second operation was performed on the 30 of the month. Just before going to sleep, on the night of October 11, Bro. A. M. Regimon, who together with Bro. K. A. Joseph kept vigil by his side, read to him a gospel passage from St. Matthew. At the end of the reading Fr. Criem said "Amen", blessed himself thrice with the Sign of the Cross and slowly fell into a slight sleep. The Lord's call came to him during that sleep, at about 2.00 a.m. on October 12.

Fr. Criem's body was brought to the Seminary and exposed in the parlour clothed in priestly vestments. Later, it was transferred to the church. Our brothers took turns keeping watch by his coffin. We had a devout and touching prayer service in our church from 7.30 p.m. to 8.00 p.m. The funeral service took place at 7.30 a.m. on October 13. The members of the Athenaeum were present in large numbers to give expression to their regard and esteem for so dedicated a professor, priest and religious. Many religious Sisters and lay people too came to pay their respects to good Fr. Criem and pray for the repose of his soul. Seventy priests concelebrated together with the Rector, Fr. Theo deSales. Father Lionel said a few words of introduction. After Mass tributes were paid by Fr. Paul Alilakuzhy, Bro. Ashikhot, SVD, Scout Master, and Bro. Linus Nelli.

Father Criem had identified himself totally with the Seminary and the future ministers of the Church. His memory will be held in blessing by those who were privileged to know him so closely and it will remain with them as a source of abiding inspiration. The number of letters that came to the Seminary after Fr. Criem's death from all over India give abundant testimoney to the veneration and esteem in which he was held especially by priests in India. (Cf. "Aumol", December 1982). On his 83rd birthday (August 26, 1982), Fr. Criem had scribbled the following note: "The Papal Seminary has been a heaven of peace, surrounded by fine superiors, amiable colleagues, and lovable students. Though all is not perfect (what is perfect in this life?), I do not know what better place I could go to except heaven, of course, where I pray I will go very soon. Amen." The good God answered the prayer of his faithful son a fort night later. May he rest in peace.

Father Carl Fonseca

A little over a year after Fr. Criem's death the Papal Seminary and Athenaeum suffered another great loss in the death of a younger member of the community - Fr. Carl Fonseca, S.J., occurred on December 11, 1983.

Fr. Carl had to be taken to K.E.M. Hospital where he had to undergo two operations. Although the surgery seemed to be successful and he was allowed to return to the Seminary, suddenly he took a turn for the worse and had to be taken back to the hospital on 10 December. There he suffered two cardiac arrests and lost consciousness. He passed away at 12.15 p.m. on December 11.

Fr. Lionel Mascarenhas had been his companion and friend in Karachi in their younger days and later in the Society of Jesusin Shembaganur and Kurseong. Fr. Lionel paid a loving tribute to his Jesuit brother at his funeral service on December 12. We feel honoured to transcribe here the main section of his funeral address: "Carl's Jesuit life and ministry after his ordination (in 1950) was composed of two chapters. The first and the longer one of his almost thirty years was devoted to the educational apostolate in school and for a short time in college. He was principal and rector of Jesuit schools in Nadiad, Anand and Baroda, rector of Loyola Hall in Ahmedabad for a year, and one of the founding group of Jesuits of St. Xavier's College, Mapuca, Goa, of which he was vice-principal.

The second chapter of his life belongs to JDV and Papal Seminary with a brief interlude between the two periods of school and seminary ministry, at the Indian Social Institute, Delhi. He was called to Pune in 1975 to be Registrar of JDV and Professor of Church History. After laying down the office of registrar in1981, he continued to teach Church History. In the Seminary he taught English to the pre-philosophy students, directed the Philosophers's Cultural Academy, supervised groups for homiletics and made himself available for sundry other services to the seminarians.

Scholar and man of letters: He had a passion for reading and was never so happy as when he was surrounded by books. He loved literature and was widely read. Along with this went a love of history and politics. Indian history, and especially Indian Church History, was a subject after his heart. He was keenly interested in Upadhyaya Brahmabandhav and his final aim and last wish was to write a book on the great Indian convert, for which he was collecting material quietly these last years.

He was a man of deep feeling and of an affective disposition, which however he hid behind a certain shyness. He loved his family, though characteristically he seldom spoke of it. He had a wide circle of friends and related easily with young people. He was proud of his former boys in school, many of whom remained bound to him by ties of friendship and affection. He valued the fellowship of his Jesuit brothers and put a premium on community life.

Above all, I esteemed and appreciated in him the priest that he was. He was a man of deep faith, which was no doubt the legacy of a saintly mother. Mass and the Eucharist were truly the centre of his life. Man of prayer that he was, he took care not to parade his spirituality. He was deeply loyal to the Church and the Society. His loyalty to the Church and the society were cast in the mould of a former age - which made it difficult for him to accept and sympathise with certain attitudes and approaches of today which disappointed and even pained him and which he tended to dismiss with a certain wry humour and irony. His living and simple faith showed itself in the fine way in which he accepted his last illness, with the sufferings and inconveniences it brought. I've rarely seen such a good patient, always grateful for the visits of friends and for the attention and care paid to him in his illness. On two occasions these last days he said to me, in a tone of calm acceptance, regarding his sufferings: "Well, if this is the way God wants it, so be it". There was neither self-pity nor Stoic indifference - just a willing "yes" to the Lord.

And so, as we bid farewell and lay him to rest, the picture I shall treasure of him is above all that of a holy and dedicated priest a living proof (if a proof were needed) of the relevance of the priesthood even in our age and day.

It may be some consolation to the members of his family and his relatives to know of the esteem and love in which Carl was held by the members of his community, which was shown simply and spontaneously by the attention and care with which he was surrounded in his illness. Today our hope and our strength lies in our Christian faith and the conviction that, if we suffer and die with Him, we shall live with Him, who is our life and resurrection."

Another death that touched the Papal Seminary very closely was that of **Fr. Pius Geisel, S.J**. As Provincial of Goa-Pune, Fr. Geisel undertook and directed the building of the Seminary and Athenaeum, in view of its transfer from Kandy to Pune. He carried out the work entrusted to him by Propaganda with the thoroughness that was characteristic of him in all his undertakings. He was also a model parish priest fully devoted to his people and much esteemed and loved by them. He was called to his eternal reward on March 17, 1984. The Athenaeum offered a Mass for him on the following day, presided over by Fr. Rex Pai, Provincial of India.

Around this time we lost the services of our active driver Mr. Gnanapragasam who passed away on November 24, 1980. His wife Rosy continued to look after the cleanliness of the house and help the community in several other ways.

Our Visitors

In the course of these years well known personalities from various corners of the world have been favouring us with their visits. It is but proper that we mention these names in love and gratitude in this historical sketch of this institution. Here they are:

- Mr. Raj Mohan Gandhi, the grandson of the Mahatma, editor of "Himmat", gave us an interesting talk on "The Socio-political crisis in India" on June 27, 1981.
- Fr. Jean Claude, the popular commentator of the French National T.V., shared with us his experience as a priest in words that made a deep impression on all. He has been accompanying Pope John Paul II in his pastoral tours, for the French T.V. (August 26, 1981).
- On September 22, 1981 Professor Naravane gave a lecture on "Mythology in the Indian Tradition", and another, on the day following, on "Freedom".
- Fr. Cecil McGarry, SJ, Assistant to the Jesuit General in Rome, paid us a visit on December 8 of the year.
- Dr. Miss Florence Hetzler, of Fordham University, USA, delivered an erudite lecture on "Philosophy and Art", illustrated with select slides (February 7, 1982).
- Archbishop Simon Pimenta, President of the CBCI and Patron of JDV came to preside over the inaugural function of the new scholastic year, on June 14, 1982.
- A group of Arunachal Pradesh Catholics entertained us with cultural songs and dances. They evoked with much feeling memories of the persecution their people had to endure in the early years of their conversion to the Christian faith.

- The "Sudds", an African Theatre Group, staged a play "The Night Before" which lasted an hour and a half (June 18).
- Msgr. Marchesano and Msgr. Cherutti of the Roman Curia dropped in for a brief visit on July 9.
- Mrs. Farah Rustom gave a talk on "The Joys of Music" to a hall filled to capacity (November 17, 1982).
- Mr. and Mrs. Billings explained the method of Natural Family Planning to an audience of interested present and future pastors and spiritual directors (February 4, 1983).
- Bishop Charlie Gomes, the former Provincial of the Goa-Pune Vice-Province, presided at our community Mass on September 28,1983.
- Henrick Dussel, the celebrated Liberation Theologian from Mexico, shared with us his views on "Liberation Theology in Latin America", and particularly Nicaragua (November 7, 1984).
- The famous "Covenant Play" troupe of Australia gave us a performance, followed by a class about dramatics in two groups. They visited us again on June 3, 1985.
- Fr. Simon Decloux, the Assistant of the Jesuit General was the main celebrant at Mass, on January 6, 1985.
- Dr. Anand Phadke gave us an instructive talk on "How Drug Industry can exploit and cheat the public".
- Fr. Paul Vaz, of Bombay, a Jesuit Priest deeply involved in the cause of slum dwellers, shared with us his views on "The implication of the Supreme Court judgement on the slum and pavement dwellers" (September 13, 1985).
- Rev. Richard Wurmbrand, a Lutheran Minister from Rumania, spoke to us of his fourteen year experience in the communist prison to which he was condemned for being Christian (January 30, 1986).
- Bishop Norbert Mtega of Iringa, Tanzania, described to us the situation of the African Church. On the day following (October 11, 1989) he ordained our Bro. Jeremiah Mhume, who belongs to his diocese. There were about 200 persons present. Jeremiah did his philosophy, theology and M.Th. at JDV while residing in the Seminary. He had many friends in the town, especially among those who had spent many years in Tanzania at the time of the British Raj. The ordination ceremony proceeded as follows. At 8.20 a.m. the community assembled in front of the "New Building" (now *Buddha Bhavan*) where Jeremiah had his room. From there he was brought in procession to the Seminary portico where Fr. Rector, Joe Thadavanal, welcomed him with a bouquet of flowers. At the entrance of the church Jeremiah was received by his Bishop. There were about four hundred persons gathered there for the ordination ceremony which lasted for two hours. A grand reception

followed. Fr. Jeremiah and his Bishop were garlanded at the entrance of the Seminary Hall. Tea and refreshments were served, while choice songs by the choir enhanced the joyfulness of the event. The festive family dinner was at 1.00 p.m. The entire community gathered around Jeremiah to congratulate him. Our African seminarian, Bro. Cleophas Mabula, presented flower bouquets to the new levite and to Bishop Norbert. Everyone contributed to make the day a truly memorable one for Jeremiah.

Pope John Paul II in Pune

Speaking of visitors, a special honourable mention is due to our late Holy Father St. who, in the year 1986, on the occasion of his visit to India, made it a point to come expressly from Bombay to Pune, to the Pontifical Athenaeum and Seminary, to gladden our hearts with his presence and encourage and guide us with his words of wisdom. In the meantime the seminary had a new Rector in the person of Fr. Joe Thadavanal, of the Patna Province of the Society. It was his privilege to welcome the Pope on his arrival at Pune by plane from Bombay, on the morning of February 10.

As soon as he arrived, the Holy Father went straight to the big campus where the entire body of the students and staff of JDV were assembled, together with a large number of the faithful of Pune, for the Pope's Mass. As he climbed the podium and took his seat there he was officially greeted by our Bishop Valerian D'Souza. Mass followed. After the Gospel the Holy Father delivered a homily addressed to all the seminarians of the nation. "Dear brothers and sons in Christ and future priests in the world you are called-he said-to be spiritual leaders with a specific identity: men of the Church, men dedicated to prayer and to the word of God, men who wish to share humbly and generously in Christ's role of mediation". Referring to India as the country where "there has always been an abiding interest inspiritual things, in the knowledge and experience of God" he exhorted the seminarians "to enter more fully into the mystery of God", "in prayer and silence to learn to listen to the voice of God". "Your first priority-he continued-must be to live in union with Christ, to be one with him at all times, faithful to his invitation: "Abide in me and I in you" (Jn 15:4). This union with Christ requires "the total acceptance of the word of God, which is communicated to us through the Sacred Scriptures and the Tradition of the Church". It likewise demands of us "adherence to the authentic Magisterium which transmits the gospel intact to each generation". The Pope concluded this part of his homily by asking the seminarians to assimilate profoundly the "unsearchable riches of Christ" in order to proclaim them with conviction in the years to come. "Your responsibility-he stressed-is to communicate Christ. But you will be able to do this only if you have first experienced his love". During the entire service our Professor Fr. Thomas Dabre (now Bishop) gave a running commentary for which the Holy Father congratulated him heartily. We had among us on this occasion a group of seminarians from Nagpur who came all the way to Pune to have a "darshan" of the Vicar of Christ.

On his way out, Pope John Paul II entered the Seminary Church, accompanied by Bishop Valerian and Fr. Thadavanal and knelt in prayer for a while at the tomb of his compatriot Msgr. Zaleski whose mortal remains lie buried in front of the main altar, and placed a bouquet of flowers on it.

During the rectorship of Fr. Theo de Sales the question of adopting an Indian name for the Papal Seminary came up again for discussion. The staff, on the whole, seemed to be in favour of the proposition, while at the same time retaining in brackets the word "Papal Seminary". It was resolved to consult the student body as well.

The reasons in favour of a change were more or less the following: 1. The term "Papal Seminary" seems to be unintelligible to a large number of our people in India. On the other hand, 2. The word "Papal" at times provokes a negative reaction among certain officials, for instance, in the rations office: at times we had to file our application for certain transactions in the name of the Athenaeum, that is Jnana-Deepa Vidyapeeth, which they easily understand. 3. This is what many Christian institutions in the country have done. Our very Athenaeum, so closely attached to the seminary, adopted an Indian name, "Jnana-Deepa Vidyapeeth, Institute of Philosophy and Religion". Why couldn't the seminary do the same so as to appear better rooted in the Indian soil? While making for a better local understanding it would in no way imply any change in its fundamental nature as the pontifical institute of training for future priests, to which the Athenaeum is attached. Besides, the term "Papal Seminary" is not as such the special name of the institution: it is a generic term. Accordingly, several Indian names were suggested: Deepti Sadan, Sadhanalaya, Samet, Bhakti Dam and others. The only reason against the change was that it might disappoint or displease our former students. However, all things considered, in order to prevent undue misunderstandings and negative feelings, the proposal was dropped. And so we continue to be known as simply the "Papal Seminary of Pune".

Panel Discussions

Besides the various lectures we mentioned in connection with several of our visitors, we have had periodically what we call "panel discussions" among ourselves. Here is a list of the topics taken up for those discussions at different times:

- "Relevance of Christ to India" (September 4, 1981).
- "Is the atmosphere in the Seminary conducive to study?" It was organized for our theologians by the Students' Council, with Fr. Subhash Anand and Bros. Lawrence Dorairaj and Paul Kattukaranas panelists.

- "The Healing Ministry" chaired by Fr. George Lobo, and the two leading Doctors from Pune as panelists: Dr. Trevor D'Netto and Dr. Durairaj.
- "Does a mature twentieth century man need God?", with the following speakers: Prof. Sundara Rajan, Head of Department of Philosophy, Pune University, Air Commodore Suri, Air Force Base, Pune, and Fr. Cyril Desbruslais, SJ, Professor of Philosophy, Jnana-Deepa Vidyapeeth.
- "The effectiveness of our formation for our future ministry". The panelists were Fr. George Lobo and Brothers Joyce, Jose Prakash, Abraham Nirappel.
- "The Christian Prophetic Role in India". Frs. J. Neuner, S. Kappen and Francis D'Sa were the speakers (July 30, 1982).
- "The Rites", with the following participants: Fr. Carl Fonseca SJ, Fr. Matthew Vellanickal and Fr. John Berchmans, OIC (December 9, 1986).
- "Diocesan Spirituality". The speakers were all diocesan priests of Pune namely, Fr. Anthony Lobo, Fr. Alex Quadros and Fr. Salvador Pinto.
- "Pastoral Ministry". The speakers this time were Fr. Eddie Fonseca: "What has helped me in my pastoral ministry"; Mr. Osy Pereira, officer at Semi-Conductors: "In virtue of my understanding of an active lay person in the parish, what do I expect from my parish priest and his assistants"; Miss. Helen Santos, youth worker of St. Xavier's parish: "My experience and my expectations of our priests in the parish". Each speaker had ten minutes at his or her disposal for the exposition of the theme. The rest of the time was left for discussion on the topic.
- "Approaches to Prayer", organized by the JDV students. The panelists were: Frs. Subhash Anand, Christian Troll and Rui de Menezes.

Jubilees celebrated

Together with the jubilees of our Seminary and Athenaeum as institutions we also celebrated joyfully the various jubilees of individual members of our community.

November 21, 1981 was the sacerdotal Silver Jubilee day of two dear members of the seminary staff: **Fathers George Lobo** and **Francis Barjau**, who was the spiritual director of theologians. Fr. George Lobo was the main celebrant at Mass and Fr. Barjau gave the homily. The "Home Herald" brought out a special issue in their honour. At lunch, the entire community greeted the jubilarians and offered them their good wishes through Bro. Lawrence Dorairaj, their spokesman. Fr. Barjau and Fr. Lobo replied in appreciation of the greetings and the good wishes they received from the community.

On January 24, 1985 it was **Fr. Carlos de Melo's** turn to celebrate his fiftieth anniversary in the Society of Jesus. It was kept up in the manner customary in our communities. The jubilarian was the main celebrant at the Jubilee Mass and His Lordship Dr. Valerian D'Souza, our Bishop, graciously concelebrated the Mass.

Father de Melo took as the theme of the celebration "Vocation and Mission". In his homily at the Gospel, after a brief reference to what he had left behind when joining the Society: "a happy, united family of parents, sisters and brothers, a deeply Christian home where he grew up in an atmosphere of peace, joy, security and love", he mentioned gratefully the Rachol Seminary, Goa, where he took his first steps towards the priesthood. He then went on to express his deep gratitude "to the Society of Jesus for the formation it gave him, humanistic, philosophical and theological, for its spiritual doctrine and tradition based on the Gospel, the Spiritual Exercises and the Constitutions, and illustrated by the life of Ignatius of Loyola, Francis Xavier and a host of confessors, martyrs and apostolic men, and confirmed by the testimony of Popes and saints; its stress on a personal attachment to Jesus Christ and to His Blessed Mother, the Trinitarian perspectives, the art of the discernment of spirits, filial devotion to the Church, the Spouse of Christ, discipline and abnegation together with a broad humanistic outlook in which action and contemplation permeate each other, contemplation leading to action and action flowing from contemplation – both fruit of love, love of God and love of humans".

"A jubilee-he said-is a typical or symbolic event. The daily life of every one of us is filled with God's gifts and favours, through persons, things, events...

> Earth's crammed with heaven
> And every burning bush a fire with God
> But only he who sees, takes off his shoes...
> (Elisabeth Barrett-Browning, Aurore Leigh, Sonnets from the Portuguese)
> Jubilees come to bring home to us this essential feature of our human
> and Christian existence".

He ended by saying: "Yes, the jubilee has come and the jubilee will go. Its one message not only to me but for all of us today is this: our life on earth is, indeed, a solemnity, a feast, a celebration, for God is the One "who comes, comes, evercomes..." (Tagore). It is this continual mutual exchange of life and love between the Heart of Jesus and our heart that is our permanent feast, the jubilee that knows no end –a prelude to Heaven..."

Our **Bishop Msgr. Valerian D'Souza** celebrated Mass for us on July 10, 1986 on the occasion of **His Sacerdotal Silver Jubilee** which occurred on June 29 of that year. The Fathers of the community together with representatives of the other houses on the campus concelebrated with His Lordship. At breakfast, a short felicitation programme was dedicated to this festive event. Bishop Vally cut the cake to the tune of an appropriate Konkani song, and in turn obliged us with a song of his own.

Hardly a week later we gathered around our dear **Fr. Lionel Mascarenhas** to celebrate his Golden Jubilee in the Society. The concelebrated Mass at 11.30 a.m. was followed by lunch during which a short programme was offered in honour of the Jubilarian. Fr. Rector welcomed the guests and read the congratulatory letter of Father General of the Society to Fr. Lionel. Fr. Carlos de Melo, a companion of Fr. Lionel in Shembaganur, Kurseong, Rome and Pune, gave a summary of Fr. Lionel's life and career, stressing his total dedication and selfless service to God and to his brothers and sisters in the mission entrusted to him by the Church and the Society as Professor of ecclesiology, Rector of De Nobili College, Rector of the Papal Seminary and Rector of the Papal Athenaeum. In addition to this, he spends his holidays giving retreats mainly to religious communities, and fulfils the office of the National Director of the Apostolic Union of the Secular Clergy which carries with it the onerous labour of editing the Apostolic Union review AUMOL. With all this heavywork on his frail shoulders he is always available to anyone who might need his services or a word of counsel or encouragement. Fr. Lionel cut the cake and said a few words of thanks full of characteristic humour.

In the evening there was a basket-ball match with De Nobili College scholastics, and a cricket match with Ramwadi youngsters. The seminarians were the losers in both. Later, we had an early supper followed by an entertainment that lasted two hours and a half. Lionel had on this occasion the pleasure of the presence of his dear sister, Sister Anne Clement, Daughter of the Cross, who came from Bombay to share in the joy of her brother - the eldest in a fine Christian home made up of parents, one brother and three sisters, all of them religious. Fr. Lionel closed the day with a word of thanks. Just before him, Sister Anne Clement, too, expressed her own sentiments on this occasion. Noting down the events of the day in his official diary, the Beadle of the theologians concludes with the following words: "All in all, it was a day to be remembered, an occasion not complete enough to express our deep appreciation and thanks to Father Lionel for his great service ableness and companionship". Quite so.

Next in the list comes the Golden Jubilee of religious life of dear **Fr. Douglas Dias**, celebrated on September 24, 1989. The Jubilee Mass was at 11.45 a.m. Present at Mass were Fr. Douggie's relatives come from Bombay on the eve. At lunch the jubilarian cut the cake and was garlanded by the beadle of the theologians. Fr. Lionel Mascarenhas said words of greeting and appreciation on behalf of the community. The refectory was full with about a hundred and seventy people, out of whom a hundred were the guests who came from Bombay in order to be with Father on this special day. Bombay, the city to which Fr. Douggie belongs, and where he spent several years as professor and Principal of St. Xavier's Institute of Education, was therefore well represented at this jubilee celebration. Education-as Fr. Lionel rightly stressed-was the major accomplishment of his working life. Education, that is, not just lecturing, but personal communication with his students, interest in their proper formation. "That's why-Fr. Lionel concluded-Fr. Douggie will be remembered with affectionand gratitude by scores of old students years after they left the Institute".

The seminarians sang songs in honour of the jubilarian, and Douggie in return contributed to our delight by singing two choice songs from his in exhaustible repertoire. It was a happy occasion for all who had gathered together to share in Fr. Douggie's joy on this beautiful day of his life.

Last in the list is **Fr. Felix Clausen**, a Swiss Jesuit of Pune Province. He has been Professor of Dogmatic Theology at the Pontifical Athenaeum since 1955, and a member of the Seminary community from the year 1982. On September 15, 1991 he celebrated the **Golden Jubilee** of his religious life in the Society of Jesus. The jubilee celebrations began with Holy Mass in the morning, during which he preached at the gospel a very inspiring homily on the Blessed Virgin Mary, based on Lk 11:27-28, which presents Mary as our Model in our service of the poor and the promotion of justice.

Fr. Clausen has spent over 40 years in India. While carrying out conscientiously his duties as professor at JDV, he found the time to devote himself whole heartedly to the service of the poor in and around Ramwadi. He built for them what is now known as the Clausen Colony. On the occasion of the jubilee his numerous friends and admirers showed their appreciation, love and gratitude to Fr. Clausen in a variety of ways. Mr. Srinivas Patel, the Collector of Pune himself came to Ramwadi to felicitate Fr. Clausen at a programme organized by the Darshak Tarun Mandal, and draped a shawl around him. The Papal Seminary conducted in his honour games and sports for about 200 poor children and shared a meal with them. Speaking on this occasion the Rector of the Seminary, Fr. Noel Sheth described Fr. Clausen as a true *karma-yogi*, working for the welfare of the people in a spirit of selflessness. St. Joseph's Colony which owes its existence to Fr. Clausen organized a cultural evening in his honour, which lasted four hours. "Fr. Clausen has shown the love of Jesus to the poor through his long years of service at Ramwadi, irrespective of caste, creed and culture".

The October 31 is the feast day of the Jesuit Coadjutor Brother St. Alphonsus Rodrigues who lived and worked in Spain and died on October 31, 1617. He was canonized by Leo XIII in 1888 and is the Patron saint of all Jesuit coadjutor Brothers. On this day (October 31, 1982) therefore we gathered around our Jesuit Brothers Aaron, Joel, Aloysius and Timothy, to felicitate them and to express to them our heart felt gratitude for their devoted services to the Seminary community. We had a devout community Mass in the morning: we prayed in a special way for our dear Brothers. We also remembered in a special way two of our seminarians who were ordained deacons on that day: Bros. Raju Selvaraj and Cherian Pulickal. At lunch, Jagdish Parmar congratulated the Brothers in the name of the community. Bro. Aloysius thanked the members of the community for making this day such a beautiful day for the Brothers.

November 1, 1982 was marked by the inauguration of a special "Procura" or shopping room in the Seminary. It was blessed by Fr. Criem who inaugurated it by selling a soap to Bro. Glen Mascarenhas. In a short speech, Fr. Rector thanked all those who worked hard towards making this Procura a reality. The following Brothers were put in charge of the "shop": Sebastian Adayantharath, Reginald Pinto, Andrew Raj and Thomas Madhavapally. The first day was marked by the sale of articles worth Rs. 400.

On the evening of All Saint's Day (November 1, 1983), Fr. Koelman blessed and inaugurated the newly converted Pre-Philosophers quarters, named "Upadhyaya Bhavan". Fr. Carl Fonseca gave a brief sketch of the life of Upadhyaya and brought out his relevance to the Church in India today. Bro. Sosai Alangaram, one of the inmates of the new building, made a speech of thanks on behalf of his companions.

On the same day, the Seminary community was shocked to receive the news of the tragic death of our younger brother Mathew Perera of the Latin Archdiocese of Trivandrum. While taking part in the Malayalam Academy Seminar at our Villa at Vitthalwadi, he was drowned while taking a bath in the canal nearby. His body was taken to Kerala by plane. He was fine member of the community and an edifying seminarian, whose death was deeply felt by all at the Seminary.

On November 2, All Souls' Day, we had a Rosary procession to the cemetery at 5.45 in the evening, followed by Holy Mass there. Some of the Fathers and Brothers of the other houses on the campus too joined in the Liturgy.

November 15 brought to us the sad news of the death of Acharya Vinoba Bhave. We had a prayer service for him. May God raise in our beloved country others who will follow in his footsteps.

Fr. Paul Parathzham returned from the States after his doctorate in Sociology, from Loyola University, Chicago. We are happy to welcome him to the Seminary as a permanent member of our community.

December 3, Feast of our Patron, St Francis Xavier, was our Community Day. We awoke to the sound of music. The feast day Mass was at 7.00 a.m. in the main hall. Fr. Rector was the main celebrant and he stressed the theme of unity in the country. Hymns were sung in different languages. The one that was specially liked by all was a khasi hymn, sung by our Brothers from the North-East. At the offertory there was a symbolic offering of the riches of our soil. From 9.30 to 12.30 we had sports on our grounds, with about twelve items, including the one reserved to our kitchen staff. During lunch Bro. George Chittadiyil spoke in Hindi voicing the gratitude of the community to our domestic personnel; Father Rector released the issue of "Kairali"- a hand-written Malayalam magazine. In the evening, Benediction of the Blessed Sacrament was followed by supper after which there was a get-together in the main hall.

As we have seen, since 1926 the Papal Seminary was empowered to grant degrees in theology and philosophy - Licentiate and Doctorate. However, not many of our students have availed themselves of this opportunity. From 1955-the year in which the Athenaeum was transferred to Pune-only five of our students did so: Fathers George Anathil, SVD, Cyril Desbruslais, SJ, Prakash Mallavarapu (Hyderabad Archdiocese) Thomas Dabre (Bombay Archdiocese) and Fr. Cyril Valiath, SJ. Three of them have since been raised to the episcopate: Bishop Anathil of Indore, Bishop Dabre, Auxiliary of Bombay (now Bishop of Poona) and Archbishop Prakash of Vijayawada. The titles of their doctoral dissertations are as follows: "Theological Formation of the Clergy in India" (Anathil); "Interpretation of Transcendence" (Desbruslais); "Bhagavata Purana: Approach to Evil" (Prakash); "The God-Experience of Tukaram" (Dabre); "The Nature of God in Ramanuja" (Cyril Veliath SJ).

On March 5, 1983 news reached us that Fr. Subhash Anand was going to move to Allahabad as Professor in the Major Seminary there. Recording this piece of news in his Diary, the Beadle of the theologians made the following entry: "All are a little sad that Fr. Subhash leaves the institution. He was really an inspiration and an example for us all". Fr. Subhash is now back in his Alma Mater teaching Indian Philosophy at the Athenaeum and helping our brothers in a variety of ways.

Fr. Theo de Sales who ceased to be the Rector of the Seminary in June 1985, left Pune on June 27. He was given an affectionate farewell by the Seminary community. He was invited to preside at the morning community Mass. The theologians' beadle gave expression to the gratitude of the community to Fr. Theo for the services he rendered during the seven years of his tenure of office. At 8.30 in the morning a cricket match began, with Fr. Theo taking an active part in the same. Rectors of the houses on the campus were invited for lunch. At 8.00 p.m., after supper, there was a variety entertainment during which Fr. Thomas Dabre spoke in the name of the staff and Fr. Antony Kollannur on behalf of the students. In his parting speech Fr. Theo, after thanking all for the generous cooperation they had given him in the course of the seven years of his rectorship, summed up his sentiments in the words of the popular hymn "All I ask of you is to remember me as loving you..."

We shall now give a brief account of some of the developments that took place during Fr. Theo's rectorship.

The top floor of the Philosophers' wing which was divided into large rooms for the pre-philosophers and the House Library, plus a living room, was conveniently modified and transformed into a staff residence with rooms for the Fathers of the communityand guests. The Library was shifted to the ground floor below the Staff corridor. As to the pre-philosophers, an additional floor was added to the out-house next to the kitchen. In this way these Benjamins of the community can be cared for more in consonance with their needs by a Prefect having his room close to their quarters. A second storeroom was built next to the kitchen, as well as new quarters for the kitchen staff, and more rooms for the guests above the storeroom.

Besides, the old "music room" near the Infirmary was converted into a T.V. room for the students. Also, both philosophers and theologians were given each group a room free for their group Masses and prayer services, as well as group meetings. In addition to this, a new Notice Board was set up on the wall behind the Fathers' dining room. It serves as a sort of "wall magazine" for the use of the students, and was named "Home Herald". It is managed by an "editor", elected from among the theologians. We know well that all good things are liable to eventual misunderstanding or abuse. Something of the sort happened here too. So, on August 3, 1985 it was made clear that the aim and purpose of the Home Herald is to foster community life, bring about a greater sense of "togetherness" and share news and views. The columns of "Home Herald" are not the place for discussing points finalized by the Superiors, nor, much less, for anonymous letters.

Another important development that took place during Fr. Theo's regime was the right given to the two Students' Councils to sit with their representatives, and some members of the staff, to discuss together matters regarding mutual relationship between the students and the staff, and regarding the running of the house.

Till this time the beadles and other officials of the Seminary were elected for one year. From the time of Fr. Theo's rectorship they began to be elected twice each year, that is, at the beginning of each term. The idea was to get more students involved in the running of the house - an experience that can be useful to them in their later life as priests.

The Seminary is indebted to Fr. Theo for another custom he introduced in the seminary routine. Up till then, - as was the custom in most, if not all the seminaries at the time – the seminarians had no responsibility in the kitchen department. Here in Pune, as we said above, it is the Sisters who ran our kitchen: first the Holy Cross Sisters, and then the Fatima Sisters of Pune. We are very grateful to them all for the relevant service they rendered to us. Much to our regret their superiors were badly in need of their services elsewhere, and so they had to leave the seminary in June 1979. May God Himself be their reward.

From then on, it is our seminarians themselves who shoulder this responsibility, in turns. They plan the menu and accordingly do the buying of the necessary material, and direct the kitchen work. This system has the advantage of giving the brothers an opportunity for getting acquainted with this material side of our life, and so, in some way, it prepares them for their future life as missionaries and pastors. In this ministry, they are accountable to Father Minister of the house and to the Brother in charge of the kitchen.

Father Theo also reinforced what we call the "group system" in the Seminary which had been introduced by Fr. Lionel Mascarenhas in 1971. With the exception of the Pre-Philosophers and the M.Ph. and M.Th. students each class or "year" is divided into two groups, each group having one of the Fathers of the staff as its "animator", who functions as their guide in matters external. The group meets twice a month to discuss common relevant issues, or just socialise.

Fr. Theo was succeeded by **Fr. Joe Thadavanal** who comes to us from the North. He is a member of the Jesuit Province of Patna. We wished him God's abundant blessings. The new school year 1986-87 began with a farewell to Fr. Devasahayam who had been a member of our community for several years and Registrar of JDV. He left for the United States for his sabbatical. He was given a warmsend-off by the community.

On June 16, after the customary seven-day retreat was over, we had the inaugural session of the new year. Bishop Valerian was the main celebrant at Mass. Fr. Perry da Silva, Rector of the Fransalian Seminary on our campus, delivered the homily. The "Lectio Brevis" was, as usual, in the main hall, presided over by our Bishop. Fr. Anthony da Silva, read a paper on "India, a nation of communities: psychological perspectives on communalism"- a theme of great actuality followed with great attention and interest by the large audience. Fr. Tony is professor of Psychology in the Faculty of Philosophy of JDV. He did his higher studies in the University of Michigan, USA, where he obtained his Doctorate. Fr. Rui de Menezes, Rector of the Athenaeum and Bro. Asirvatham read reports of JDV and the Students' Council respectively, and His Lordship wound up the meeting with a message.

On August 3, in a short ceremony after breakfast, the Seminarians bade farewell to our cook Mr. Rebello, who is retiring from service, and presented him a gift of their own, as a token of their gratitude.

On February 25, 1987, Fr. Thomas Dabre's book "The God-experience of Tukaram" was officially released during a public function that lasted two hours. Fr. Dabre gave a summary of his book and was warmly applauded for his scholarly work.

On July 29, 1991, Fr. Joe Thadavanal was succeeded by **Fr. Noel Sheth**, who is a Sanskrit scholar and a member of the Bombay Province. At his installation, Fr. Noel said that he would lay emphasis on diocesan spirituality, Indian values, an openness to other religions and cultures, integral formation, and a greater participation by the students in the decision-making process.

Fr. Gaspar Koelman was one of the senior-most members of the Seminary community. In March 1991 he left Pune to be back in his own Province (Ranchi) where in his old age-he was 83 years old-he could be more carefully attended to in the Province Infirmary. However, four months later he had to be transferred to the Mandar Hospital run by the Medical Mission Sisters. He had a severe stroke during the second week of September. On receiving this news two members of the Seminary community were expressly sent to Ranchi to see Father Koelman: Fr. Lionel Mascarenhas and Bro. Dominic Joseph, the house beadle. Travelling by plane they reached Ranchi on September 13, in the afternoon and proceeded from there immediately to Mandar. Fr. Koelman was by then unable to speak, but they felt some how that he did recognize them in spite of his apparent impassivity. On September 15, Sunday, Father Lionel offered Mass in his room by his bedside. Father Koelman breathed his last on Monday, around 2.00 a.m. The funeral was at 2.00 p.m. in the Mandar Parish Church. The Papal community was well represented by Fr. Lionel, Bro. Dominic and Bro. Hilarius of Ranchi who had been a member of the Seminary community for four years, looking after the kitchen. What is more striking is that, providentially our Bishop Valerian D'Souza was present, and he presided at the funeral service. His Lordship had just finished a retreat for the clergy of the diocese of Ranchi and was about to start his journey back to Pune. He postponed it in order to be present for the funeral of the one who had been his professor and friend.

As Fr. Lionel recalled, speaking at the Gospel "Fr. Koelman was a model of DEDICATION to God and to his brothers and sisters for God. This dedication was shown in his life of prayer and spiritual life. He taught for 47 long years with competence and hard work. He put himself and his talents at the service of all. In addition to teaching, he devoted a lot of time in the spiritual direction of the many who sought his help: students, priests, sisters. For 16 years he was chaplain of the Franciscan Missionaries of Mary in the town. He spent much of his time during the holiday months in giving retreats and missions allover'. "What were the main springs of his personal life and ministry? Three loves: the Eucharist, the Trinity, Marian devotion".

Fr. Lionel concluded by saying: "Generations of Papalites and JDV students - not to mention sisters all over India and Sri Lanka - will cherish the memory of this holy, dedicated Jesuit priest, professor and guide, who spent his whole life truly" doing good to so many. I feel sure that in God's eternal Today, he is already in the possession of that joy of the Lord whom He served as a "good and faithful servant".

Bishop Vally spoke briefly at the beginning of the liturgy, and Bro. Dominic, representing the students of the seminary, spoke at the end. May the good Lord bless him with his well-deserved, eternal reward.

The Catholic Bishops' Conference of India held its annual meeting in Pune, at Ishwani Kendra, in January 1992. On January 5, the President of the Conference, Archbishop Alphonsus Mathias of Bangalore, visited the seminary, together with Bishop Mar Ephraem, to see to the arrangements. The inaugural Mass was celebrated in the Seminary Church with Archbishop Mathias as the main celebrant. One night Their Lordships, the Seminary staff and the students had supper together in the students' refectory. On January 8, His Excellency the Delegate Apostolic Archbishop George Zur had lunch with the Fathers. He also celebrated Mass for our community on the morning of January 9 in our Church. Next day, Papalite Bishops offered Mass in our Church together with our community and joined us for breakfast. On January 11, four Bishops of the Malankara Rite celebrated Mass for our students in our church. That same day we had the bishops with us for dinner. A Cultural programme followed, in honour of our revered guests, in the seminary hall, offered by the Jnana-Deepa Vidyapeeth. On January 13, our community Mass was in the Syro-Malabar Rite. Fr. Rector thanked the Bishops in the refectory.

In August 1991 the Seminary constituted a Ministry Coordinating Team, consisting of staff and student members. The purpose of this team is to co-ordinate, streamline and organize the various ministries undertaken by the seminarians. The team also arranges discussions and sharing with those who are already working in the pastoral field, and conducts an evaluation of the students' ministries. It also promotes theological and pastoral reflection on the ministries in which the students are engaged. In this way the ministry becomes a learing experience that is both relevant and fruitful. In the summer of 1992, in addition to the optional thirty-day retreat, the seminarians were also offered an optional course on Vipassana or Insight Meditation, which helps to develop concentration, calmness, inner silence and spiritual depth. There introduction of yoga classes as well as initiation into some Indian forms of prayer at periodic prayer workshops, and the encouragement to learn Indian music have promoted greater inculturation and interest in the spiritual and cultural heritage of India. Another new venture that has been introduced is the five-day formation programme for the seminarians just before the academic year begins. The programme includes the Intensive Journal, Enneagram, Value Clarifications, etc. Greater impetus and encouragement has also been given to the regional languages by providing rooms and funds for regional language libraries, subscribing to dailies and periodicals, organizing language seminars, etc. The Statutes of the Students' Councils were revised. One of the important changes is the greater participation of the students in the decision-making process. Student representatives now not only participate in staff meetings, but also have a vote. Of course the vote (both of the students as well as of the staff) is only indicative, since the final decision rests with the Rector.

The Centenary Year

We now come to the year 1993. It is our centenary year: the Papal Seminary which was inaugurated on May 4, 1893, completed a hundred years of its existence on May 4 of this year. The centenary year was officially inaugurated on November 7, 1992.

It began with the Eucharistic celebration of which the theme was: "With grateful hearts, unto new horizons". The main celebrant was our Bishop Valerian D'Souza. The homily was given by Bishop Gali Bali of Guntur, Chairman of the CBCI Commission for Clergy and Religious. The two readings were very appropriate for the occasion: Colossians 3:11-17, and John 15:12-17. They beautifully placed before the members of the seminary and the Athenaeum the idea that should animate them in their daily relationship with God and among themselves.

The theme for the Centenary Year is: *sarva-jiva-sukham, sarva-dharma-sakhyam*: the happiness of all living beings and friendship among all religions. As the folder explaining the theme tells us: "All finite life is a reflection of the Divine Life. We should therefore be concerned not only for human welfare but also for the good of all living beings, including plants and animals. Indeed our concern should extend even to the material world since everything in the universe is interrelated. Thus our theme also has ecological significance. On the one hand religion has been the cause of rabid communalism and savage wars but, on the other hand, it has also inspired heroic sacrifice and selfless service. True friendship among religions will be an effective antidote to the communal virus that has infected so many of us".

The members of the JDV staff, Rectors from the various Houses on the campus, student representatives and those specially invited joined us for lunch. Fr. Noel welcomed the guests with an apt quotation from Tukaram to the effect that whenever holy and saintly people come to visit our home, that day is Diwali and Dasara, therefore, a feast, a celebration. Fr. Varkey Perekkatt, the Jesuit Provincial who is in charge of the "common houses", rose to congratulate the Seminary for its contribution to the progress of Christian life in the country, by its openness to the signs of the times and its adaptability to change.

The evening function was graced by the presence of **Sri Sudhakarrao Naik, Chief Minister of Maharashtra** and other guests. He lighted the huge lamp symbolising the aim and purpose of the Papal Seminary and the Athenaeum. Fr. Noel Sheth welcomed the Chief Guest and all present, and gave an explanation of the centenary theme. He also announced that as part of the centenary programme, the Seminary would host in the coming month of Augustan international seminar on JESUS CHRIST AND THE ENCOUNTER WITH RELIGIONS, organized by the Pontifical Council for Inter-religious Dialogue, Rome. The last speaker of that day was Bishop Valerian. "Religion and politics should not be mixed up – he said. Yet, the Catholic priest cannot stand neutral when human rights are transgressed".

Fr. Lionel Mascarenhas proposed the vote of thanks and presented the Chief Minister with a gift packet containing books on Indian Religions and culture and also with a set of slides on Hinduism - all published by the Seminary staff.

The Cultural programme consisted of a Prayer dance, some musical items and a presentation of several of our Folk Dances:

Tribal Dance - Chotanagpur
Koli Dance - Maharashtra - Parish Youth group
Kol-Oyil Attam - Tamil Nadu

Dekhani - Goa
Oarichamuttu Kali - Kerala
There was also a One-Act Play: "Two Blind men and the Donkey".
The centenary celebrations will be climaxed later in October of this year.

This is our centenary year. It is gratifying for us to know that the Sri Lanka National Seminary which succeeded the Papal Seminary in Kandy celebrated this event with due solemnity on June 3 of this year. We are particularly grateful to the Reverend Rector of the Seminary, Fr. Emmanuel Fernando, for courteously inviting us to their celebrations. Accordingly, Pune was represented at Kandy by our Rector, Fr. Noel Sheth and Fr. Lionel Mascarenhas. We wish the Kandy Seminary a future filled with God's generous blessings.

"Jesus Christ and the Encounter with Religions" (Theological Colloquium)

As we said above, on the occasion of the inauguration of the centenary year, the Rector of the Seminary, Fr. Noel Sheth, had announced that an international seminar on "Jesus Christ and the Encounter with Religions" would be held at the Papal Seminary, integrated into our centenary celebrations, under the auspices of the Pontifical Council for Inter-Religious Dialogue, Rome.

This international meeting did actually take place in the Seminary from 24 to 29 August of this year (1993) under the presidency of His Eminence Cardinal Francis Arinze. The following distinguished theologians from different parts of the world participated in this "theological colloquium": Fr. Angelo Amato (Italy), Fr. John Aniagwu (Nigeria), Fr. Jaroen Atitya (Thailand), Dr. John Borelli (USA), Dr. Horst Burkle (Germany), Fr. Alex Dassanayake (Sri Lanka), Prof. Gavin D'Costa (UK), Fr. Joseph Doré (France), Bishop Patrick D'Souza of Varanasi (India), Fr. Jacques Dupuis (Italy), Fr. Bruno Forte (Italy), Dr. Elizabeth Johnson (USA), Fr. Edward Kuukure (Ghana), Fr. Edward Malone (Hong Kong), Archbishop Giacinto Marcuzzo (Jerusalem), Fr. Laurent Mpongo (Cameroon), Fr. Albert Nambiaparambil (India), Prof. Drago Ocvirk (Solvenia), Fr. Kuncheria Pathil (India), Dr. Israel Selvanayagam (India), Fr. Noel Sheth (India), Fr. Paul Tan Chee Ing (Italy), Fr. Felix Wilfred (India), Fr. Prosper Grech (Italy), Fr. Sebastian Karotemprel (India), Fr. Remi Hoeckman (Italy), together with the following representatives of the Pontifical Council for Interreligious Dialogue: Bishop Michael Fitzgerald and Felix Machado.

Rt. Rev. Valerian D'Souza, Bishop of Poona, and Fr. Noel Sheth, our Rector, welcomed the delegates and participated in the sessions of the international conference. Cardinal Arinze stated in his inaugural discourse that the purpose of this meeting was to increase communion and collaboration in the field of religion and to propose concrete suggestions for the promotion of inter-religious dialogue in universities, seminaries and other areas of encounter. The occasion for this meeting was the Centenary of the World Parliament of Religions and the Centenary of the Papal Seminary of Pune. Pope John Paul II – Cardinal Arinze informed the participants - was happy to learn of this meeting and assured them of his prayer that it may give a fresh impulse to the improvement of relations between believers.

The Colloquium then proceeded with the discussion of the papers that had been circulated before hand among the participants. These were "The unique Mediation of Christ as Lord and Saviour", by Angelo Amato; "Some Tentative Reflections from an Indian Perspective on the Language of Christian Uniqueness" by Felix Wilfred; "The Mediation of the Church" by Paul TAN CHEEING; "The Mediation of the Church" by Joseph Doré; "The Role and Value of Different Religious Traditions" by John ANIAGWU; "Revelation and Revelations: The Role and Value of Different Religious Traditions" by Gavin D'Costa.

During the second part of the Colloquium the participants were divided into three groups: Apostolate of Dialogue; Seminaries and Houses of Formation; Universities and Faculties of Theology.

As the Report on the "International Meeting on Religions" informs us "During the sessions, the participants declared that human kind constitutes one family of the children of God, and our relationship as members of one family is maintained by continuous dialogue, self-communication, and the resulting communion which is an unending process in history and beyond it. Humankind is facing today an existential crisis, which can be overcome only by the collaboration of people of different faiths, cultures and ideologies. The participants discussed dialogue on three levels: first there is the dialogue in life, where by all strive to dwell in an open and neighbourly spirit, sharing their joys and sorrows; second, dialogue in action, in which Christians and other collaborate for the integral development and liberation of people from poverty, injustice etc.; and third, the dialogue on the intellectual level, by deepening our understanding of different religious traditions and appreciating and respecting each other's religious heritage and values.

Hence, the Report concludes, the training of our religious leaders should be in the light of the cultural, philosophical and religious heritage of the country, always maintaining mutual collaboration and enrichment. This would imply an inter-disciplinary approach in the methodology of study emphasizing human virtues and openness to the truth. Exposure programmes will initiate the students in universities, seminaries and schools for a contact with people of other faiths, as well as with their rituals, festivals, scriptures, devotions, etc".

Inter-Religious Meeting

On this occasion, and integrated into the Papal Seminary centenary programme, there was a special inter religious meeting at Gulati Hall, in the town, on August 21.

The meeting was open to the general public and was attended by persons of all religions. It opened with a Prayer Song by the Papal Seminary choir and discourse by the Rt. Rev. Dr. Valerian D'Souza, Bishop of Poona, on "Peace Through Religions". Other distinguished speakers followed: Prof. Mrs. Leela Arjunwadkar on "The Hindu Approach to other Religions"; Fr. Noel Sheth, S.J., Rector of the Papal Seminary, on "The Buddhist Approach to other Religions"; Shaik Abdul Razak Shah Biyabani on "The Islamic Approach to other Religions". The meeting ended with Cardinal Arinze's reflections on the "Contribution of Christianity in promotion of Justice and Peace", and a Vote of Thanks by Mr. Talib Khambatta.

In the course of this centenary year the Papal Seminary also organised two "Refresher Courses" intended mainly for our former students by way of further updating of their ecclesiastical studies. Due stress was laid on Modern Trends in Scripture Studies, Ecclesiology, Christology, Sacramental Theology and Moral Theology. The problems of Religious Pluralism, Ecology and Pastoral Questions were discussed and followed with great interest. All through the sessions, the challenge of the Indian situation was taken into account. A special lecture was given on Buddhism and a Slide-show on Hinduism.

Our Centenary Year also provided an opportunity for a three-day Seminar for the Papalites who are teaching in Major Seminaries or Scholasticates and the JDV Staff. It was held at the Athenaeum from August 13 to 15, 1993. **The Seminary** offered to meet the expenses of board and lodging as well as the travel to and from Pune. Our M. Th. students were also invited to participate in it. The theme chosen for the Seminar was "Our Christian Commitment to a United India". Some thirty-five Professors attended the Seminar and took part in the discussions that followed the exposition of the topics presented.

The Seminary has started a Computer Centre for the seminarians. It is the first such centre on the campus, and it is a sign and symbol that this hundred-year old institution is relevant to the times and is preparing itself for the 21st century. As part of a comprehensive renovation of the house and its surroundings, the infirmary as well as the staff and guestrooms have now been made self-contained. This is a great boon especially to the older staff members.

The Centenary Celebrations

The concluding Celebrations of the Centenary were scheduled for October 25-29, 1993, both days included. The alumni of Papal Seminary and other guests were to arrive on October 24. Some 450 priests, 10 bishops and two Cardinals arrived on that day. Accommodation for this motley crowd was arranged in the seminary and the other houses on the campus.

A Pavilion was put up in the Papal Seminary football ground. The main meals - breakfast, lunch and dinner - were served in the pavilion. An outside caterer, a Catholic gentleman from Pune, undertook the preparation and serving of these meals during the days of the centenary celebrations.

The actual celebrations began with an inaugural mass in the Latin rite. Archbishop George Zur, Apostolic Pro-Nuncio, was the main celebrant and Archbishop Henry D'Souza of Calcutta preached the homily. At the beginning of the Mass Fr. Noel Sheth, the Rector of Papal Seminary welcomed all the participants: "On the historic occasion of the centenary of the Papal Seminary, I warmly welcome each one of you to the celebrations". Then he explained the theme of the Mass: "Filii Tui, India, Administri tibi salutis" Your sons, India, will be the minsters of salvation to you. This is the motto of the seminary and is inscribed in its coat of arms and was given by Pope Leo XIII to the seminary which he founded in May 1893". Then Bishop Valerian D'Souza welcomed all the guests to the diocese of Poona.

Late in the morning, that is , from 10.30 am to 12.30 pm, an academic session was held in the seminary. Father Errol D'Lima, SJ, and Fr. Kurien Kunnumpuram, SJ, gave brief talks on the conciliar and post-conciliar changes in the understanding of the mission of the Church in India. Many participants intervened in the session asking questions and making comments about the Church's mission. It was altogether a lively session.

At 5.00 in the evening of the same day there was a public meeting. Mr. Bharat Sawant, the Mayor of Pune, was the chief guest. While inaugurating the Centenary celebrations the Mayor said: "The Christian community spreads love and peace along with national integration." Welcoming the distinguished guests and all the other members of the audience, Fr. Noel Sheth, SJ, the Rector, said that he was happy to have so many of the alumni of the Papal Seminary here for the concluding celebrations of the centenary. He added: "We are fortunate to have with us former Rectors of the seminary and they deserve our appreciation". These Rectors are: Fr. Lionel Mascarenhas, SJ, (1967-1972), Fr. Theo de Sales, SJ, (1978-1985); Fr. Joseph Thadavanal, SJ, (1985-1991) and Fr. Noel Sheth, SJ, the present Rector. These rectors were felicitated by the Pro-Nuncio Archbishop George Zur who also offered each of them a shawl.

Father Noel Sheth stated that the freedom, which the seminarians enjoy here, enables them to grow into mature persons. By way of conclusion he added: "As we stand on the threshold of the next century, we ask ourselves what contribution we can make to build up a united India".

Archbishop George Zur, the Apostolic Pro-nuncio, paid warm tributes to Archbishop Ladislas Zaleski, who, as Apostolic-delegate of the East Indies, organized the Papal Seminary in Kandy, thus fulfilling the earnest desire of Pope Leo XIII. The Pope and his delegate were greatly interested in the formation of Indian Catholic priests, and thus give fuller impetus to the indigenisation of the Church. Both of them wanted the Indian priests to be respected as much as the foreign missionaries. Archbishop Zur spoke highly of the great Father Silvanus

Grosjean, the Founder-rector, and all the Jesuits who were professors of the seminary. He concluded his speech by saying: Jai Hind! Jai Jesus.

Bishop Valerian D'Souza who spoke next regaled the audience with his witty remarks. He said that he was happy to be here in the midst of the students of the seminary, past and present. He mentioned that he owes a lot to this seminary, his alma mater.

Fr. Varkey Perakkat, SJ, Jesuit Provincial of India and Vice-Chancellor of Jnana-Deepa Vidyapeeth, paid rich tributes to the staff and students of the Papal Seminary which is the only all India Institute for the training leaders of the Catholic community. Cardinal Antony Padiyara, who spoke last, was all praise of this august institution which has imparted a relevant formation to thousands of priests in India and the neighbouring countries. The Cardinal also said kind words to the local bishop, to the rector, the staff and students who have organized these centenary celebrations.

On this memorable occasion Mayor Sawant released a book titled "The Papal Seminary of Kandy-Pune" which was the history of the first hundred years of this institution and was written by Fr. Carlos de Melo, SJ. The author of this book was honoured by Archbishop Zur who also gave him a shawl.

During the second part of the public meeting there was a cultural programme which included a Naga Folk dance; Keraliyam which is a cluster of Kerala's cultural dance; a street play "oru kelvi" based on the traditional folk theatre of Tamilnadu; "Janapada Geyam", a folk dance of joy from Andhra Pradesh; a Mando-Dulpod a traditional Goan folk dance and a Maharastrian "Koli" dance depicting the life of the firsherfolk. This was altogether a delightful programme.

The meeting came to an end with a vote of thanks proposed by Fr. Paul Parathazham who was the chairman of the Centenary committee.

On Tuesday, October 26, the Mass was offered for the benefactors of the seminary. Cardinal Anthony Padiyara, the Major Archbishop of Syro-Malabar Church, celebrated the liturgy in the Syro-Malabar rite. Fr. Joseph Thadavanal, SJ, gave the homily.

From 10.30 a.m. to 12.30 p.m. there were academic sessions in different language groups. During these sessions the students of the seminary got an opportunity to interact with their elder brothers who are now involved in missionary activity or pastoral ministry in different parts of the country. At 3.30 p.m. the Rector, Fr. Noel Sheth, spoke to the papalites. He gave them an idea of what was happening these days in the seminary. The participants had a lot of questions to ask and some comments to make. It was by and large an interesting meeting. From 6.30 to 8.00 p.m. there was a get-together of the Papalites in different language groups. As the concluding event of the day there was a half-an-hour multi-media presentation on mission and formation, titled "The Beginning and the Beyond".

Wednesday, October 27, was the third day of the concluding celebrations. In the morning Holy Mass was celebrated in different language groups. From 10.30 a.m. to 12.30 p.m. there was an academic session held in the seminary hall. Fr. John D'Mello of the Archdiocese of Bombay had, at the request of the Seminary authorities, conducted a survey of the former students of the Papal Seminary engaged in pastoral work in different dioceses of India and the world. This study looked at formation and pastoral effectiveness. It was meant to be an evaluation of the formation imparted in the Papal Seminary. Some 450 priests who had passed out of the portals of the seminary participated in the study by filling out the questionnaire and the data was collected in 1992.

During the Academic session Fr. John D'Mello shared the findings of the study with the staff and students, both past and present, of the seminary. He went on to make some reflections and comments on the findings of the study.

In the light of his studies Fr. D'Mello believes that the key process transpiring in the seminary is the production and transmission of a culture "According to him the four characteristics of seminary culture that can be gathered from the scientific study of the formation imparted in the Papal Seminary are:

1. A culture which is deficient in the pastoral dimension.
2. A culture which emphasizes a theoretical (and cognitive) orientation.
3. A culture which lacks the horizontal dimension of spirituality.
4. A culture which exhibits some elements of rule-consciousness, conformity and fear.

Fr. John D'Mello gave the following explanation of these four characteristics. According to the respondents of the study the most outstanding element missing in their formation was pastoral experience. More than 52% of them expressed this view. The respondents also pointed out that the formation they received in Papal Seminary had an abstract, theoretical orientation. Academic excellence meant the mastery of conceptual knowledge. The spiritual formation imparted in the seminary lays great stress on one's relationship to God but not enough stress on one's relationship to fellow human beings and the cosmos. As a result, there is very little commitment to the poor, very little concern for social justice. Finally, the seminary seems to foster a culture which shows some elements of rule consciousness, conformity and fear. If a person does things out of a sense of conformity to the rule or because he is afraid that he will be punished, then to that extent there is no socialization for commitment. Only in freedom can a seminarian grow into maturity.

John D'Mello concluded the talk by saying: "In short, one might say that one reason for fear among the students is the report that is sent about them at the end of the year by their superiors – either to the Bishops or to the Provincial Superiors. Here there is a problem". The authorities of the Seminary believe that the Bishops and Provincial Superiors have a right to know how their students are profiting by the formation in the seminary and that, hence, they have a duty to give them an honest report. (In order to lessen the fear of the seminarians Papal Seminary has made a decision to do two things: 1. To formulate the report carefully so that the Bishop or the Provincial Superior does not misunderstand it; 2. To show the report to the seminarian concerned so that he can raise objections to points in the report which he thinks are not quite correct).

Fr. Paul Parathazham, who had conducted many scientific studies on the priesthood and priestly formation in India, also spoke of the need to update seminary formation so that those priests who come out of seminaries will be able to face the challenges to priestly ministry in India today.

In the evening from 6.00 to 8.00 p.m. there was a wonderful performance by the St. Louis Orchestra of the Blind, Chennai. The audience found it quite enjoyable.

On Thursday, October 28, the morning Eucharist was celebrated in the Syro-Malankra rite. Bishop Mar Baselios of Bathery was the main celebrant. He also preached the homily on the theme: "*Jesus Our Life, Now and Always*". During the academic session from 10.30 a.m. to 12.30 p.m., a team of former students of the seminary shared with the audience their experience of the ministry. Many priests and seminarians asked questions for clarification and made their own comments.

On Friday, October 29, the morning liturgy was in the Latin rite with the theme: *Sarva-jiva sukham, sarva-dharma sakhyam.* Cardinal Simon Pimenta, the Archbishop of Bombay, was the main celebrant. Archbishop Alan de Lastic of Delhi delivered an inspiring homily.

During the academic session from 10.30 a.m. to 12.30 p.m., Father Jacob Parappally, MSFS, and Subhash Anand gave short talks on the spirituality of the diocesan priest. There was a lively discussion after the talks.

In the evening from 4.00 p.m. to 6.00 p.m., there was a family get-together in the seminary Hall. All the participants - students of the Seminary past and present – thoroughly enjoyed this get-together.

Reflecting on the concluding celebrations of the centenary of Papal Seminary, Fr. Noel Sheth, SJ, the Rector, made this significant comment: "We now come to the final celebrations of the Centenary Year held from 25 to 29 October, 1993. The occasion was graced by the presence of two cardinals and 12 bishops (who were present on different days) and a motley gathering of about 450 alumni of our Seminary. Though the days were filled with a variety of interesting programmes, religious – in the three main Rites – and cultural, what our alumni enjoyed most was the "Family Gathering" of Papalite priests and seminarians of different generations from various places in India, with a sprinkling of former students from Sri Lanka, Bangladesh, Pakistan and Canada. All experienced "how good and how pleasant it is when brothers live in unity"! The high point of this 'experience' was the final day of the concluding celebrations, kept as a 'Family

Day'. The tone of the day was set by a liturgy of the Papalites present, celebrated by Cardinal Simon Pimenta of Bombay. One of our alumni from Sri Lanka delivered the homily. The day, and the year's celebrations, were brought to a close by a unique Family Gathering, at which Bishops, priests and seminarians mingled freely and joyfully. *Ex tempore* items kept us all happily entertained. Our Poona Bishop, Valerian D'Souza, widely known as the 'Singing Bishop', delighted the gathering with a song which he himself accompanied on the guitar! The evening was a fitting conclusion to the five-day celebrations, during which we lived in an intense way the spirit of this seminary, which has long been known as the "Home of Love".

On the occasion of the Centenary of the Papal Seminary the Government of India issued a special commemorative postal stamp. It was released on December 16, 1993, by the Honourable Shri Sukhram, Union Minister of State for Communications, in the presence of Mother Teresa, the Chief Guest, Rt. Rev. Valerian D'Souza, Bishop of Poona and a large number of staff and students of Papal Seminary.

If the centenary celebrations of Papal Seminary were a wonderful experience for all of us, it was largely because of two people: Fr. Noel Sheth, SJ, the Rector of Papal Seminary, and Fr. Paul Parathazham, the Chairman of the Centenary Committee. Fr. Noel Sheth had to write to hundreds of dignitaries, civil and ecclesial. He also had to make several speeches on various occasions. Given the character of the man, these speeches were carefully composed and beautifully delivered. As for Paul Parathazham, he did an enormous amount of work. First as Convenor of the Committee for planning the Jubilee Celebrations, he had to formulate a comprehensive plan for the inauguration of the centenary year and the programmes to be conducted during the year. And then as Chairman of the Centenary Committee he meticulously planned the concluding celebrations. This meant that he had to arrange accommodation for about 450 priests and a dozen bishops. He had to chalk out a detailed programme for the five days of the concluding celebrations of the Centenary. He also had to see to it that the meals were prepared well and served in time. Without the hard and painstaking work of Fr. Noel Sheth and Fr. Paul Parathazham the centenary celebrations would not have been an unforgettable experience for all those who participated in them. It is also true that both these men got the whole-hearted support and cooperation of the staff and students of the Papal Seminary.

On October 26, 1993, the Mar Thoma Malayala Samajam celebrated its centenary. Speaking on the occasion Fr. Noel Sheth, the Rector, said: "It is a great joy for us all that we are celebrating the centenary of the Malayalam Academy together with the Centenary of the Papal Seminary. The academy has indeed been an intrinsic part of the Seminary from the very first year of its existence. As Rector of the Seminary, therefore, I heartily congratulate all the members, both past and present, of the Malayalam Academy!

"The Academy has always been making a significant contribution to the welfare of the Seminary. At times it also comes up with creative suggestions for the community. For the last few years it has been organizing optional courses in Malayalam literature in JDV. I must say that in many ways the Malayalam Academy has been in the fore front not only in the seminary but also in the Church in India. It has produced a Cardinal and over 20 Archbishops and Bishops. Several priests have been doing pioneering and dedicated work in different parts of India, and indeed of the world".

Father George Lobo, SJ

When in compliance with the request of Fr. Noel Sheth, the Seminary Rector, we began to collect material for this historical sketch of the Papal Seminary in India, never could it occur to our mind that we would have to include in the list of our deceased brethren a dear colleague, present member of the community. And yet, that is what we have perforce to do.

Fr. George Lobo had been Professor of Moral Theology allthrough his life, since the end of his time of formation, first for nineteen years, at St. Mary's College, the Jesuit Theologate of Kurseong, and Delhi, and since the year 1980 at the Papal Seminary, here in Pune. He died in harness, quite unexpectedly, in the train (Jhelum Express), on his way back via Delhi, from Naini Tal where he gave a retreat and a course to the Ursuline Sisters of Mary Immaculate. After a few days of rest in Pune, he intended to proceed to Bangalore for another course to religious, but death came during the journey, on his way home, to the surprise and dismay of us all in Pune.

The funeral Mass was held in the Seminary Hall (as the chapel was getting ready for the centenary celebration) and Fr. Lobo was buried in the Papal Seminary cemetery, on May 2, 1983. The months of April and May are closed for the summer vacation, so no more than a few students could be present for the funeral of such a dear master and friend. To make up for this deficiency there was a special Mass for the whole of Athenaeum on August 2, after the reopening of the Seminary. In homage to Fr. George were produce here the text of Fr. Lionel Mascarenhas' beautiful "homily" on this occasion:

"Familiarity may not always breed contempt, as the saying would have it, but it certainly tends to dull our perception of persons and events. Having lived with and so close to Fr. George Lobo, not a few of us - and I can say this first of myself – may have fallen short in our appraisal of him. Yet I can confidently assert that he was an outstanding person in many ways. I shall touch briefly now on only two aspects of his personality and work.

1) To all who heard of him or met him, here and there, in the course of his work, Fr. George came across, first and foremost, as a scholar and professor. In this field of intellectual work, he had the makings of a genius. Breadth of information and knowledge, quick assimilation, a remarkable memory and a sharp critical

mind were elements of his intellectual make-up. Moral theology, of course, was his field of specialization, to which was added the social teaching of the Church. Fr. George contributed in a big way to the advancement and renewal of Moral Theology in the light of Vatican II, and he was an authority in the important and difficult area of medico-moral problems. The Association of Moral Theologians of India honoured him in 1991 by dedicating to him the volume "Social Sin, Challenge to Christian Life" (published in Bangalore that year). But his expertise was acknowledged far and beyond the confines of our country, as evidenced by the number of invitations he received to participate in seminars and conferences in countries as far apart as Bangladesh, the Philippines, Japan and Australia. George was a prolific writer, too, and one is astounded by the volume of books, articles and book reviews that flowed from his pen, all with remarkable speed.

2) Secondly, as a Jesuit priest, Fr. George was totally dedicated to his vocation and mission. His intellectual and pastoral activities were his mission, and he successfully integrated them both. In fact this pastoral outlook remained adominant concern in his studies.

In the line of direct priestly apostolate, one should mention his work as chaplain of the Catholic Hospital Association of India. He was also much sought after for renewal courses and retreats to the diocesan clergy, religious and lay people. George was truly "a man for others", always available to those who asked for his help, be it for a retreat, or a seminar, or for personal counselling. His life was an untiring round of service to others, often involving long, tiring journeys, across the country.

In conclusion, while we honour his memory, we thank God for the gift he made in Fr. George Lobo to our country, to the Church, and to us here in Jnana-Deepa. We shall render the best and most fitting tribute to him, I feel, if emulating his example, we can make our own his dedication to serious intellectual study in the context of the problems of today's world and of our country; his spirit of unremitting, disciplined work; and his pastoral concern and ready availability to all whoneed his help". R.I.P.

EPILOGUE BY CARLOS M. DE MELO SJ

In the preceding pages we have tried to give a brief but sufficiently comprehensive historical sketch of the "General Seminary" for the whole of India which through the initiative of Pope Leo XIII was first established in Kandy, Ceylon, a hundred and twenty-two years ago, in 1893. The history of this ecclesiastical institution can clearly be divided into two distinct parts: the first sixty-two years of its existence in Ceylon (Sri Lanka), and the following sixty years in Pune, India.

A hundred and twenty-five years is not too long a period in the life of an institution. However, this particular portion of the history of the world in which our life is cast is witness to radical changes in humans' way of thinking, judging and acting. We are living in an age that is marked by clashes between different cultures, languages, races and religions, and the consequent uncertainty they give rise to, particularly in the minds and hearts of the young - uncertainty regarding the truths they should believe in, the direction they ought to give to their life, the paths they are called upon to choose in view of the future... It is enough to go through our dailies to realize how far this is true even in an otherwise traditionally slow-moving society as ours is in India.

Such thoughts crossed our mind as we glanced back at the two parts of our history: the Papal Seminary in Kandy and the same Seminary in Pune.

In Kandy the Seminary was one community, the only one on the campus, closely knit together as one family. The young men who had gone to Kandy to prepare themselves for the grace of the priesthood lived and grew up in an atmosphere of peace, serenity, security and mutual fellowship. Such an atmosphere was both necessary and helpful for their human and spiritual growth as Christ's chosen ones getting ready for their mission as the messengers of His "Good News" in this vast country well known for its ancient civilization and its rich spiritual heritage.

The situation was significantly different in Pune. Here they were "newcomers" to a campus where other young men from all over the country, Indians, Europeans, Americans... had preceded them and set the pace, though all united in the pursuit of the same high ideal of announcing Christ to those to whom they were to be sent. The campus in Pune was made up of a number of different houses or communities in which religious of various Orders or Congregations lived under their respective Rule but frequenting a central College for their classes and academic lectures. This central College – "De Nobili" as it was called - had no power to confer academic degrees in theology. Those who were to take such degrees obtained it through the Jesuit theologate at Kurseong - St. Mary's College, to which De Nobili was affiliated. With the coming to Pune of the Kandy Athenaeum, they were enabled to secure the degrees both in philosophy and theology from this Papal Athenaeum of Kandy now established in their midst. Besides the Jesuits residing in "De Nobili College", there were the CMIs, the SVDs, the MSFs and the OICs living in their own houses or communities spread around the campus. This was the setup of which the Kandy Pontifical Seminary and Athenaeum now became a part in 1955.

The shift from Kandy to Pune did entail a certain loss to the Papal Seminary community, but it also brought to the seminarians coming to India definite advantages. The bulk of these seminarians were Indians. The transfer meant for them a "homecoming" all to their advantage. Their training could hence forward be more directly geared towards their future ministry in their respective dioceses. Communication with these home dioceses was thereby made more easy and direct, while there remained the advantages of a relative distance that could help them to approach problems with a certain detachment and a greater objectivity.

Nearer home the daily contact with their young companions from the various other houses on the campus could be an enriching factor both for the personal life of the seminarians and for their future apostolate or work in their vast country. It helped them to broaden their mind and enlarge their vision enabling them to embrace the reality as it is lived by the people of the country, while at the same time offering them opportunities for getting acquainted with the ways of thinking and acting of those coming from foreign countries. This much about the transfer of the Seminary to Pune, six decades back.

While we express to God our deep gratitude for so much that this institution has received from Him till now we have to ask ourselves how the Papal Seminary is carrying out today its mission of forming priests who can truly make Jesus present to our brothers and sisters by the way they live their life. The intellectual or academic side of the priestly formation is catered to by the Jnana-Deepa Vidyapeeth. It is the task of the Seminary to help our young students to be men of God, prayerful, united with God, self-controlled, dedicated to their duty, humble and cheerful, loving and devoted to their companions, men of character, happy in their life of study, prayer, obedience, service... The Papal Seminary in Pune is trying to come up to the expectations of the People of God and of our worthy Prelates who send their candidates to us, the hope of their dioceses.

Writing about Kandy in 1923 such a keen observer as Archbishop Alban Goodier, of Bombay, made this judicious remark: "I have seen men trained in Kandy and I have seen men trained in Rome and if it has to come to a choice between the two I have no hesitation whatsoever on which I would decide. Moreover Kandy has a hold upon its past students which I would not for anything see relaxed: that is an aftermath better than any degree". If we ask ourselves what might have been the secret of it, we can perhaps find an answer or an explanation from another distinguished Prelate who had his formation in Kandy. Speaking on the occasion of the 75th anniversary of its existence, Archbishop Mar Gregorios said: "The young candidates should have a clear and integral vision of the ideal of the priesthood as a service of God's people, as a call to self-denial and sacrifice". And immediately he proceeded to speak about his own experience of life in Kandy: "Whatever its disadvantages, life in Kandy was supremely conducive to this kind of formation. It raised you above banalities and petty strifes and placed you in the heart of a family in which selfless and universal love was the rule of life; where there was an abundant measure of freedom in which the spirit expands and grows; where there was instilled into everyone a sense of responsibility which created moderation, circumspection and consideration for others; where the rules were observed more out of love for virtue than out of fear of punishment". Mar Gregorios ended by saying: "This may perhaps look too ideal to be true. But no doubt this is an approximate sketch of life in Kandy. The life and work of generations of priests have proved the true wisdom of such a training. The memory of the days in the seminary has sustained them in time of trials and inspired them with generosity in the service of Christ".

The Papal Seminary of Pune is a continuation of the one of Kandy. Our Jubilee celebrations are a call on everyone of us to thank our heavenly Father for all that He in His divine providence has deigned to bless us with in the course of these hundred and twenty-two years and to go ahead with humility and trust striving generously towards the ideal so vividly recalled for us by Archbishop Mar Gregorios - an ideal to which we are all sincerely committed.

POSTSCRIPT

The following have been my source for this History of the Kandy-Pune Papal Seminary:

- Sylvain Grosjean, SJ, *Historia Fundationis Seminarii Kandyensis*
- Silver Jubilee Souvenir of the Papal Seminary, 1918
- "Golden Jubilee Celebrations", Papal Seminary, Kandy (1893 – 1943)
- The Diaries kept by the Beadles of the Theologians of the Papal Seminary, Pune
- Unpublished documents – Letters, Reports, Notes, etc. Preserved in the Archives of the Papal Seminary, Pune.
- Souvenir of Centenary Celebrations
- Souvenir of Golden Jubilee Celebrations

☼☼☼

I am grateful to Fr. Noel Sheth, SJ, my Rector, for entrusting me with the task of writing this historical sketch of this Seminary which has been my HOME for the last thirty years, that is, since June 1963. It has been for me a labour of love. I also wish to express my thanks to Mr. Francis Mariadoss, our clerk, who typed the manuscript for the press and to our seminarian, Bro. K. Anthiah, of the diocese of Nellore, who has taken a lot of trouble in connection with the printing of this book.

Last but not least, I feel particularly grateful to our Bishop, Rt. Rev. Dr. Valerian D'Souza, for graciously accepting to write the Foreword to this centenary memorial of this Pontifical Seminary of which he was a most distinguished alumnus, years ago.

Carlos M. De Melo, SJ

Papal Seminary
Pune 1993

[In the light of sixty years of Papal Seminary in Pune, the Papal Community decided to celebrate its dimond jubiliee with simple and meaningful celebration. One of the activisties was to revise and edit the History of Papal Seminary by Carols M. De Melo. The Rector of Papal Seminary requested one of the senior emeriti and the longest staying person, Fr. Kurien Kunnumpuram, to do the needful. He was ably assisted by Charles Davis and Kuruvilla Pandikattu and some committed students.]

Diamond Jubilee

2015 is the Diamond Jubilee of the Papal Seminary's existence in Pune. It was transferred from Kandy, Sri Lanka, to Pune in May 1955. It is the considered view of the staff and students of the seminary that there will be no big, noisy celebration of the jubilee. Instead they have decided to do seven things as part of the jubilee celebrations and have appointed committees of staff and students for each of these activities.

Committees	Animators	**Convenor**
(1) Souvenir & Brochure Commitee	Fr. Stephen Jayard Fr. Francis Gonsalves, SJ	Bro. Rhakho George
(2) Papal Seminary History Committee (Editing & Updating the book by Fr. Carlos)	Fr. Kuruvilla Pandikattu, SJ Fr. J. Charles Davis	Bro. Zacharias Cyriac
(3) Blood Donation Committee	Fr. Prasad Lankapalli SJ Fr. Joyce Kaithkottil	Bro. Ravi Joseph
(4) Public Relations & Fundraising Committee	Fr. Kuruvilla Pandikattu, SJ Fr. J. Charles Davis	Bro. Sebastian
(5) Competitions & Documentary Committee	Fr. Nishant A. Irudayadason	Bro. Edwin Raj
6) Plantation Committee	Fr. Francis Ezhakunnel, SJ Fr. Patras Kujur, SJ Fr. George Karuvelil, SJ	Bro. Elisha
(7) Archives Committee	Fr. V.M. Jose Fr. Paul Raj Fr. George Cordeiro	Bro. Tony Jose

Besides there is a Diamond Jubilee Core Committee with Fr. J. Charles Davis as Chairperson and Bro. Romel Saldanha as Convenor.

☼☼☼

The Last Decade of 20th Century

On October 6, 1994, **Father Michael Alosanai, SJ,** took charge as Rector of the Papal Seminary. He belongs to Madurai Province of the Society of Jesus. He has had some experience of formation: He was Novice-Master in his Province and spent some years in De Nobili College, Pune, as Superior of the Philosophers.

During the years of his rectorship three significant things took place which have a bearing on the formation imparted here and the administration of the Seminary. First of all the introduction of **Living Group System** among the students. There is an historical background to this system. In the 1970's and 1980's we had two prefects: the prefect of the philosophers and the prefect of the theologians. It was quite difficult for the prefects to get to know students deeply. Without a deep knowledge of the seminarians it would not be possible for the prefect to accompany them effectively. Hence the seminary began to have animators for each class of theologians and philosophers. After a few years it became clear that a class of 24 to 26 students was still too large a group. That is why it was decided in March 1995 to go in for a living group system. Now each class would be divided into two groups with a staff animator for each group. The members of the group will live in close proximity to each other. Hence the name Living group. For example, the first half of the ground floor of the theologians will be allotted to Group A of the 3rd year theologians. The second half of the floor will be allotted to group B of the third year. Similar arrangements were made for each class of the theologians and the philosophers. In a meeting of the Papal Seminary Staff held on March 15-16, 1995, it was stated:

(a) that the Living Group System enables the development of close, inter-personal relationship between an individual student and his animator with all advantages that flow from such a relationship;
(b) that it fosters communion of the group members with one another in the spirit; and,
(c) that it builds up character and fosters leadership qualities and team spirit.

The staff went on to assert that sound and integrated formation is best achieved when seminarians live and interact with one another in a small group with an animator as the facilitator of the group.

The formation of the groups was left to the students. They had to keep in mind that each group should be inter-linguistic, inter-diocesan, inclusive of north-south dioceses. The first year theologians should remember that there should be a healthy mixing up with old-timers (those who did philosophy in Pune) and the new comers (those who joined the seminary only after doing philosophy elsewhere). All have to take note of the fact that ours is a national seminary.

With regard to the choice of animators the students have a say. Each living group can give to Father Rector a list of three names of staff members available to them – six for the theologians and four for the philosophers. Fr. Rector will finalize the assignment of the animators keeping in mind the wish of each group.

The various activities of the house will be managed at the group level – liturgical celebrations (weekly community Mass, evening prayers, etc.); manual works, scullery and various celebrations. Once a week there will be an Eucharistic celebration in the Living Group. Evening prayer will be in the group once a week. Every living group will meet at night after supper for personal sharing, discussion, etc. once in two weeks.

Each group has an animator. He will accompany each student of the group in his attempt to achieve his integrated growth (human, emotional, intellectual, pastoral and spiritual) – all in the external form. He is normally present in all group meetings, actively animates them, while respecting the freedom of each student.

In June 1995 Living Group System became a reality in life of the seminary and has continued to exist till 2015. All the staff and students are happy with this system.

In order to animate living groups effectively the animators need to acquire new skills and learn to adapt themselves to the needs of the group. To help them to acquire new skills some sessions were held for the animators with the help of resource persons who were competent in these areas.

In June 1996, a new form of **midday prayer** was introduced. For many years the seminary faced a difficult problem. It was customary for students to spend about 15 minutes just before lunch in the chapel for examination of conscience, etc. Now when Jnana-Deepa Vidyapeeth introduced a new schedule the students had to attend four lectures from 9.10 a.m. to 12.45 p.m. Sometimes they had an additional lecture at 8.20 am. When the students came back to the seminary tired, they were not in a mood to go to the chapel to pray. Some of the older fathers on the staff used to complain that the students are talking with one another after the morning lectures and not going to the chapel to pray.

It was in this context that Fr. Rector decided that there would be no prayer in the chapel after morning lectures; instead the staff and students will gather in the refectory for lunch five minutes before 1.00 p.m. At noon we shall recite the Angelus and say the prayer before meals. This practice has continued to exist till now (2015).

Vitthalwadi (Villa) Property

On September 14, 1994, there was a staff meeting in the presence of the Provincial of India (POI) and the Assistancy Delegate for Formation (ADF) which discussed the question the disposal of our property in Vitthalwadi. In early 1960's the Seminary bought a property in Vitthalwadi and a villa was built on it. In the 1960's all the seminarians spent their summer vacation (April-May) there. Gradually the Seminary adopted a new policy which stipulated that all the seminarians would spend their summer vocations in their own dioceses. Most of the staff members felt that the seminarians should spend time in their homes and in the dioceses if they are to grow in an integrated way. As a result, the villa in Vitthalwadi was used very little. The Pre-Philosophers spent 15 days every year there having group dynamics and making a retreat. During the October holidays different language academies had a short (for two or three days) seminar in the villa.

Besides, it was always difficult to look after the Vitthalwadi property which was about 15 kilometres away from the seminary. Different people in the neighbourhood began to encroach on our property. Hence, after consulting the Provincial of India and getting the permission of the Roman Congregation for the Evangelization of Peoples, it was decided to sell the property in Vitthalwadi – 8 acres and the villa to the Bishop of Poona, 2 acres to the Jesuit Provincial of Pune, 2 acres to the Assumption Sisters; 5 acres to Dr. M. Durairaj and 4 acres to the Investment in Man (IIM) Trust. However, because Papal Seminary is a trust it is not possible to sell its property. And also it is not possible to alienate trust property without the permission of the Charity Commissioner.

Fr. George Soares-Prabhu, an outstanding Scripture scholar and professor of JDV met with an accident on July 22, 1995, and died immediately. The funeral service was held on Sunday, July 23, in the Seminary Chapel. Bishop Valerian D'Souza was the main celebrant of the funeral Mass. The Provincial of India and the Provincials of Bombay and Goa participated in funeral service. About 2000 people including the staff and students of JDV were present at the services.

In June-July 1996 floods wreaked havoc in some parts of Assam. Jnana-Deepa Vidyapeeth decided to send a group of ten students from various campus houses to participate in the relief work. Four seminarians joined the team. They left for Assam on July 20, 1996.

An **Apostolic Team** consisting Archbishop Ivan Dias of Bombay, Bishop Joe Rodrigues of Jamshedpur, Bishop Thomas Dabre of Vasai and Fathers Bede McGegor and Agnelo Gracias came here for the visitation of the Papal Seminary. This team was authorized to do so by the Holy Father John Paul II.

On January 23, 1999, we got the news that Fr. Noel Sheth, SJ, has been appointed Rector of Jnana-Deepa Vidyapeeth. In June 1999 Father George Karuvelil, who teaches philosophy at JDV, joined the Seminary community. Earlier he was residing in De Nobili College. In the same month Fr. Reinhold Kiess, SJ, of Goa Province, the new spiritual director, arrived here. On June 25, 1999, the seminarians under the leadership of Father Joseph Ovelil, the Minister of the House, started teak plantation. This is the way the beadle of the house described the event: "Today is a memorable day in the history of the Papal Seminary. All the brothers together planted 500 teak seedlings near the football court". During the next three years the seminarians in different groups watered the young plants so that they were able to take root in the soil.

In the last years of the 20th century we had several visitors. On September 27, 1996, Fr. Peter Kurukula Arachi, the Jesuit Provincial of Sri Lanka, paid a visit to the Papal Seminary. Next day, Fr. Julian Fernandes, SJ, one of the Assistants of the Superior General of the Society of Jesus, was our guest. Then on October 16, 1998, Mar Koorilos, Bishop of Thiruvalla and Mar Joshua, Auxiliary Bishop of Trivandrum Malankara Archdiocese, visited the Seminary. Next morning Mar Koorilos celebrated Mass with the Papal community. On that day, during lunch, Mar Koorilos and Mar Joshua were felicitated.

On January 12, 1997, **Fr. Antonio Sabino** died in the hospital. On the night of January 2, he had an accident and got burnt partially. He had also a thigh bone fracture. On January 12, we got the news of Sabino's death at about 8.15 p.m. After supper most of the staff and students were standing in front of the seminary, waiting for his body to be brought from the hospital. A good number of students were weeping unashamedly, because they loved him so much. There is no doubt that Fr. Sabino was the best loved member of the seminary staff. Fr. Sabino's funeral was on January 13. Besides the staff and students of Papal Seminary, many people from the campus and from the town attended the funeral service.

Chapter 9

The First Years of the 21st Century

Fr. Joe Mathias, SJ, of Ranchi Province, was installed as the new Rector of the Papal Seminary on June 9, 2000. The installation ceremony began with a Holy Mass at 11.45 a.m. Rt. Rev. Valerian D'Souza, the Bishop of Poona, was the chief guest. Before the festive lunch at 1.00 p.m., there was a short function to bid farewell to the outgoing Rector, Fr. Michael Alosanai, and welcome the new Rector.

In 2002, Jnana-Deepa Vidyapeeth planned to build a **Post-Graduate Block** which would have lecture halls and other facilities for the resident post-graduate students. For this purpose, Fr. Noel Sheth, the President of JDV, approached the Rector of Papal Seminary with a request for some land beyond the football ground. In an official letter to the Papal Seminary, the President of JDV wrote: "Since the land was originally bought for the purpose of the Athenaeum too, there would be no need to ask for Vatican's permission to formally alienate the land requested by JDV.... It would merely be an internal adjustment among ourselves. Of course from the civil point of view, the actual separation or the utilization of the land by giving JDV power of attorney will have to be effected".

A Seminary staff meeting was held on October 30, 2002, to discuss the issue of land for the JDV building project. It was pointed out by some staff members that, since the boundaries of the properties of Papal Seminary and JDV have already been fixed, giving land to JDV will be an alienation of seminary land. Besides, land was a financial security for the seminary in the future, especially since we cannot always depend on foreign subsidies. It was suggested that we need to get a clearance from the Roman Congregation for the Evangelization of Peoples. Further, since the authorities of the seminary and JDV are periodically changed, it was important to have everything clearly spelt out in writing, so as to avoid any future misunderstanding. The Rector of the seminary finally decided to hand over a plot of land to JDV for building the PG Block.

There was a request from the Students' Council of the theologians that the students be allowed to have **access to the internet** which would help them to send and receive e-mails. It was also pointed out that internet can be of some help in the preparation of class assignments. After discussing the request in the Formators' Forum, on August 14, 2000, the Rector decided to grant the request.

The Apostolic Visitation Team had recommended that the seminarians should do some **manual work**. "The seminarians should be engaged in some manual work. It could be considered as an extra-curricular activity and would be a concrete expression of their identification with and option for the poor".

The question of manual work was discussed in the meeting of the Formators held on August 14, 2000. While the Formators were for introducing manual work on a regular basis, they thought it worthwhile to consult the students in Living Groups and take into account their points of view. At present all the students are asked to do one hour of manual work every week. Some of the students do much more than that.

On October 27, 2002, Fr. Carlos de Melo passed away at the infirmary of De Nobili College. The funeral service was held at 4.00 p.m. in the Seminary chapel. Fr. Lionel Mascarenhas, SJ, delivered the homily at the funeral Mass. He began by saying: "Rather than give a formal homily, I have elected to offer a tribute of appreciation, gratitude and love to a fellow Jesuit who was more like a brother to me". He added: "I would like to remember and celebrate Carlos first as a scholar, and writer, then as person and finally as a Jesuit priest and apostle". Fr. Lionel went on to describe the manifold activities Carlos was engaged in as well as his sterling qualities as a person. By way of conclusion he stated: "But behind and below these rich qualities and multifarious activities was the deepest level of the Jesuit priest. To anyone who knew him, Carlos came across as eminently a "man of God". Prayer was his very life, the atmosphere he breathed".

On July 28, 2003, Fr. Francis D'Souza, SJ, was given a send-off as he was leaving the seminary for a new assignment. He was the treasurer of the seminary for about four years.

In June 2004, **Father Ornellas Coutinho, SJ**, of Gujarat Province, took charge as the Rector of Papal Seminary. Right at the beginning he was faced with a serious financial problem. This was caused by two factors. 1. The rising cost of living; 2. The decrease in the income. On the one hand, the Congregation for the Evangelization of Peoples started cutting down the subsidy that it used to give to the seminary. Because of the drastic fall in the interest rates we were receiving much less from our savings deposited in the banks.

In order to deal with the situation there were discussions among the staff and the students. As a result of these discussions we were able to find some ways of cutting down our expenses. Formerly all the living groups had their group dynamics in different places outside the seminary. Now it was decided that only two living groups of the second year philosophers and two living groups of the third year theologians will have their group dynamics outside the seminary. All the other groups would have their group dynamics in the seminary. It was also decided that the Seminary would no longer meet the expenses of the Goa pilgrimage of the third year theologians. Further, the language academies would have their seminars on the campus and not in the villa at Vitthalwadi.

But gradually as the financial situation of the seminary improved, some changes were introduced. Now all the living groups, except the two living groups of the first year philosophers and two living groups of the first year theologians, have their group dynamics outside the seminary. Besides, the seminary gives a subsidy, which is quite substantial, to the third year theologians for their pilgrimage to Goa.

Golden Jubilee of Transfer to Pune

In 2005 Papal Seminary completed 50 years of existence in Pune. Already in March 2004, the Seminary staff discussed the plan for the **Golden Jubilee Celebrations** of the transfer of Papal Seminary to Pune. The plan was prepared by a committee consisting of Frs. Lionel Mascarenhas, Lorenzo Fernando and Kurien Kunnumpuram. According to the plan, the inauguration of the Jubilee year will be on October 2, 2004 and Fr. Kuruvilla Pandikattu was appointed the main organiser by the rector. It was decided that there would be a solemn Mass in the evening followed by dinner. Only people from Pune, including Bishop Valerian D'Souza and priests who are former students of the Papal Seminary, will be invited.

A number of activities were planned for the Jubilee year. A Refresher course in theology for the former students of Papal Seminary will be conducted twice – once in the second half of January 2005, then once in October 2005, just before the concluding celebrations of the jubilee – October 25-27. It was also planned that the staff and students of the seminary will undertake some concrete work for the poor and the needy in our neighbourhood.

It was felt that the gardens and immediate surroundings of the seminary should be beautified. Fr. Isaac Padinjarekuttu undertook this task and did it wonderfully well, i.e., the circle garden (lawn) outside and the gardens inside the seminary.

The **Concluding Celebrations** of the Jubilee began on October 25, with a solemn liturgy celebrated by our Bishop Valerian D'Souza. Four Latin rite bishops and four oriental rite bishops concelebrated the Mass. A large number of our alumni were concelebrants. During the Mass, Fr. Hector D'Souza, SJ, Provincial of South Asia, preached the homily. In his homily Fr. Hector said: "We recall today the incalculable and heroic efforts those stalwarts both in Kandy and Pune made in the initial and early stages of the transfer and transplantation of the seminary into new location in Pune.

Once transplanted fifty years ago, Papal Seminary blossomed into a new state of invigorated existence as happens to a transplanted seedling in the agricultural setting. In the course of the half century of its life here, Papal Seminary has become a formidable force to be reckoned with in the Indian Church. It has time and again demonstrated an innate resilience and resource fulness to adapt and adjust itself to the winds of change".

After Mass there was a coffee break. Then all of us assembled in the seminary auditorium for the Inaugural Session which was presided over by the Bishop of Poona. Fr. Rector, Ornellas Coutinho, delivered the welcome speech which was spiced with humorous anecdotes from his rich repertoire. He said: "I know for all of you Papalites this is a joyous occasion. I can also sense a swell of emotions that is flooding back upon all of you, and that is as it should be, typical of the spirit of this jubilee..."

"I feel elated as I mention the names of Cardinals Valerian Gracias, Joseph Parecattil and Joseph Cordeiro, all three students of the Papal Seminary. Added to the pantheon is a list of 32 living Bishops, all Papalites. If we consider the 35 or so Bishops who have gone to their eternal reward, it would be approximately 65 bishops nurtured by the Papal Seminary."

"Gratitude, respect and pride sum up how I feel about the Papal Seminary".

Bishop Valerian then delivered the keynote address. He spelled out the significance of the transfer of the seminary and its half a century of life here. "All this made for a remarkable widening of the Seminary's life and horizons, resulting in an all round enrichment for both the staff and students – academically, culturally, socially and spiritually...."

After this Fr. Alex Dassanayake of the National Seminary of Sri Lanka gave us a complementary address. Since he was an eyewitness of the memorable exodus from Kandy he was able to give us an account of the complicated preparations for the transfer. For the staff and students of the Papal Seminary it was a painful experience to leave Kandy with its beautiful surroundings and to come to the Pune campus, which then resembled a dry, hot wilderness. Yet, mingled with these first unpromising impressions, was the expectation of entering the Promised Land, which was rich in opportunities for growth and fulfilment".

The early afternoon of that day was devoted to Academy gatherings of different language groups. These brought home to our alumni both the cosmopolitan nature of our community as well as the efforts of our seminarians to master the regional languages and to become familiar with the cultures and aspirations of the people among whom they are to work later – an important dimension of pastoral formation. The evening was filled with a delightful programme titled "Those were the days..." This was a recall of life in our seminary by representatives of three generations: Fr. Terence Franz of Bangalore, a veteran of the exodus group; Fr. Joseph Abraham of Bangalore, speaking of a later generation and finally Fr. Francis Alphonso of Calcutta, representing the latest generation. Commenting on the programme Fr. Lionel Mascarenhas said: "It was instructive and inspiring to see how one theme ran through the spontaneous and sometimes humorous presentations like a uniting silver thread, viz., the homely, democratic, fraternal and open attitude that have marked the "Home of Love" down the years".

Then, there was a unique item, "Inspired by the Past, Involved in the Present", a Multimedia Presentation on the history and life of the Papal Seminary. It brought alive the vibrant past of our institution with a galaxy of representative greats from the Kandy era down to Poona times, with typical shorts (clips) depicting the various activities of the seminarians (liturgical, academic, social outreach and recreational); and the seminary buildings against new verdant landscapes. Referring to this item Fr. Mascarenhas remarked: "All very creative, imaginative and comprehensive and well appreciated by the Papal audience. Considering that our students are not pros in the line, they did a very creditable job within the time constraints, which speaks well of their talent and hard work".

October 26 opened with a solemn liturgy in the Syro-Malabar rite. Mar James Pazhayattil of Irinjalakuda was the main celebrant and Mar Jacob Manathodath of Palghat was the homilist. He shared with us some inspiring reflections on the theme of the jubilee: "Rooted in Christ and Committed to Serve". In the morning academic session there was a panel discussion on the relevant topic of Priestly Formation. Fr. X.D. Selvaraj of Tuticorin Diocese and at present Director of the CPCI office in Bangalore was the first speaker. He described for us an outline of the priestly formation, he envisages, which calls for a rethink along the lines of a contextualised formation in mission rather than the traditional – largely western – pattern we have inherited from centuries past. The two other speakers were lay people: Mrs. Melanie Fernandez, a widow actively involved in lay ministry in the parish; Mr. Luke Lobo, a family man devoted to lay witness. Their presentations were quite challenging as they frankly pointed out the desiderata in priestly formation and their sometimes unfortunate lack in priestly life today. There was then a lively interaction between the speakers and the audience which raised many questions and made some relevant comments.

The early afternoon was devoted to a 10 generation Batches Meet in various places which gave the participants an opportunity to share their experiences and ideas. This session was appreciated by all.

In the evening there was an enjoyable cultural programme consisting of a medley of lively, well executed regional dances performed by our seminarians assisted by outsiders. "Their variety of content and form opened a window on the richness of our multi-cultured country, and was also a living tribute to the beauty and expressive power of *natya*, one of our characteristic art forms. Witnessing this succession of variegated dances made one feel proud of India's rich cultural heritage" (Observations made by Fr. Lionel Mascarenhas).

The final day, October 27, began with a solemn liturgy in the colourful Syro-Malankara rite. The main celebrant was Mar Timotheos, the bishop-emeritus of Tiruvalla. Isaac Mar Cleemis, the present bishop, gave us an inspiring homily.

The morning session was meant to give us an understanding of the specialized ministries some of the alumni are engaged in. Fr. S.A. Louis (Pune) shared with us his experiences as Coordinator of Youth Ministry in the Western Region. Fr. Kuriakose Mampilly (Ernakulam) described for us the unique experiment in social work which he has started. Fr. K.J. Thomas (Jalandhar) was unable to come to make his presentation. He has initiated a project called "Roshini" for the help of children disabled by polio.

At 11.15 a.m., there was a family get-together chaired by Fr. Rector. At the beginning the Rector introduced the members of the seminary staff, several of whom were new-comers.

The afternoon session was devoted to an overview of "The State of the Church" by regional representatives. Fr. Robert Majaw described the state of the Church in the Northeast and spoke about some of the problems the Church faces there. Fr. Lourdes Daniel (Pune) dealt with the Church in the Western region. Fr. Stephen Gomes of Tuticorin made some pertinent observations on the Church in the South. Finally Bishop Julius Marandi of Dumka spelt of the promise and the special problems of the tribal Church.

In the evening there was a basketball match between the alumni and the present students. It was a delight for both the winners and the losers.

The Jubilee celebrations concluded with a brief thanksgiving service for our seminary's 50 years in Pune and the jubilee reunion of Papalites.

This is what Fr. Lionel Mascarenhas had to say about the Jubilee celebrations: "Musing on the Jubilee celebrations, two things stand out prominently: On the one hand, the palpable, heart-warming joy of the Papalites of all generations in their return to their alma mater and their enduring attachment to our seminary which neither the passing of the years nor their pastoral preoccupations have diminished. On the other hand, equally striking is the generosity with which both the students and the staff, under an enthusiastic Rector, gave their time and energy and gave themselves for the meticulous preparation and the carrying out of the celebrations, all in a family spirit of give and take. Both sides seemed to compete in keeping alive that elusive but very real "Poo-Kandy spirit" that is the hallmark of our Seminary, a legacy for which we cannot thank God enough".

The Statutes of the Papal Seminary

After the Apostolic Visitation of the Papal Seminary on November 5-6, 1988, a Special Commission of the Bishops was appointed by the CBCI in 2003 to assist this national inter-ritual seminary, in keeping with the principle that local Bishops are to be more responsibly involved in the care and administration of seminaries. It was felt that, like other seminaries, the Papal Seminary also should have its own proper Statutes which define the principles of the close collaboration of the Society of Jesus with the CBCI, the Roman Congregation of the Evangelization of Peoples (CEP) and Jnana-Deepa Vidyapeeth (JDV) in the administration of the Papal Seminary.

As a result, Rome set up a Commission consisting of Archbishop Oswald Gracias of Agra, Bishop Thomas Dabre of Vasai, Fr. Noel Sheth, SJ, a member of the Seminary staff, and Fr. Ralph D'Costa, SJ, the Rector of De Nobili College. While the Commission was preparing the statutes, the seminary staff was asked to formulate a Vision Statement for the Seminary which would eventually be incorporated into the Statutes of the Papal Seminary. A committee consisting of Fathers Lionel Mascarenhas, Kurien Kunnumpuram and Noel Sheth (convenor) was set up by the Rector. This is the Draft of the Vision Statement prepared by this committee:

> Papal Seminary takes as its ideal and inspirational goal the vision of its founder, Pope Leo XIII, expressed in his memorable words, "Filii tui, India, administri tibi salutis" (Your own sons, India, will be the ministers of salvation for you).
>
> Mindful of its national and pioneering character, the seminary aims at providing, in communion with the local churches, an inculturated priestly formation, with a view to preparing ministers of the Word and Sacrament for our land: men imbued with the mind and spirit of Jesus Christ; deeply rooted in the multi-cultural and multi-religious traditions of India; capable of providing intellectual leadership for the people of God; men, too, who will reach out in humble, fraternal dialogue to the men and women of other faiths; and, in Christlike solidarity and compassionate service to the poor and marginalized people of our country, bringing to all the Christian message of peace, love, hope and joy.

In the meantime the Commission produced the first draft of the Statutes of the Papal Seminary. This document was sent to Rome in July 2004. After a few years came Rome's reply which pointed out that the Statutes need to be thoroughly revised according to the guidelines Rome gave. The Commission once again set to work on the revision of the statutes. By now Fr. Ralph D'Costa had gone back to his province (Karnataka). Hence, with Rome's permission, Fr. Pradeep Sequeira, SJ, the then Rector of Papal Seminary, was co-opted into the commission. The commission worked hard and revised the Statutes. They were sent to Rome after a few years. The finally approved Statutes have not yet been made public.

The **Centenary Computer Centre (CCC),** needed more computers and more space. So the centre was shifted to the corridor between the philosophate and the theologate. Now there will be 24 computers, three of which have internet facilities. This was done under the supervision of Fr. G. Alex, SJ, who was the Minister of the Seminary from 2006 to 2007. He also renovated the library and made it more user-friendly by creating space for students to sit and study there.

In June 2007, **Fr. Pradeep Sequeira, SJ**, of the Karnataka Province took charge as Rector of the Papal Seminary. With his vast experience in administration, he did a good job as Rector. The main entrance to the Seminary was beautified and a new arch and gate were installed during his tenure. He took the initiative, along with Fr. Alex, of tackling all property matters which were neglected for long years.

In a staff meeting on June 13, 2007, some staff members pointed that it is not safe for the Papal Seminary to have so much land unused when the city is rapidly expanding in this direction. Hence, it is advisable to have a Master-Plan for the seminary campus, showing further developments and constructions.

In June 2007, Father Anand Prabhu, SJ, who was a member of the Papal Seminary community and the Registrar of JDV went back to his Karnataka Province.

Fr. Lionel Mascarenhas, SJ, who was ailing for some years died of a cardiopulmonary arrest on the morning of December 28, 2009. It was a quiet, peaceful death without troubling anyone. The funeral was on December 30. Bishop Thomas Dabre was the main celebrant. But four more Bishops – Valerian D'Souza, Alwyn Barreto, Lourdes Daniel and Franco – concelebrated. So, too, Fr. Edward Mudavassery, SJ (POSA), and Fr. Bertie Rosario (the Provincial of Pune). Fr. Noel Sheth, SJ, preached the homily. He began by saying that Fr. Lionel Mascarenhas "had to his credit the hat trick of having been rector of De Nobili College, Papal Seminary and Jnana-Deepa Vidyapeeth". Noel went on to describe the manifold activities Fr. Mascarenhas was engaged in both on the campus and outside of it. He concluded the homily by summering of Lionel's life: "In a nutshell Fr. Lionel was a perfect gentleman, gifted writer, lively humorist, accomplished musician, able administrator, inspiring teacher, compassionate counsellor, caring superior, committed Jesuit and holy priest".

Property Matters Again

In 2009 we got information that the Pune Municipal Corporation has notified that some part of our Vitthalwadi property would be reserved for some public services like education, health care and so on. The Seminary had already allotted this land to several people. Now the Rector called a meeting of Dr. Durairaj, IIM Trust, Assumption Society and St. Anne's Society to study the implications of the notification and take necessary action.

Even though the Seminary had given this land to these people some 15 years ago, they were not able to start any construction work till now. The reason was that, since Vitthalwadi property belongs to the Papal Seminary trust, it cannot be alienated. They also found it difficult to get the necessary permissions from the Municipal Corporation.

There was yet another problem. As our lawyer Advocate Joachim Reis pointed out, the Charity Commissioner would not allow large chunks of property to be given to others. If people or institutions wish to get land from the seminary, their aims and objectives should be consonant with the aims and objectives of the Papal Seminary Trust.

After some years of negotiation, the seminary has signed a Memorandum of Understanding with all these parties. As a result the Seminary will give them land on lease.

Spiritual Formation in the Seminary

On January 5, 2010, the Formators' Form had a Brain-storming session on the spiritual formation in the Papal Seminary. These are some of the points that came up. For the interiorization of spiritual values a suitable atmosphere of silence is necessary. Such an atmosphere of silence is lacking even during recollection days. It appears that better silence is observed during examination days than during recollection days. It was also suggested that in a spirit of inculturation we should adopt and personalize Indian methods of prayer. It was pointed out that the essential dimensions of spirituality such as personal integrity, honesty, fairness, concern for the poor, etc. are not necessarily fostered by the mere observance of routine spiritual exercises. Hence creative ways must be found to foster a genuine spirituality.

There was an observation about the Living Groups. They were originally meant for planning and implementing formative programmes like faith sharing or depth sharing of personal experiences. But over the years they have become mere social gatherings. This needs to be looked into.

At the end of the Brain-storming, group animators and spiritual directors were invited to enhance the spiritual formation imparted in the Seminary by making use of some of the ideas that have surfaced in this meeting.

There was a felt need in the Seminary to have a community Recollection on July 10 and 11 on the theme: "The Special Character of the Papal Seminary". Fathers Kurien Kunnumpuram, Paul Parathazham and Mathew Jayanth have been asked to organise it. There were five sessions: 3 common sessions and 2 group sessions. Whatever has been discussed in the groups will be taken up and deepened in the common sessions. The recollection began in the evening of July 10 and ended with Holy Mass on July 11 at 4.15 p.m. The members of the community were quite happy with the recollection.

In April 2010, Fr. Pradeep Sequeira, the Rector of the Papal Seminary wanted to go back to his Karnataka Province. Hence, the Provincial of Sough Asia, Fr. Edward Mudavassery, SJ, appointed **Fr. Jose Thayil, SJ**, of Patna Province, Acting Rector. It was only in December 2010 that the Congregation for the Evangelization of Peoples officially appointed Fr. Thayil Rector of Papal Seminary.

One of the new things Fr. Thayil as Rector did was to get some competent religious Sisters as **spiritual directresses** of our seminarians. In April 2011 when one of the spiritual directors of the seminary, Fr. Kulandairaj, had to go back to his Andhra Province, the Provincial of South Asia found it difficult to find a replacement for him immediately. At that time Fr. Jose Thayil suggested that we could try and get some religious Sisters as spiritual guides. Fr. Edward agreed with Fr. Thayil's suggestion. So, Fr. Rector contacted some Sisters who were competent in spiritual direction and counselling. Most of them happened to be novice mistresses. In June 2011, these Sisters were called to the seminary. They introduced themselves to the newcomers of the seminary as well as those who were going to Fr. Kulandairaj for spiritual direction. Then it was left to the seminarians to choose their spiritual guides either from the spiritual directors of the seminary or from the religious Sisters. In June 2011 some 30 seminarians chose the Sisters as theirs spiritual directresses.

In the first year there were some problems and difficulties. 1. Since the seminarians normally went to their spiritual director for confession, they had to find a priest to hear their confession; 2. Some found it difficult to disclose to the spiritual directress their sexual problems; 3. As these Sisters were not living in the seminary, the seminarians could not easily meet them in case of an emergency. But from the second year onwards the seminarians did not have any of these difficulties. After four years now the seminarians feel quite comfortable to go to religious Sisters for spiritual direction. During this year 2015-16, 32 brothers have opted to go to the Sisters for spiritual direction.

The Brothers feel that they are well understood by their spiritual directresses. They have no hesitation to disclose to them all their personal problems and difficulties. They believe that these Sisters are quite competent in spiritual direction and counselling. They find the Sisters very regular and demanding. Sisters on their part are quite willing to contribute their mite to the formation of future priests for India. Getting spiritual direction from women helps the seminarians to overcome their prejudices against women. This experience will enable them to respect women and treat them as equal partners in their mission as priests and not to look upon them as subordinates.

Seminary Newsletter

During the academic year 2011-12, Papal Seminary started a Newsletter in order to communicate some of the important activities and significant initiatives of the

Papal Seminary to the campus houses, dioceses, archdioceses and Jesuit provinces of India. At the beginning it was published once a year. Now it has become a biannual feature. During the last two academic years, the Papal Seminary brought out two issues, one at Christmas time and the other at the end of the academic year. Response from the bishops and the provincials have been quite encouraging. They said that they were very happy to receive news of what has been happening in the Papal Seminary. We hope to continue to publish the Newsletter which has been an initiative of the Rector Fr. Jose Thayil, SJ.

Land Dispute Almost Solved'

For some years now there was a case filed against us by one Laxman Deokar. In the early 1950's the Provincial of Pune, Fr. Geisel, had bought some land from two Deokar brothers for the seminary. After sometime a third Deokar Laxman claimed that he too had a right to the land and so must be paid. After some time the dispute died out. A few years ago his grandson also called Laxman went to court claiming that he has a right to a big chunk of the seminary property. At that time the authorities of the Seminary did not take the case seriously. About three years ago our Treasurer, Father Alex, hired a good lawyer to plead on our behalf. After more than two years we won the case and Laxman Deokar has filed an appeal. During our search for documents related to the property of the Seminary we came across a letter which the grandfather Laxman wrote. In this letter he makes it quite clear that he has absolutely no right to any part of the seminary property.

Staff Community

During the last twenty years there have been many changes in the staff community. In June 1995 Fr. William Beck, SJ, of Madhya Pradesh Province, joined the Papal Seminary community as Moderator of the Philosophers. Frs. K.P. George, SJ of Delhi Province (teaching staff at JDV), Fr. Thomas Quadros, SJ, of Karnataka Province (Spiritual Director), Fr. Joseph Minj, SJ, of Ranchi Province (Spiritual Director), and Fr. Jef Lombart, SJ, of Madhya Pradesh Province (Librarian at JDV) too were on the staff during this time. In October 1996 Fr. Kuruvilla Pandikattu, SJ, of Dumka Province, joined the Seminary as a teaching staff at JDV philosophy faculty. Fr. Dudley Mendonca SJ, of Bombay Province, joined the Papal Seminary community in June 1998 as spiritual director of theologians and Fr. Lourdes Daniel of Poona Diocese (now Bishop of Nashik) as spiritual director of Philosophers for three years. Also in the same month Fr. Joseph Ovelil, SJ, of Gujarat Province took charge as Minister of the House. Fr. Britius Ekka, SJ, of Madhya Pradesh Province, joined the seminary as Moderator of the Philosophers. Fr. M. Arokiasamy, SJ, and Peter D'Cruz, SJ, were in the Seminary as spiritual directors for a short while. On March 3, 1999, Bro. Joseph Cana of Goa Province, who was assistant treasurer for a few years, passed away in the seminary due to a cardiac pulmonary arrest and the funeral was on March 4. In June 1999 Fr. George Karuvelil, SJ, became a member of the staff community. He teaches in the faculty of philosophy at JDV. Fr. Francis D'Souza, SJ, of Darjeeling Province, joined the Seminary staff as Treasurer in June 2000 followed by Fr. Ambrose D'Souza, SJ, of Karnataka Province as Minister in 2001.

Fr. Anand Prabhu, SJ of Karnataka Province came to the Papal Seminary as Registrar & Treasurer of Jnana-Deepa Vidyapeeth in 2003. Fr. Marianus Kujur, SJ, of Ranchi Province was with us just for two years as a member of the teaching staff of JDV. Bro. A. Antony, SJ, of Kohima Province succeeded Fr. Ambroseas Minister and Treasurer in June 2003. In October 2003, Fr. Douglas Dias went back to his Bombay Province. Fr. Pravin Severakar, SJ, of Bombay Province, joined us as Spiritual Director in 2003 followed by Fr. Stephen Ekka, SJ, of Madhya Pradesh Province, also as Spiritual Director in June 2004. Father P. S. Arul, SJ, of Madurai Province, came to Papal Seminary in June 2004 as Moderator of Philosophers for one year followed by Fr. P. Arokiadoss of the same Province as Moderator of Philosophers and Professor at JDV. Due to cancer he could not survive for long. Fr. James Ponniah of Sivagangai Diocese, a Papalite, joined his *alma mater* as a teaching staff of philosophy faculty in 2005 and he continued in the same faculty till June 2014. He was appointed as professor in Madras University in June 2014. Fr. Albert D'Silva, SJ, of Kohima Province, came to the Papal Seminary as Spiritual Director in June 2006 and remained here till April 2010. Fr. Arul Jeevan, SJ, of Madurai Province came to Papal Seminary as Librarian in JDV in June 2006. Due to some serious health problem she could not continue his work for long and returned to his province in 2010. Fr. Isaac Padinjarekuttu of Kohima Diocese, at the request of his bishop, returned to his diocese in March 2006. In the same year Fr. Jose Thayil, SJ, of Patna Province joined the staff as Moderator of the Philosophers as well as teaching staff at JDV. Fr. Maria Arul Stephen of Sivagangai Diocese and Mathew Jayanth, SJ of Calcutta Province too joined the staff in 2007. Both were with us only for a few years. In June 2006, Fr. G. Alex, SJ, of Jamshedpur Province succeeded Bro. Antony as Minster and Treasurer, but since he is very comfortable with accounts, he relinquished the job of Minister and continued as Treasurer of Papal Seminary and JDV.

In June 2007 Fr. Jacob Kulangara, SJ, of Gujarat Province, young and a vibrant personality, took charge as Minister of the House. In the year 2009 Fr. Paul Fernandes, SJ, of Jamshedpur Province, Fr. Nishant Alphonse Irudayadason of Palayamkottai and Peyyala Mariadoss of Vijayawada (both Papalites) joined the staff. Fr. Paul Fernandes left us after two years to be the Vice-Chancellor of Xavier University in Bhubaneswar. Fr. Mariadoss returned to his diocese after two years. Fr. Anil Gomes, SJ, of Calcutta Province and Fr. M. Kulandairaj, SJ, of Andhra Province, joined us as Spiritual Directors replacing Frs. Albert D'Silva and Stephen Ekka. Father Prasad Lankapalli, SJ, of Andhra Province joined the Seminary in June 2011 as Moderator of the Philosophers and teaching staff at

JDV, and Fr. V.M. Jose, SJ, and Paul Raj of Sivagangai diocese in June 2012. Father Stephen Jayard became a member of the Seminary staff in April 2008, and Fr. Nishant Alphonse Irudayadason in February 2009. Both of them teach philosophy at JDV. Father J. Charles Davis joined the Seminary in November 2013 and Fr. Joyce Kaithakottil in June 2014. Father Davis teaches Moral Theology and Fr. Kaithakottil Sacred Scripture at JDV. In June 2014, Fr. Arun Kumar SJ, of Karantaka Province came to Papal Seminary as Moderator of the Philosophers. In September 2011, Fr. Lorenzo Fernando went back to his diocese, Tuticorin after becoming emeritus at JDV.

Repairs & Renovation

Papal Seminary buildings are more than fifty years old. They are in need of serious repair. With the support of the Rector, Fr. Jose Thayil, Fr. Jacob Kulangara, our young and energetic Minister, did a lot of repair work. He thoroughly renovated the kitchen and the toilets on both sides of the philosophers' and theologians' wings. He repaired the underground water-tank which provides us with water security. He constructed two new courts – one for basketball and the other for volleyball. He built two wash rooms in the parlour – one for men and the other for women. He also installed a new cooking system in the kitchen using steam boilers which is very fast and economic.

Then finally during March-June 2015 he initiated a thorough renovation of the Seminary chapel including the roof which had started leaking. The financial assistance for the chapel renovation was obtained from German Jesuit Mission, Nuernberg, Pontifical Foundation of Church in Need, Koenigstein and Archdiocse of Cologne, by the effort of Frs. Jose Thayil SJ, and J. Charles Davis.

New Staff

During the course of the year 2012, the Provincial of South Asia informed the staff that he would like the professors who are emeriti to go back to their provinces or dioceses. So, in May, 2013, Fr. Francis Pereira left for Mumbai (he died in the Vinayala Infirmary, Mumbai, on May, 10, 2014) and Fr. Paul Parathazham went back to his diocese Kothamangalam. Now he is the Director of St. John's Medical College, Bangalore. In August of the same year Fr. Kurien Kunnumpuram returned to his Kerala Province. In May-June 2015, Frs. Noel Sheth, Anil Gomes and Arun Kumar left the seminary for their respective provinces.

In June 2015, Fr. Jacob Kulangara was transferred to De Nobili College as Minister of the House. In the same month Fr. Karunaidass, SJ, of the Andhra Province, took charge as Minister of the Seminary. Further, the Seminary also got three new staff members: Fr. George Cordeiro, SJ, spiritual director of the seminarians; Fr. Francis Ezhakunnel, SJ, as Moderator of the Philosophers and Fr. Francis Gonsalves, SJ, Professor of JDV and animator of a Living Group of theologians.

Papal Seminary Journal

The Papal Seminary publishes a periodical: *Asian Journal of Religious Studies* which is a bimonthly. It has a long history of about sixty years. It was started by Fr. Robert Criem, SJ, in 1955, as the mouthpiece of than association of priests called: Apostolic Union of the Missionaries of Our Lord. Hence, the periodical was called AUMOL. It was a monthly with one or two articles in it together with sermon notes for the Sundays of the month. It was a small little journal of about 30 pages. Fr Criem edited it for about thirty years. Then Fr. Lionel Mascarenhas, SJ, became the editor of the Journal in 1986. He changed the name of the periodical to AUC, since the priests' association was then known as the Apostolic Union of the Clergy. Fr Lionel did not change the format and length of AUC.

At the beginning of 2003 Fr Lionel Mascuenhas found it difficult to continue to edit AUC because of age and infirmity. Hence, Fr. Kurien Kunnumpuram, SJ, volunteered to edit AUC. He changed the nature of AUC, gave it a new name and made it bigger in size with 48 pages. Now the journal is called *Asian Journal of Religious Studies*. It has a spiritual-pastoral orientation and has four or five articles in each issue, besides the sermon notes. Originally the Journal was meant only for priests but it is now for priests, religious and Christian leaders.

In 2013 Fr. Kuruvilla Pandikattu, S.J., took over the editorship of the Journal. It is generally well appreciated by many priests because of the thought-provoking articles and the helpful sermon notes in it.